Ethnography

Understanding Social Research

Series Editor: Alan Bryman

Published titles

Unobtrusive Methods in Social Research
Raymond M. Lee

Ethnography
John D. Brewer

Ethnography

JOHN D. BREWER

Open University Press
Buckingham · Philadelphia

Open University Press
Celtic Court
22 Ballmoor
Buckingham
MK18 1XW

email: enquiries@openup.co.uk
world wide web: www.openup.co.uk

and
325 Chestnut Street
Philadelphia, PA 19106, USA

First Published 2000

A catalogue record of this book is available from the British Library

ISBN 0 335 20268 3 (pb)   0 335 20269 1 (hb)

Library of Congress Cataloging-in-Publication Data
Brewer, John D.
   Ethnography / John D. Brewer.
     p. cm. — (Understanding social research)
   Includes bibliographical references and index.
   ISBN 0-335-20268-3 (pb) — ISBN 0-335-20269-1 (hb)
   1. Ethnology—Methodology. 2. Ethnology—Research. I. Title. II. Series.
GN345.B74 2000
305.8'001—dc21   00-035625

Typeset by Type Study, Scarborough
Printed in Great Britain by Biddles Limited, Guildford and Kings Lynn

Contents

Series editor's foreword

This Understanding Social Research series is designed to help students to understand how social research is carried out and to appreciate a variety of issues in social research methodology. It is designed to address the needs of students taking degree programmes in areas such as sociology, social policy, psychology, communication studies, cultural studies, human geography, political science, criminology and organization studies and who are required to take modules in social research methods. It is also designed to meet the needs of students who need to carry out a research project as part of their degree requirements. Postgraduate research students and novice researchers will find the books equally helpful.

The series is concerned to help readers to 'understand' social research methods and issues. This will mean developing an appreciation of the pleasures and frustrations of social research, an understanding of how to implement certain techniques, and an awareness of key areas of debate. The relative emphasis on these different features will vary from book to book, but in each one the aim will be to see the method or issue from the position of a practising researcher and not simply to present a manual of 'how to' steps. In the process, the series will contain coverage of the major methods of social research and will address a variety of issues and debates. Each book in the series is written by a practising researcher who has experience of the technique or debates that he or she is addressing. Authors are encouraged to draw on their own experiences and inside knowledge.

John Brewer's book on ethnography exemplifies these features well. It is more than a textbook about ethnography in that it reveals valuable insights into his experiences with this approach in a variety of contexts. Brewer is especially well known for his research into the Royal Ulster Constabulary and he draws on this work on many occasions. Making use of such experience allows the reader to relate general principles of ethnographic fieldwork to actual practice. Not only does this approach give life to methodological principles, it also demonstrates how ethnography is more than simply a set of axioms to be followed. There are so many contingencies to be dealt with, perhaps especially in the fraught circumstances associated with the troubles in Northern Ireland, that ethnography is better thought of as an accomplishment than a case of following methodological rules. As such, the book is very much in tune with the reflexivity that has inspired much writing on ethnography in recent years. It reflects a concern with the role and significance of the ethnographer in the construction of ethnographic knowledge and with a recognition of the part played by a multitude of unforeseen events in arriving at an ethnographic knowledge.

One of the most significant developments in ethnography in recent years is the growing recognition of the importance of viewing it as a text as much as a method. This recognition entails an acknowledgement that an ethnography is written as much to persuade readers of the credibility of the account offered as to present 'findings'. One feature of this trend has been the examination of ethnographic writing conventions. The impact of postmodernist thinking can be seen in this growing interest in ethnographic writing, though the degree to which postmodernism is solely responsible is debatable. Brewer does not shirk these issues and indeed confronts them head on. Consequently, the book provides a valuable mixture of discussions about practical issues, like the use of computer-aided qualitative data analysis packages, and the more heady debates about what ethnographers are doing when they write. Readers may be surprised also to encounter a discussion of ethnography in relation to globalization but the examination of these issues further serves to identify the distinctiveness of the ethnographic imagination and its contribution.

Brewer's book, then, brings together the excitement of ethnography with the frustrations (including negative book reviews!) and methodological precepts with the unanticipated contingencies. He never loses sight of what it means to be an ethnographer. It is the combination of insight from experience as an ethnographer with an extensive knowledge of the literature on the craft that will prove valuable to a wide constituency of readers.

Alan Bryman

Acknowledgements

First, I would like to thank Alan Bryman for the invitation to contribute to this series, and record my appreciation to Open University Press for patience in waiting for the final manuscript. This book represents years of experience as an ethnographer on a number of different projects, and owes much to all the people associated with my previous qualitative research. I would like to thank the Research Assistants who have worked with me in the past, Kathleen Magee, Paula Rodgers and Gareth Higgins, and all the organizations which gave me permission to do research on them and their members: Action Party (the former British Union of Fascists), the Royal Ulster Constabulary and the South African Police. Ordinary people have been kind in allowing me to interview them, and I record my thanks to the people of East and West Belfast, conservative evangelicals in Northern Ireland, the family of the men I interviewed in the Royal Irish Constabulary and the adults and children involved in several day-care centres and schools for people with learning difficulties. I also wish to record my thanks to several ethnographers with whom I have had many years of contact and association, and who have helped me in numerous and previously untold ways: Chris Jenks, Steve Bruce, Sam Porter, Tank Waddington, Nigel Fielding and Ray Lee. The Conclusion is based on a conference paper delivered at the American Society of Criminology in Toronto, November 1999, and I am grateful to Paul Rock for the invitation and his comments on the original paper. Finally, I would like to record my thanks to Bronwen and Gwyn – now long since grown up – for being such wonderful children.

John D. Brewer

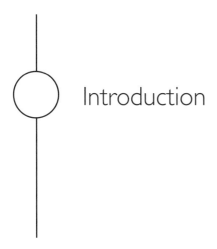

Introduction

The centrality of method in the social sciences

As a relative newcomer to the family of disciplines, the social sciences had to work out their identity against that of two older and more popular cousins, the humanities and the natural sciences, which were well established as family members, possessing a longstanding acceptance and status. Lesser known cousins quite often struggle to establish themselves, and can feel marginal to the wider family. They can feel unloved, unwelcome and generally resentful towards popular cousins. But newborns can also sometimes use older relatives as role models and establish themselves in the family by copying the popularly acclaimed and well liked members. So it was with the social sciences in the family of disciplines. The social sciences modelled themselves on the humanities and the natural sciences, but took different things from each, and in the process the social sciences resolved their identity crisis by becoming preoccupied with subject matter and method.

With a subject matter close to the humanities, the social sciences distinguished themselves from this popular and well liked cousin by the different methods adopted for doing research. They borrowed these methods from the natural sciences, in order to be like this most popular of cousins, despite having a subject matter very unlike that of the natural sciences. Identity for the social sciences thus partly became reduced to method; hence the centrality of methods to the social sciences. Janesick (1998: 48) recently referred to this obsession as 'methodolatry', in that method has become a form of idol-atry, in which the slavish devotion to method has excluded the substance or the interest of the story being told in the research.

What is 'method'?

Ask students what a 'method' is and they will list questionnaires, interviews, personal documents, experiments, surveys and the like, although they will tend to neglect some of the more recent innovations in data collection aris-ing from cultural studies (see Box 1). This is partly correct, but methods of data collection are only one type of method. There are methods of data analysis, such as statistical inference, sampling and new forms of computer-based qualitative analysis, which are used to interpret and analyse the data; and methods of research enquiry, used to formulate the research, such as the methods for constructing hypotheses, concepts, theories and propositions.

Couched in this way, methods are merely technical rules, which lay down the procedures for how reliable and objective knowledge can be obtained. As procedural rules they tell people what to do and what not to do if they want the knowledge to be reliable and objective. Thus, they lay down the procedures for constructing a hypothesis (methods of research enquiry), for designing a questionnaire, conducting an interview or doing **participant observation** (methods of data collection), for working out some statistical formulae or for using computer packages to analyse quantitative or quali-tative data (methods of data analysis). People are not free to design their questionnaire, do their observation or work out correlation coefficients any old way they want; or, at least, not if they want their research to be seen as reliable. The research community has endowed certain procedural rules with the authority to certify knowledge as reliable and objective. If these rules are not followed, the knowledge can be impugned as unreliable; and one sure way to undermine results is to criticize the methods used to obtain them. Hence methods, of whatever kind, are central to research practice because they lay down the procedural rules to follow for obtaining certifiably objec-tive and reliable knowledge.

What is 'methodology'?

If 'methods' are technical rules that define proper procedures, 'methodol-ogy' is the broad theoretical and philosophical framework into which these procedural rules fit. It is because these procedural rules reflect broader theoretical and philosophical ideas about the nature of knowledge, expla-nation and science that the research community gives them authority to endow knowledge as reliable and objective. The study of the 'fit' between

Box I

Imagine a role play, and you are standing in front of a class of students on their first research methods lecture. How would you start to talk about methods? Perhaps . . .

Who here eats polyunsaturated margarine? What brands do you eat? Why is it that they're called 'Flora', 'Sun', 'Olivio'? Close your eyes and think of tubs of 'Olivio' margarine. What does the name conjure in your mind? Go on, close your eyes; by the time this course is over you'll be glad of occasions to close your eyes in class. So, what does 'Olivio' conjure? I suggest you're thinking of rows of sun drenched olive trees, a Mediterranean vista, blue skies, purple seas and a pretty shepherdess or shepherd. We are now able to see why this blob of yellow coloured fat in a plastic tub is called 'Olivio' or 'Flora' or 'Sun', because the names conjure up such images of pastoral scenes, the countryside, things natural, healthy and strong. They tap, in other words, into a powerful cultural image in our society that associates health, naturalness and happiness with the countryside. This is why we watch *Ballykissangel*, *Emmerdale*, *Glenroe* or the *High Road* or listen to the *Archers* – real community, real happiness and healthiness are not found in the city. Why not call this blob of yellow fat smog, grime, or dog turd infested pavement? It wouldn't sell if you did. Our society is replete with this image – seen in children's stories, soap operas, television advertisements and so on.

What's this got to do with a module on research methods? Let us say I was interested in doing research on public attitudes towards the building of a nuclear waste dump in Ballymena. One thing I may want to do as part of this research is undertake a questionnaire-based survey of what people in the area think. I would conduct a large survey, subject the results to statistical analysis and provide some impressive figures and tables describing people's attitudes. Another part of my research, however, may examine the great sense of affection people feel for the countryside, what it means to people and why they want so strongly to protect and preserve it. The cultural images which it conveys to them therefore form part of this research. Data from this part of the study could comprise things like long quotations of natural language, extracts from personal documents, records of old videos, photographs and other memorabilia, newspaper cuttings, fictional stories, television advertisements and so on. What people in Ballymena think of great blobs of fat, for example, can thus be serious social research because, among other things, this reveals their images and meanings of the countryside, which bears upon their feelings towards the building of nuclear dumps in the place.

research methods and the methodology that validates them is called 'the **philosophy of social research**' by John Hughes (1990). It should be distinguished from the philosophy of social science, which is a more ancient concern with general epistemological and philosophical issues as they bear on the social sciences. In the philosophy of social research, the focus is on the authorization and validation of these procedural rules (research techniques, practices and methods) by the broad methodological context in which they fit. The flow of causation is:

methodology → procedural rules = methods → knowledge

As long as these philosophical ideas are unchallenged, the validity of the procedural rules will not be impugned. In this circumstance, there is great consensus about the methods to use to obtain reliable and objective knowledge, and results people disagree with are criticized for the application of the procedural rules (that is, the methods applied) rather than the validity of the rules themselves. Thus, debate about method within the social sciences is umbilically linked to issues of philosophy, science and the nature of knowledge and explanation: method and methodology cannot be separated.

Debate about methods in the social sciences

A number of trends are discernible in the current discussion of method and methodology in research method textbooks in the social sciences. First, a concern with technical issues has shifted towards theoretical ones. The early attention given to clarification and perfection of the procedural rules we know as methods has given way to a concern with methodological issues about the nature of knowledge, evidence and how it is that we know what we know. Early methods texts were essentially 'cook books', which suggested that research was like following a recipe, which is no more than a set of procedural rules for the preparation of meals. So students were told the steps to follow in research as if they were making dinner. Now research methods books no longer just outline technical advice about what procedural rules to follow in what circumstance and how to apply them properly, but also concern themselves with theories of knowledge and the nature of social reality. Some authors may do this reluctantly, but it is still done. Thus, Seale (1999: ix) opened his book on qualitative methods by writing:

> this book starts from the premise that methodological writing is of limited value to practising social researchers, who are pursuing a craft occupation in large part learned 'on the job'. Methodology, if it has any use at all, benefits the quality of research by encouraging a degree of awareness about the methodological implications of certain decisions

. . . it can help guard against more obvious errors. It may also offer ideas. Reading methodology, then, is a sort of intellectual muscle-building exercise.

Accordingly, the first part of his text covered methodological debates and issues.

A second trend in the methods literature is the perception of research as a process as much as practice. This means two things. Research is no longer presented as a set of discrete and logical steps or stages – planning, access, data collection, analysis, writing up, dissemination of the results – but as a whole event occurring over time, in which stages merge and are not sequenced. Many modern textbooks thus stress the importance of locating procedures in the larger **research process** and of seeing the enterprise as a messy one rather than a series of neat hermetic stages. The other consequence of the attention on process is that narrative tales about the 'research process' involved in any study or series of studies are as common as textbooks outlining good practice and procedure. There is a long tradition of books which have collected together authors to write about the research process involved in some well known work with which they are associated. At first this was done to illustrate the range of processes that bore upon famous works (Hammond 1964; Bell and Newby 1977; Bell and Roberts 1984), but it has since developed a stronger methodological impulse associated with the need for researchers to be 'reflexive' and identify, honestly, some of the social, biographical and practical contingencies that helped to produce the data. Some such accounts are used to exemplify a particular research method, such as ethnography (Hobbs and May 1993), to illustrate a particular research task, such as qualitative data analysis (Bryman and Burgess 1994), or the methodological problems posed by particular types of research, such as 'sensitive research' (Renzetti and Lee 1993).

A third trend in methods textbooks is a focus on research styles as much as on specific techniques. 'Feminist research' (see Harding 1987; Stanley 1990a), 'dangerous fieldwork' (Lee 1995) and 'sensitive research' (Lee 1994) are styles of research rather than techniques, and identification of the problems and procedures associated with such styles broadens our understanding of what research is. Two familiar and older styles of research were 'quantitative' and 'qualitative' research, and another noticeable trend in methods textbooks is the emergence of qualitative research out of the shadow of its partner. Qualitative research has become popular, reflecting some dissatisfaction with quantitative research and improvements in the systematization of qualitative research. This expresses itself in the greater use of qualitative data by researchers, students and, significantly, policy makers. Methods textbooks come to reflect this latter development when they address what is called 'applied qualitative research' (Walker, 1985) and outline its relevance to policy issues and policy making.

Within the focus on qualitative research there are also some noticeable trends. The first is a concern with the techniques and problems surrounding the **analysis** and **interpretation** of qualitative data (see Dey 1993; Bryman and Burgess 1994). The second is the attempt to define the opportunities computers offer to qualitative data collection and analysis (see Fielding and Lee 1991, 1998). Finally, there is a preoccupation with systematization in an attempt to avoid the stereotypical allegation that qualitative research is 'mere journalism'. This concern with systematization also shows itself in many ways. These include attempts to deconstruct the art and skill of writing up qualitative research (Clifford and Marcus 1986; Atkinson 1990, 1992; Wolcott 1990), a stress on **reflexivity,** by means of which researchers reflect on the contingencies during the research process which bore upon and helped to produce the data (Hammersley and Atkinson 1983; Woolgar 1988a; Williams 1990), clarification of the strengths and limits of qualitative data, a concern with the methodological and theoretical base on which qualitative research is founded, especially its ability to 'represent' reality accurately (especially see the critique of Hammersley 1989, 1990, 1992), and attempts to build **generality** and representativeness into qualitative research in order to overcome the limits of the single **case study** approach. Much of this debate is engaged in by qualitative researchers themselves rather than by critics hostile to qualitative research. This might be termed 'the ethnographic critique of ethnography' (Brewer 1994), and it led Altheide and Johnson (1998: 283) to argue that qualitative researchers have met the enemy, and it is within themselves, for they have become their own worst critics.

Purpose and outline of this book

This volume defines **ethnography** as follows:

> Ethnography is the study of people in naturally occurring settings or 'fields' by methods of data collection which capture their social **meanings** and ordinary activities, involving the researcher participating directly in the setting, if not also the activities, in order to collect data in a systematic manner but without meaning being imposed on them externally.

Defined in this way, it is one of the principal research methods in the social sciences, and foremost in the repertoire of qualitative researchers. Among all the methods available to qualitative researchers it has been subject to the most criticism by ethnographers themselves, it has seen the greatest debate about its theoretical and methodological suppositions, and it has been the object of many of the processes of systematization. Thus, it is an excellent example to illustrate the shifts in our understanding of methods that were described above.

This book locates the method of ethnography in the context of the methodological debate surrounding it. Ethnography is a **method** for collecting data, but this cannot be distinguished from the broader theoretical and philosophical frameworks that give authority to this way of collecting data. Because method and **methodology** are so intertwined some authors describe ethnography as a perspective rather than a means of data collection (Wolcott 1973), although its features as a method and a methodology need to be distinguished. While the 'procedural rules' of ethnography are described, the discussion goes beyond the technical level in order to locate ethnography within the different methodological positions that compete for the intellectual legitimation of ethnography. Technical advice on how to do and write ethnography is matched with consideration of theoretical issues raised by the practice of the method, such as reflexivity, representation and **realism**. The book confronts the ethnographic critique of ethnography and rescues it from those postmodern critics who deconstruct it to the point where it dissolves into air, leaving everyone uncertain as to the value of the data collected by it. A vigorous defence is made of ethnographic data. This involves guidelines for the systematic use of ethnography, an outline of the strengths of the data and of the ways to minimize their weaknesses, and illustration of the uses to which ethnography can be put practically.

Chapter 1 addresses the question of what ethnography is, given some of the common-sense misrepresentations of it, dismissing the parodies of ethnography as 'mere journalism', and tabloid journalism at that, which suggest that it is unable to move beyond descriptive images of the exotic and the erotic. By way of clarifying what ethnography is, a distinction is drawn between 'big' and 'little' ethnography. In the former, ethnography is seen as synonymous with qualitative research, whereas, more properly, it should be understood as 'field research'. Finally, the first chapter introduces the two major critiques of ethnography, the natural science and postmodernist critiques, addresses the case for and against ethnography and outlines the possibility (and desirability) of systematic ethnography. This defence goes on to structure the rest of the volume.

In Chapter 2, we outline the philosophy of social research, locating ethnography in the context of competing methodological premises underlying it, the imperatives for social research which follow on from these methodologies and its characteristic form of data. This chapter also addresses some of the characteristic features of the data collected in field research, and considers the debate around **'thick description'**, which is the central characteristic of ethnographic data. It also addresses issues surrounding the accuracy, **reliability**, **validity** and **relevance** of ethnographic representations of reality. Chapter 3 looks at how to make ethnography systematic, and offers technical advice on doing ethnography. This covers negotiating access, the issue of informed consent, **triangulation** and multiple methods, recording the data, developing trust and managing relations in the field, gender and social biography in the field, ethics and the problem of sensitive research and dangerous fieldwork. It offers advice on sampling within ethnographic research and on how to overcome the problems of the single case study approach in order to introduce breadth and generality into ethnographic research. The chapter suggests that **research design** is as important in ethnographic research as in more quantitative styles of research. An account is also provided of the methods of data collection in field research: observation, in-depth interviews, documentary analysis and studies of natural language. The strengths and weaknesses of field research methods are outlined, and a stress is placed on triangulation and the use of multiple methods.

Chapter 4 explores issues in the analysis, interpretation and **presentation** of ethnographic data. **Inductive analysis**, insiders' accounts and what Alfred Schutz calls 'the postulate of adequacy' are suggested as ways of verifying and validating one's findings. Advice is given on how to develop a category system to analyse the data, on the role of computer-assisted qualitative data analysis and on writing up an ethnographic text. The issue of **reflexivity** is addressed and advice given on how an ethnographer can be reflexive. Various debates around ethnographic texts are addressed. Chapter 5 looks at the uses of ethnography, contrasting the styles of ethnographic research and their different uses. The chapter focuses on the role of ethnography in **theory** generation and on applied ethnographic research, where it has applications for the study of social policy and relevance to policy makers. The Conclusion summarizes the case for ethnography in the context of **postmodernism** (which denies the possibility of objective research) and globalization (which denies the relevance of the local and small-scale).

There are numerous textbooks on ethnography, and it features in many more general textbooks on research methods. The case for another textbook is twofold. It cannot be left out of a series on social research that attempts to provide an 'understanding of social research', since it is an integral part of the research enterprise and the series would be the worse for excluding ethnography. The distinctiveness of this textbook, however, comes from its being research led, and the incorporation of examples from ethnographic research into the text. In this way, it will be associated with the author's strong defence of ethnography from its postmodernist critics, and his extensive experience of doing qualitative research in difficult, sensitive and even dangerous settings. Much of the illustrative material in the text is drawn from ethnographic research in Northern Ireland and deals with sensitive and dangerous topics. As C. Wright Mills once wrote, 'it is better to have one account by a working student of how he is going about his work than a dozen "codifications of procedure" by specialists who often as not have never done much work' (Mills 1959: 195). It should be noted, however, that the extent of codification into 'how-to textbooks' is much less for ethnography than survey research, and some traditional ethnographers remain obstinately antagonistic to attempts to formalize their procedures for those engaged in teaching and learning the practice of field research. I am not one.

Suggested further reading

As a general introduction to issues of method and methodology read:

Bryman, A. (1988) *Quantity and Quality in Social Research*, London: Allen and Unwin.
Hughes, J. (1990) *The Philosophy of Social Research*, 2nd edn. Harlow: Longman.
Seale, C. (1999) *The Quality of Qualitative Research*. London: Sage.

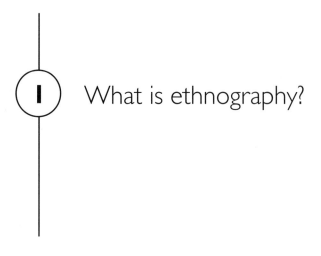

What is ethnography?

Introduction

This chapter answers the question of what ethnography is, and the corollary of what it is not. It confronts the common-sense misrepresentations of ethnography, defending it against the allegation that it is journalism in another guise. By way of clarifying what ethnography is, a contrast is drawn between two ways of defining ethnography, referred to here as 'big' and 'little' ethnography. The former equates it with qualitative research as a whole; the latter restricts its meaning to 'field research'. A definition of 'little' ethnography – 'ethnography-as-fieldwork' – is suggested.

> Ethnography is the study of people in naturally occurring settings or 'fields' by means of methods which capture their social meanings and ordinary activities, involving the researcher participating directly in the setting, if not also the activities, in order to collect data in a systematic manner but without meaning being imposed on them externally.

Two forms of criticism of ethnography are then outlined, the natural science and the postmodern forms, the first of which abuses it or sees it merely as an adjunct to the serious stuff of quantitative research, while the latter tries to deconstruct it to the point where it almost dissolves. This chapter claims that it is desirable and still possible to undertake systematic ethnography, a claim that the following chapters support and defend. First, it is necessary to note briefly from where ethnography came historically, since a legacy of its past is the pejorative common-sense stereotype that it deals with the foreign, strange and exotic.

The history of ethnography

Ethnography is not one particular method of data collection but a style of research that is distinguished by its objectives, which are to understand the social **meanings** and activities of people in a given 'field' or setting, and its approach, which involves close association with, and often participation in, this setting. It is premised on the view that the central aim of the social sciences is to understand people's actions and their experiences of the world, and the ways in which their motivated actions arise from and reflect back on these experiences. Once this is the central aim, knowledge of the social world is acquired from intimate familiarity with it, and ethnography is central as a method because it involves this intimate familiarity with day-to-day practice and the meanings of social action. To access social meanings, observe behaviour and work closely with informants and perhaps participate in the field with them, several methods of data collection tend to be used in ethnography, such as in-depth interviewing, participant observation, personal documents and discourse analyses of natural language. As such, ethnography has a distinguished career in the social sciences. There have been 'travellers tales' for centuries, going back even to antiquity, which count as a form of ethnographic research in that they purported to represent some aspect of social reality (in this case, a country, group or culture) on the basis of close acquaintance with and observation of it, although often they reflected the cultural and political prejudices of their own society (see Box 1.1).

Ethnography begins properly only with the twentieth century and two entirely independent intellectual developments, one British, the other North American. The first was the emergence of the classical tradition of social anthropology in Britain, with people like Malinowski, Boas, Radcliffe-Brown and Evans-Pritchard. That most were British or worked in Britain (with the obvious exception of Boas) can be explained because of the close association between social anthropology and British colonialism. And while social anthropology might no longer be the handmaiden of colonialism, its origins were tied to the needs of the British Empire to understand the cultures and groups it was seeking to rule once the period of colonial conquest was completed and assimilation in the 'British family of nations' was possible. This explains why it emerged at the beginning of the twentieth century rather than in the heyday of colonial conquest in the nineteenth century. These anthropologists pioneered an approach that involved close acquaintance with pre-industrial groups and cultures by close immersion and observation.

The second development was the work of the Chicago School in sociology,

Box 1.1

Giraldus Cambrensis, *The Topography of Ireland, Part III,* 'The Inhabitants of the Country'.

> For given only to leisure and devoted only to laziness, they think that the greatest pleasure is not to work . . . This people is, then, a barbarous people, literally barbarous. Judged according to modern ideas, they are uncultivated . . . All their habits are the habits of barbarians . . . This is a filthy people, wallowing in vice. Of all peoples, it is the least instructed in the rudiments of the Faith . . . Moreover, I have never seen among any other people, so many blind at birth, so many lame, so many maimed in body and so many suffering from some natural defect. And it is not surprising if nature sometimes produces such beings contrary to her ordinary laws when dealing with a people that is adulterous, incestuous, unlawfully conceived and born outside the law and shamefully abusing nature. It seems a just punishment from God.

Cambrensis (1147–1223) was a Welshman at the English Court of Henry II when he first went to Ireland in 1183. It was Henry who first conquered Ireland. Cambrensis finishes his *Topography* with a eulogy to Henry and the 'manner in which the Irish world was added to the titles and triumphs' of England. Cambrensis visited Ireland twice, and then only travelled around Cork and Waterford.

which used observational techniques to explore groups on the margins of urban industrial society in the United States in the 1920s and 1930s. With the occasional exception, the focus was on the dispossessed, the marginal and the strange, a focus Erving Goffman later came to characterize as an attempt to address 'the standpoint of the hip outsider rather than the dull insider'. They bequeathed sociology with important studies of numerous deviant sub-groups, like prostitutes, drug dealers, street gangs, various unusual urban occupations, such as taxi dance hostesses, jack rollers, janitors and the hobo, and relatively unknown social worlds, like those of flop houses and burlesque halls, Polish immigrants, Jewish ghetto culture and the culture of the slum (as well as that of the wealthy Californian Gold Coast elite). In every case, investigators actively participated in the setting or the way of life under study, being mindful that, as Robert Park, the foremost of the Chicagoans, used to put it to his undergraduates, for 'real research' first-hand observation was necessary (see Box 1.2).

While social anthropology called this approach 'ethnography', sociologists tended to call it participant observation or field research, but it meant much

Box 1.2

Robert Park, speaking to undergraduate students at the University of Chicago in the 1920s.

You have been told to go grubbing in the library thereby accumulating a mass of notes and a liberal coating of grime. You have been told to choose problems wherever you can find musty stacks of routine records. This is called 'getting your hands dirty in real research'. Those who counsel you thus are wise and honourable men. But one thing more is needful: first hand observation. Go sit in the lounges of the luxury hotels and on the doorsteps of the flop-houses; sit on the Gold Coast settees and in the slum shakedowns; sit in the orchestra hall and in the Star and Garter Burlesque. In short, gentlemen, go get the seat of your pants dirty in real research.

the same thing in the way research was conducted. There are some differences between these two intellectual pillars (see Berg 1998: 120), but many similarities. The task of each was, in Wolcott's (1973) phrase, 'cultural description', and while social anthropology sought to explore pre-industrial groups and cultures, requiring ethnographers to adopt an initial research role as an outsider, the groups studied by the Chicagoans were only slightly less unfamiliar and strange to middle-class, Middle Western Americans, and their research role as an 'insider' was not guaranteed. Since then, of course, ethnography has moved into other social sciences, notably education, health studies and social work, and the differences between sociological and social anthropological uses of ethnography have widened, despite the fact that social anthropology now parallels sociology in a focus on urban and industrialized settings. But this heritage has left one particular legacy for ethnography that dogs it to this day: the common-sense notion that it offers mere description of things foreign, exotic and peculiar. Within sociology, this just adds to the distortions about the discipline within common-sense knowledge.

Ethnography, sociology and common sense

Sociology is unique among academic disciplines, including other social sciences, in having a subject matter of interest to most ordinary people. The social institutions that interest sociology, like the family, community, the education system, the class structure, the state, the organization of work, law and order, religion and many others, form the fabric of the lives of ordinary people, and lay members of society spend considerable time thinking and talking about these institutions. This is a tremendous advantage, for sociology begins with a subject matter that is intrinsically interesting to many people; ordinary people in the street want to know about the things sociology knows about.

The disadvantage is that sociology sometimes competes with ordinary common-sense views of the same things. People develop lay knowledge by which they understand the world, make judgements and decisions, and guide their conduct and behaviour. This lay knowledge is called 'common sense', and the very term describes its two enduring qualities: lay people believe it to be shared and intersubjective (it is 'common') and true (it makes 'sense'). Because social institutions form the fabric of the lives of ordinary people, a lay knowledge is inevitably developed about them, and people are only too keen to share views on them. People are confident that they know why the family is declining, or why crime or unemployment has risen, or what is wrong with the church, morality, the police or whatever. In this respect, the natural sciences have it relatively easy. When astronomers, for example, are producing new theories to explain the orbits of the moons of Jupiter or the existence of super novas, they do not have to argue with taxi drivers or hairstylists, who feel confident to tell astronomers that super novas are super novas because their mothers went out to work and neglected them. Or at least, insofar as ordinary unqualified people try to argue with astronomers, not many people take them seriously. But every lay member of society has a common-sense pet theory about why some people rather than others commit crime, or what causes unemployment, divorce and so on, or what the link is between race and employment, or what lies behind the years of civil unrest in Northern Ireland. However, people's common-sense knowledge of the world is derived from the small part of the world they know about and inhabit, so that explanations are partial and generalized from personal experience. Moreover, lay people often fix upon explanations derived from common-sense knowledge which best suit their personal beliefs and views, and never work at their explanations, or continually try to improve them. This means that sociology's explanations have to confront habitual common-sense beliefs about phenomena that are often wrong and resistant to change (see Box 1.3).

Sociology is not able, therefore, to demarcate a subject matter that is 'professional', in the sense that it does not have a subject matter about which ordinary people feel ignorant and uninformed, which they take little interest in or rarely discuss. This is not the case for the natural sciences and most other social sciences, which are accorded, superficially, a competence and professionalism because their subject matter is beyond the realm of understanding and interest of lay people. It follows from this that critics of sociology can easily parody it as common sense – and many do. For these critics, sociology can win neither way. If it comes up with explanations that seem to

---

Box 1.3

Interview with a member of Ian Paisley's Free Presbyterian Church, for research published in J. D. Brewer, *Anti-Catholicism in Northern Ireland 1600–1998* (London: Macmillan, 1998), with G. Higgins.

I feel churches today are more interested in themselves than preaching the gospel, and I feel ecumenism [cooperation between and integration of the denominations] is the whole purpose of some of the churches. The ecumenical movement is set on a one-world church, and under the ecumenical movement there'd be no other leader than the Pope. The Roman Catholic Church is a political organisation. The Vatican is a political state. I've studied the thing. While I've nothing against Roman Catholics, the system [of Roman Catholicism] sets out the Pope as Christ on earth. That's why the country's in the state it's in. You've ecumenism, all these ecumenical services where it doesn't matter what you believe – anything goes. I mean law and order has broken down in the home, in the schools, it's broken down everywhere because man has tried to go his own way and forgotten the teachings of God.

---

confirm common-sense knowledge, critics retort that this was known all along without the need for sociologists to tell us, and findings which contradict or dispute common-sense knowledge are dismissed as counterintuitive and simply not true. As Giddens (1996a: 4) wrote in his defence of sociology, it is the fate of sociology to be seen as less original and less central that it actually is, and much sociological research and many concepts and theories are so much a part of people's everyday repertoire as to appear as 'just common sense' (see also Bauman 1990: 8–10, for the similarities and differences between sociology and common sense).

Ethnographers, however, find themselves in a double bind. Sociological explanations of all kinds confront considerable resistance, but the common-sense parody of qualitative research and the kind of data it collects gives additional problems. Many proponents of the natural science model of social research, as well as lay people and policy-makers, parody qualitative data as 'mere journalism', providing highly descriptive and non-analytical accounts of people droning on about this or that topic, with so-and-so saying this followed by so-and-so saying that. And not only are we 'mere journalists', we are tabloid journalists at that, providing interesting details of the exotically unusual, the peculiar, odd and strange, copy that titillates but does not inform. Thus, ethnographers are seen as simply hanging loose on street corners or in bars, going with the flow, waiting for tittle tattle, the exotic and the erotic, like a hack from the tabloids, doing our ethnography unrigorously and unsystematically. Qualitative data are interesting, they say, but mere anecdote, hearsay and essentially unproven. It is evidence that reflects the artful, deceitful skill of the investigative journalist or documentary maker, not the serious researcher; real research requires numerate, statistical data (see Box 1.4).

Journalism shares some similarities with qualitative research writing (Seale 1999: 15), but there are important differences based on the researcher's commitment to greater depth of thought, more sustained periods spent on investigation and a more rigorously self-critical approach. And while some extreme postmodern ethnographers deconstruct their work to claim it has no difference from fiction or journalism, post postmodern ethnography takes us beyond this scepticism. This parody, however, does not lie solely in prejudice against humanistic models of social research, for some ethnographers do very poor qualitative research. Qualitative research is very easy to do, but it is very hard to do well. There is no defence for poor qualitative research, yet the notion that qualitative

---

Box 1.4

Professor Brice Dickson, discussant on Brewer, Lockhart and Rodgers, 'An ethnography of crime in Belfast', a paper presented to the Statistical and Social Enquiry Society of Ireland, and published in *Journal of the Statistical and Social Enquiry Society of Ireland*, vol. 27, part 3, 1995–6. Professor Dickson's response (pp. 199–201) opened:

> The authors of the paper we have just heard have done us all a service in providing such an original and insightful contribution to the debate concerning urban crime in Northern Ireland. I do, however, retain some reservations about the ethnographic method. Although it makes for interesting reading, it does not present a representative picture in the way that a more statistically-based project would do. As a lawyer, I have some difficulty accepting the evidence – which is anecdotal and hearsay – as satisfying the burden of proof. It seems to me that there is a tendency on the part of ethnographers to accentuate the unusual at the expense of the mundane. I am reminded of the kind of documentary journalism which makes excellent television by providing good soundbites and startling images but which leaves the viewer not quite sure what is fact and what is fiction. The ethnographic method certainly provides an alternative perspective but it is a supplementary one.

research cannot be systematic is years out of date. As Seale (1999: 17) argues in the title of his recent book, quality in qualitative research is possible. Some time ago, I undertook an ethnographic study of the Royal Ulster Constabulary (RUC) (Brewer 1991a) and one of the few criticisms made – at least in writing – was that some people doubted the capacity of qualitative data to support the comments made, although dislike of the findings led to some personal abuse (see Box 1.5). I naturally defended ethnographic data and later published a set of guidelines, by means of which ethnographers can do systematic qualitative research and display this fact when writing up the results, which have since become widely known and used (Brewer 1994). These guidelines, discussed in later chapters, paralleled similar discussions by many authors, before and since, which have sought to show how rigorous and systematic qualitative sociology can be (for example, Hammersley 1989, 1990, 1992; Silverman 1989; Stanley 1990b). Readers of the methodological literature on qualitative research have thus been aware for many years that common-sense parodies are increasingly difficult to support by reasoned argument. The prejudice against qualitative data persists only because the parodies are common-sensical and thus resistant to change.

'Big' and 'little' ethnography

In common-sense knowledge, ethnography is understood as descriptively 'telling it like it is from the inside'. More reasoned judgements can be offered. These are two sorts of definitions. One uses 'ethnography' as a synonym for qualitative research as a whole, and virtually describes any approach as ethnographic that avoids surveys as the means of data collection. This can

---

Box 1.5

Ed Moloney, journalist on *The Sunday Tribune*, reviewing *Inside the RUC* for *The Sunday Tribune* 24 February 1991.

> Sociologists have a unique gift to make any subject boring – the mind-boggling jargon, the cloaking of the obvious in pseudo-science. John Brewer's book is not a book for the public to read. They'll be lucky to stay awake after the first chapter. John Brewer's are contentious conclusions. The RUC will be pleased with them, nationalists sceptical. Others might have been happier had the conclusions been tested by wider research. Policing is also about the sort of things empirical research cannot always discover.

be called 'big' ethnography or 'ethnography-understood-as-the-qualitative-method', and is represented well by Wolcott's (1973) view that ethnography is really a perspective on research rather than a way of doing it. Others define ethnography to mean the same as 'field research' or 'fieldwork', and this can be called 'little' ethnography or 'ethnography-understood-as-fieldwork'. In this definition, ethnography becomes one particular way of doing qualitative research. This 'way of doing things' is best summarized by Burgess (1982: 15):

> Field research involves the study of real-life situations. Field researchers therefore observe people in the settings in which they live, and participate in their day to day activities. The methods that can be used in these studies are unstructured, flexible and open-ended.

However, even in this case, ethnography involves both method and methodology, in that it is more than just a way of collecting data. 'Little' ethnography is thus still not all that small. This is perhaps best illustrated by the definition of ethnography adopted in this volume (see p. 10). Defined in this way, 'little' ethnography still involves judgements about: the object of the research, which is to study people in naturally occurring settings; the researcher's role in that setting, which is to understand and explain what people are doing in that setting by means of participating directly in it; and the data to be collected, which must be naturally occurring and captured in such a way that meaning is not imposed on them from outside. These issues of technique derive from a set of theoretical and philosophical premises – a methodology – so that 'ethnography-understood-as-fieldwork' still describes more than just a set of procedural rules for collecting data (that is, ethnography is more than a method of data collection). This is why it is unsound to equate ethnography with one particular technique of data collection, say participant observation, although this may be one of the principal methods of data collection in ethnography. 'Little' ethnography uses several methods that access social meanings, observe activities and involve close association with, or participation in, a setting or 'field'.

The accounts of ethnography proffered by Hammersley and Atkinson, who along with Burgess comprise Britain's foremost authors on the topic, capture its quality as both method and methodology (see Hammersley and Atkinson 1983; Atkinson and Hammersley 1998; see also their separate work: Hammersley 1989, 1990, 1992; Atkinson 1990, 1992; Burgess 1982, 1984). In a succinct definition, Hammersley (1990: 1–2) describes what is here called 'ethnography-understood-as-fieldwork' or 'little' ethnography in embracing terms, making references to data collection techniques as well as broader methodological issues. According to Hammersley, ethnography is research with the following features:

- people's behaviour is studied in everyday contexts rather than under unnatural or experimental circumstances created by the researcher;

- data are collected by various techniques but primarily by means of observation;
- data collection is flexible and unstructured to avoid pre-fixed arrangements that impose categories on what people say and do;
- the focus is normally on a single setting or group and is small-scale;
- the analysis of the data involves attribution of the meanings of the human actions described and explained (see also Atkinson and Hammersley 1998: 110–11).

Hereafter, it will be this form of ethnography that will be referred to throughout this volume as 'ethnography', rather than 'ethnography-understood-as-the-qualitative-method'.

Critiques of ethnography

Leaving aside common-sense parodies, there are two major critiques of ethnography within the social sciences, emanating from almost opposite sources. The natural science critique comes from advocates of the natural science model of social research, and accuses ethnography of falling below the standards of science, which form the proper measure for the social sciences. The postmodern critique comes essentially from within the humanistic model of social research, as ethnographers themselves come to reflect critically on their practice under the impulse, *inter alia*, of postmodernist theories. In its extreme form this critique deconstructs ethnography to its constituent processes, and accuses ethnography of melting into air and dissolving into nothingness, or, to use an older analogy, of being like Hans Christian Andersen's emperor in having no clothes (an analogy used in Brewer 1994). However, less extreme versions of postmodern critique exist, which retain some form of realism. Each critique is worth addressing.

The natural science critique

Mainstream social science has been governed by what Giddens (1996b: 65–8) calls the 'orthodox consensus', which is that the social sciences should be modelled on the natural sciences (a position known as '**positivism**' but which Giddens, rather confusingly, calls '**naturalism**', a term normally reserved for the very opposite position). Three beliefs follow from this (see also Giddens 1974: 3–4; Platt 1981: 73–4): the social sciences address problems similar to those of the natural sciences; they should search for social causation when explaining human activity and aspire to deductive explanations; they should deal with systems and wholes. As Giddens (1996b: 68) is himself aware, this is a consensus no more. Yet the last home of the orthodox consensus is methodology textbooks in the social sciences (Box 1.6). Here a conception of natural science is advanced that

---

Box 1.6

Louise Kidder, *Selltiz, Wrightsman and Cook's Research Methods in Social Relations*, 4th edition (New York, Holt-Saunders, 1981), p. 13.

> Practising science is one of the many ways of exploring social worlds. Practising art and religion are other ways. Why learn research methods and why practice science? One reason is to be able to predict correctly how people and nations will behave, to foresee the future. Another reason is to understand how the social world works by discovering the causal connection. We understand how something works when we can both predict what will happen and explain why. A third reason is to control events and produce intended effects.

---

philosophers of science would not recognize any longer (this notion of science is, according to Platt (1981), now more of a 'social construction'). However, this is our model of 'scientific method' in the social sciences according to these textbooks, and ethnography falls short of its standards.

Four salient features of ethnography are worth re-emphasizing to show the offence they offer to natural science models of social research. Ethnography focuses on people's ordinary activities in naturally occurring settings, uses unstructured and flexible methods of data collection, requires the researcher to be actively involved in the field or with the people under study and explores the meanings which this human activity has for the people themselves and the wider society. Couched in these terms it breaches several principles held dear by the natural sciences. Some principles have to do with the role of the researcher. The natural science model of research does not permit the researcher to become a variable in the experiment, yet ethnographers are not detached from the research but, depending on the degree of involvement in the setting, are themselves part of the study or by their obtrusive presence come to influence the field. If participant observation is used in data collection, ethnography can involve introspection, or what Adler and Adler (1998: 97–8) call auto-observation, whereby the researcher's own experiences and attitude changes while sharing the field has become part of the data, something criticized since Francis Bacon as being unscientific. Other principles concern the methods of data collection. Methods that are unstructured, flexible and open-ended can appear to involve unsystematic data collection, in which the absence of structure prevents an assessment of the data because differences that emerge in the data can be attributed to variations in the way they were collected. The rationale behind the highly structured methods of the natural sciences is to minimize extraneous variations in order to isolate 'real' differences in the data. This is why procedural rules within natural science models of social research are designed to eliminate the effects of both the researcher and the tool used to collect the data.

Ethnography also breaches dearly held principles in science concerning the nature of data. The natural science model of social research seeks to describe and measure social phenomena, but both description and measurement are achieved by assigning numbers to the phenomena. In short, it deals with quantity and collects numerate data. Ethnography also describes and measures, but it does so by means of extracts of natural language (long quotations from interviews, extracts from field notes, snippets from personal documents) and deals with quality and meaning (see Bryman 1988; Dey 1993: 10–14). As Dey (1993: 12) indicates, meanings may seem shifty, unreliable, elusive and ethereal. Such data can appear as 'too subjective' and contrast unfavourably with numerate data, which appear to be more objective.

For all these reasons ethnography is criticized by proponents of natural science models of social research. If it is accorded a role in research at all, it is as a sensitizing tool to collect preliminary data at the pilot stage, before the topic is pursued properly by means of quantitative research. The response to the natural science critique has been threefold: defending the natural science model, rejecting it and, finally, transcending it. This gives us what we might call, respectively, 'scientific' or 'positivist ethnography', 'humanistic ethnography' and 'postmodern reflexive ethnography'. This is a distinction returned to throughout this volume, but the salient differences can be outlined here.

In order to meet some of the standards of the natural sciences, some ethnographers have refined and improved their procedural rules, claiming their practice was scientific (Denzin and Lincoln (1998: 13–22) distinguish between positivist, post-positivist and modernist phases of the 'scientific' mode of ethnography). Early textbooks on ethnography reflected this phase, such as Becker (1970), Lofland (1971), Bogden and Taylor (1975) and Lofland and Lofland (1984). Rigour made these ethnographers like scientists in the accuracy with which they wanted to capture reality, and like scientists they believed in a fixed reality, which rigorous method could uncover, describe and explain. This is not entirely extinct. Thus, in a recent textbook, Fetterman (1998: 2) declares that ethnographers are both storytellers and scientists, in that if their practice is systematic, the more accurate is the account given and thus the better the science. There is still a commitment in this style of ethnography to in-depth studies of people in natural social settings or fields, and a search for meaning, but the practice of ethnography was systematized and made rigorous and formal. Not only could ethnography ape the natural science model, it was part of it, for these ethnographers recognized its adjunct role. It was accepted that ethnography could be used as a preliminary and pilot phase in quantitative studies. It was also suggested that ethnographers could give causal accounts, use structured methods of data collection in addition to the usual repertoire and present some data in a numerate and statistical form.

Other ethnographers responded to the natural science model of social research by asserting aggressively the primacy of alternative models which did not seek to appropriate the methods and approach of the natural sciences, advocating instead what Hughes (1990) calls the humanistic model of social research, much as Goffman (1961) did in his ethnography of a hospital (see Box 1.7). While the natural science model of research saw human beings as acted upon by external social forces, so that behaviour was the outcome of social causation, the humanistic model reasserts the idea of people as active, creative, insurgent and knowledgeable. These capacities are summarized in the notion that people are 'meaning endowing'; they have the capacity to endow meaning to their world. These meanings are always bounded by the structural and institutional location of the person, but people possess a 'practical consciousness' – that is, a body of knowledge that enables them to know social life from the inside – and they possess the discursive capacity to articulate this understanding. 'Interpretative sociologies', like Goffman's dramaturgical approach, Schutz's social phenomenology or Garfinkel's ethnomethodology, have shown the complicated knowledge necessary for ordinary people routinely to manage and accomplish social behaviour, and 'humanistic ethnography' is a style of ethnography that seeks to explore these 'reality construction' abilities. It is antithetical to science and valorizes the social meanings which ethnography attempts to disclose and reveal; indeed, 'ethnography-understood-as-fieldwork' is often portrayed by these adherents as the most reliable means to disclose these meanings. Stress is laid on the advantages of research into naturally occurring behaviour by means of direct first-hand contact over artificially created

---

Box 1.7

Erving Goffman, *Asylums* (London: Penguin, 1968 [1961]), pp. 7–9.

My immediate object in doing fieldwork was to try to learn about the social world of the hospital inmate, as this world is subjectively experienced by him . . . It was then, and still is, my belief that any group of persons – prisoners, primitives, pilots or patients – develop a life of their own that becomes meaningful, reasonable and normal once you get close to it, and that a good way to learn about any of these worlds is to submit oneself in the company of the members to the daily round of petty contingencies to which they are subject. Desiring to obtain ethnographic detail, I did not gather statistical evidence.

experiments, and on the necessity to reflect in research the meaning-endowing capacities of human beings, who are not inanimate but can understand, interpret and construct their social world. 'Humanistic ethnography' thus sees itself as producing a very privileged access to social reality and is often associated with the forceful assertion that social reality is constituted by people's interpretative practices, claims common in ethnomethodology, phenomenology and what Denzin (1989) calls 'interpretative interactionism'. In this view, ethnographic research must disclose people's reality-constituting interpretative practices rather than concerning itself with the interests of natural science models of social research. Advocates of this position include classic statements of ethnography like Blumer (1969) and Filstead (1970), and more recent accounts by Hughes (1990) and Holstein and Gubrium (1998).

The third response is to try to transcend the old dichotomy between natural science and humanistic models of social research, and the associated antinomies between quantity and quality, numbers and meaning. This transcendence is achieved by drawing on themes within postmodernism. 'Numbers' and 'meaning' are interrelated at all levels (Dey 1993: 17–28), often requiring each other or being implicit in each other. Elementary forms of enumeration (such as counting) depend on the meanings of the unit reckoned together, and social meanings are often better understood when articulated in relation to the number of observations referred to or the number of the experiences they describe (on the use of various forms of counting in qualitative research see Bryman 1988: 131–51; Seale 1999: 119–39). But 'postmodern reflexive ethnography' goes further than stating that the two poles are compatible; it deconstructs the terms of the debate to say a plague on both houses. This involves a rejection of both natural science models of social research and the claims by some humanistic ethnographers that it has 'special' and 'privileged' access to insider accounts of people's world-views, a view described by other ethnographers as 'naive realism' (Hammersley 1990, 1992). In this view, ethnography should be rigorous and systematic, but science is not held up as the model, and while ethnography is still seen as suited to satisfying the interpretative and humanistic injunction to study people in natural settings, its knowledge is not privileged and unproblematic. Drawing on social studies of science, these ethnographers point to the fact that the natural science model of social research fails to meet its own standards. As Dey (1993: 15) argues, all data, regardless of method, are 'produced' by researchers, who are not distant or detached, since they make various choices about research design, location and approach which help to 'create' the data they end up collecting. Thus, it is claimed, all research is subjective, in that it is personal and cultural, including science (Hammersley 1990: 9). These ethnographers question the ability of any method to represent 'reality' accurately on three grounds: there is no one fixed 'reality' in the postmodern understanding of nature to capture 'accurately'; all methods are cultural and personal constructs, collecting partial and selective knowledge; and since all knowledge is selective, research can offer only a socially constructed account of the world. These ethnographers appropriately turn the lens on themselves and criticize the claim that ethnography is a privileged method. This postmodern ethnographic critique of ethnography provides a serious challenge to ethnography.

The postmodern critique of ethnography

Postmodernism began as a body of theory associated with Lyotard and Baudrillard and some writings from post-structuralists like Foucault. However, the term was first used by Lyotard in 1979 to describe a social condition of advanced capitalist society rather than a set of theoretical ideas (for one of the best sociological treatments of postmodernism, see Harvey 1989). This social condition is characterized by the realization that two great Enlightenment ideas (called 'meta-narratives') have been myths and illusions. The idea of progress and liberation is a myth, as witnessed by twentieth-century examples of genocide, and so is the idea that knowledge can be objective and truthful. In this latter respect, scientific knowledge is relative (as argued much earlier by Feyerabend and Kuhn), so there are no guarantees as to the worth of the activities of scientists or the truthfulness of their statements. Science is simply a 'language game'. The deconstruction of both ideas into myths implies the disintegration of all the symbols of modern capitalist society, and specifically in relation to truth claims, postmodernism denies the existence of all universal truth statements, which are replaced by variety, contingency and ambivalence, and plurality in culture, tradition, ideology and knowledge. Everything solid melts into air, every structure dissolves and every truth statement is contingent and relative; we are left merely with rhetoric, discourse and language games about knowledge and truth. 'Truth' can be deconstructed to talk about truth, or 'truth claims', which are themselves reducible to language and are merely games. The effects of this approach are felt everywhere by everything, including ethnography.

This 'moment' in the history of ethnography is referred to as the 'double crisis' (Denzin and Lincoln 1998: 21–2). Under the impulse of postmodernism, some ethnographers challenge the claim that ethnography can produce universally valid knowledge by accurately capturing or representing the nature of the social world (in anthropology see Clifford and Marcus 1986; Clifford 1988; in sociology see Hammersley and Atkinson 1983; van Maanen 1988; Atkinson 1990; Hammersley 1990, 1992; Denzin 1997; Atkinson and Hammersley 1998; Richardson 1998). All accounts are constructions and the whole issue of which account more accurately represents social reality is meaningless (see Denzin 1992; Richardson 1992). This is called the crisis of representation. Inasmuch as ethnographic descriptions are partial, selective, even autobiographical in that they are tied to the particular ethnographer and the contingencies under which the data were collected, the traditional criteria for evaluating ethnography become problematic, as terms like 'validity', 'reliability' and 'generalizability' are deconstructed. This is called the crisis of legitimation.

As we shall see in Chapter 2, these crises have deep effects on ethnography. The crisis of representation, for example, has implications for how we should understand ethnographic accounts: they do not neutrally or impartially represent the social world (but, in this view, nor does anything else). There are implications for the claims ethnographers are able to make about their account, which is no longer a privileged description of the social world from the inside (what Geertz once called a 'thick description' in order to emphasize its richness and depth). And there are implications for the written text, which attempts to represent in writing the reality of the 'field', for ethnographers should no longer make foolish authority claims in order to validate the account as an accurate representation of reality but be 'reflexive', in which they reflect on the contingencies which bore upon and helped to 'create' the data as a partial account. Ethnographers should produce 'tales of the field' (van Maanen 1988) rather than attempt spurious realist accounts of some setting. However, as we shall see in the next chapter, some postmodern ethnographers have responded to this challenge and developed a kind of post postmodern ethnography, which takes on board these criticisms but responds in ways that reassert some of the certainties and realism of earlier types of ethnography.

Conclusion

The postmodern critique presents four chief problems for ethnography, attacking its representation of the field, the value it places on 'thick description', the reliability and validity of its data and the construction of the ethnographic text. These criticisms are addressed in later chapters of the volume as we defend ethnography and make a case for its continued use. It is sufficient here to end with a general few remarks on the postmodern critique of ethnography and the defence against it.

'Realist' ethnographies survive among ethnographers who have not gone down the postmodern path and hold steadfastly to the validity of humanistic and interpretative approaches to studying people in natural settings. Realist ethnographies also continue among those ethnographers who subscribe to 'critical realism' as a methodological base, which asserts the objectivity and reality of some material structures, evidence on which it is possible accurately to uncover ethnographically (as well as by other means). Good examples of critical realist ethnography are Willis's (1977) work on class reproduction, which addresses ethnographically the objectivity of the class system and how it imposes itself on school children, and Porter's (1995) ethnography of the nursing profession, which confronts the reality of power relations in hospitals and objective structures like sectarianism and racism on critical realist ethnographies (see Porter 1993; Davies 1999).

Other ethnographers have sought to rescue ethnography from the excesses of postmodernism by incorporating some of its criticisms in order to defend ethnography and meet the challenge of postmodernism (Silverman 1989; Stanley 1990b; Brewer 1994; Seale 1999). This is not the extreme form of postmodern ethnography espoused by someone like Denzin (see Denzin 1988, 1992, 1994, 1997), where the method becomes a form of fiction or journalism, whose work represented for one critic 'a somewhat elaborate review recording his personal responses' (Seale 1999: 4). The attempt to reconcile postmodern ideas with the practice of good ethnography is clear in Hammersley's own work (1990, 1992), where he criticizes the failings of 'naive realism' only in order to advocate a more robust form of ethnographic representation which he calls 'subtle realism', and his use of 'relevance' as an alternative way of assessing ethnographic data under the attack on their validity and reliability. These responses, which defend ethnography from its critics, constitute a kind of post postmodern ethnography and are discussed in the chapters that follow.

Suggested further reading

The following are good general textbooks on ethnography:

Burgess, R. (1984) *In the Field*. London: Routledge.
Davies, C. A. (1999) *Reflexive Ethnography*. London: Routledge.
Fetterman, D. (1998) *Ethnography*, 2nd edn. London: Sage.
Hammersley, M. and Atkinson, P. (1983) *Ethnography: Principles in Practice*. London: Tavistock.

Ethnography as method and methodology

Introduction

As argued in Chapter 1, methods are presented in research textbooks as procedural rules for obtaining reliable and objective knowledge. One kind of method concerns procedural rules for collecting data, of which ethnography is an example. Ethnography tends to rely on a number of particular data collection techniques, such as naturalistic observation, documentary analysis and in-depth interviews. While these methods are used on their own as well, what marks their ethnographic application is that they are used to study a people in a naturally occurring setting or 'field', in which the researcher participates directly, and in which there is an intent to explore the meanings of this setting and its behaviour and activities from the inside. This is what 'ethnography-understood-as-fieldwork' means. However, the procedural rules that lay down how this is properly done, and which thereby certify the knowledge as reliable and objective, obtain their legitimacy and authority as procedural rules because the community of scholars and researchers endorses them. According to John Hughes's (1990) arguments in developing what he calls the philosophy of social research, this endorsement itself derives from the fact that the procedural rules 'fit' with and reflect a broader theoretical and philosophical framework for which researchers and scholars have a preference. This framework is called methodology, and, in short, methods-as-procedural-rules are given the authority to certify knowledge as reliable and objective because they are legitimated by a methodological stance. Method and methodology are thus inextricably linked.

This chapter explores the different methodological frameworks in which ethnography is located and which go towards explaining the particular procedural rules that are endorsed as the 'way to do' ethnography properly. The procedural rules themselves are outlined in greater detail in Chapter 3. Here, we outline the philosophy of social research, describing the methodological premises underlying 'little' ethnography, the imperatives for social research which follow on from this methodology, the typical techniques of data collection used and the characteristic form of data. Differences in methodological preferences highlight the divisions between ethnographers about theory and practice, and this leads on to a debate about the current contested terrain among ethnographers. Two debates are addressed: that around 'thick description', which was once seen as the central characteristic of ethnographic data; and that around the accuracy, reliability, validity and relevance of ethnographic representations of reality.

The philosophy of social research

The philosophy of social research can be defined as the study of the theories of knowledge which validate particular research methods. Conventionally, social research methods courses offer examination of the data collection techniques by which research is undertaken. That is, they offer practical training in how to do research. However, developments in social theory and philosophy have made us realize that these techniques or procedural rules exist within a broader philosophical and theoretical framework, which can be called a 'methodology'. This was presented in the Introduction, and can be reproduced again:

methodology → procedural rules = methods → knowledge

These methodological positions involve researchers in commitments whether or not they are aware of it, for they entail assumptions about the nature of society (called 'ontological' assumptions) and assumptions about the nature of knowledge (called 'epistemological' assumptions). These methodological positions can also entail different sorts of research practices, since they predispose the use of different data collection techniques. They thus end up producing quite different kinds of data. The study of this broader methodological context to research methods has been called the philosophy of social research (Hughes 1990; see also Ackroyd and Hughes 1981).

The most contentious claim in this argument is not that research methods get their authority and legitimacy from particular theories of knowledge, but that researchers choose the data collection techniques to employ in any piece of research because of a prior commitment to this methodological position rather than out of practical expediency. It is possible to envisage that this preference can be scientifically based – in that researchers believe one methodology and the set of methods and techniques to be more scientific than another – or it can be subjective and personal. The researcher may lack the competence to understand and apply one or other technique: since we cannot count or are frightened by computers, or do not like talking to people, we avoid those methods that involve our shortcomings. But whatever the reason, we have biases. According to Hughes:

- the data collection methods used to make the social world amenable are not neutral tools that somehow exist within a vacuum, but operate within a given methodological position;
- since methodologies lay down the procedural rules by which reliable and objective knowledge is said to be obtained, the choice of data collection technique is not dictated by the problem at hand, but largely by prior preferences in the researcher for a given methodological position with which those techniques or rules are associated;
- the differences in the kinds of data produced have to be located in methodological choices by the researcher rather than decisions about the problem at hand;
- at a technical level it may be desirable, even necessary, to combine multiple methods, but at an ontological and epistemological level this can result in marrying incompatible methodological positions;
- in a state where there are competing methodological positions, validating different procedural rules for collecting data, there will be no consensus about the value or merit of particular research methods and the use of particular methods can become a source of contention.

In his explication of the philosophy of social research, John Hughes outlined two models of social research which were premised on two different methodological positions, the natural science model based on positivism and the humanistic model based on naturalism. These were counterposed as mutually exclusive (indeed, as if they were in a 'paradigm war') and set up almost as ideal types. His argument can be made more concrete by describing the two models and their respective methodological justifications in his ideal type terms, although most attention here is naturally devoted to the humanistic model. Table 2.1 summarizes the differences between the two.

The natural science model of social research

The natural science model of social research is premised on positivism. The essential attributes of this methodological position are summed up in the

Table 2.1 The two models of social research

	Natural science	*Humanistic*
Methodology	Positivism	Naturalism
Methods	Questionnaires, surveys, experiments	In-depth interviews, ethnography, personal documents
Style of research	Quantitative	Qualitative
Type of data	Numerate, 'hard'	Natural language, 'soft'

word 'positive', which in the English language conjures up an image of 'certainty', 'precision' and 'objectivity'. And its principal characteristic is that the methods, concepts and procedural rules of the natural sciences can be applied to the study of social life. This involves ontological assumptions about the nature of society, for social life is perceived to comprise objective structures independent of the people concerned, and to consist of wholes and systems which go beyond the consciousness of individuals. There is thus a 'real world' out there independent of people's perceptions of it: the social world is revealed to us, not constructed by us. It thus follows that objective knowledge is possible, for there is a fixed and unchanging reality which research can accurately access and tap. Further epistemological assumptions follow: knowledge of social life can reveal only that which is externally observable through the senses, and it can disclose the causal relationships that exist within social life. From this follows the epistemological assumption that it is possible and desirable to develop law-like statements about the social world by means of the hypothetico-deductive method and using nomological-deductive explanations. These phrases essentially mean the **deduction** of general statements from a theory or law, from which hypotheses are formed, which are then tested against prediction and observation.

The best example remains Durkheim's theory of suicide (Durkheim [1905] 1951). His general statement was that suicide varied inversely with the degree to which individuals were integrated with the group. From this he deduced less general statements, to the effect, for example, that Catholics have lower suicide rates than Protestants because Catholicism is a more communal religion and integrates believers into a more collective group. Factual statements could be deduced from this which could be tested against prediction and observation, to the effect that the suicide rate will be lower, for example, in Catholic countries than Protestant ones. Suicide statistics for Italy compared to those for Holland could then confirm or refute the original general law-like statement. It is the original law-like general statement or theory that is the explanatory variable, below which come descriptive data that are revealed through sense-experience observation. Confirmation or refutation cannot be achieved by data revealed through people's interpretative or mean-ing-endowing capacities (in Durkheim's case by studying the meanings of vic-tims as revealed, say, in their suicide notes; see Jacobs 1979) but only data revealed externally through the way the world is observed and experienced via our senses (in this case 'objective', 'official' statistics).

Data for the natural science model of social research are thus called 'hard', wishing to imply that they are untainted by the interpretative and meaning-endowing processes of people, whether these people are the subjects of the research or the researchers themselves. And such data are numerate, seeking to measure and describe social phenomena by the attribution of numbers. This gives an elective affinity, as Weber would say, between the natural sci-ence model of social research and those data collection techniques which give best access to sense-experience data, notably questionnaires, surveys and experiments. Positivism believes the world to be an external, knowable entity, existing 'out there' independent of what people believe or perceive it to be. In a world made known to us through our sense experience, people contribute very little to knowledge in this way, simply receiving the sensory stimuli and recounting the response. Questionnaires and surveys are exemp-lary at doing this. They collect numerate data that supposedly render social phenomena 'objective' and untouched by people's interpretative and reality-constructing capacities. Hence, for example, textbooks identify the pro-cedural rules for, say, constructing and applying a standardized interview schedule (advice on prompting and probing by means of standardized phrases to be used by the interviewer, the elimination of the 'interviewer effect' and practices to standardize the instrument), the following of which supposedly allows researchers to eliminate personal and interpersonal vari-ables that distort what is seen as a simple and unproblematic relationship between stimulus (the question) and response (the answer). Since the stimu-lus takes the same form for everyone, if respondents give different responses the differences are assumed to be 'real', not artificially created by variations in the way the question was asked. The data thus become 'real', 'hard' and 'objective', since they are seen as untainted by the personal considerations of the interviewer or the respondent (see Box 2.1).

The humanistic model of social research

From the 1960s onwards there has been an intellectual attack on positivism, from people like Thomas Kuhn, Karl Popper and various kinds of interpre-tative sociologies, such as phenomenology and ethnomethodology. This has resulted in an intellectual attack on the natural science model of social research and also on its procedural rules for certifying knowledge as reliable and objective. So there was an attack on the very idea of questionnaires, for

---

Box 2.1 Standardization of the interview

Standardization of the interviewer effect
This relates to all kinds of interview.

1 Have one person do all the interviews so that respondents are subject to a constant interviewer effect (or at least use a homogeneous set of interviewers).
2 Randomize the effect by picking a random sample of interviewers.
3 Minimize any inequalities between interviewer/respondent (such as sex, age, class, social status, religion).
4 Institute control by assessing/supervising the interview/interviewer.

Standardization of the interview as an instrument
This particularly relates to formal interviews with a rigid schedule.

1 Ensure the respondent is nominated by the sampling procedure, not the interviewer (except with quota sampling).
2 Standardize introductory statements about the purposes/sponsors of the research – there should be a standard reply to any query for further information.
3 The interviewer should not try to persuade/influence respondents either in what to say or whether to say anything at all.
4 There should be precise instructions about when and how to prompt/ probe.
5 Try to keep recording by the interviewer to a minimum.
6 Ensure there is no modification or variation in the instructions given to respondents.
7 Leave controversial/sensitive questions until the end.
8 Wording of the questions. Ten basic rules:
   (a) use familiar words which are class/culture fair;
   (b) use simple words free from jargon/technical phrases;
   (c) be specific and unambiguous;
   (d) be concise and to the point;
   (e) be precise, especially avoid double negatives;
   (f) keep it short;
   (g) avoid leading questions which suggest a response;
   (h) avoid hypothetical questions;
   (i) avoid presumptuous questions which assume a response;
   (j) avoid double-headed questions (two questions in one).

---

example, as reliable methods for collecting data, no matter how well they were operated. Familiar and old methods were impugned to their core, with a level of vitriol that approached what Pawson (1999: 29–32) called a paradigm war. A new tradition emerged, or, more properly, was rediscovered, since its ideas were longstanding, which gave legitimacy to new procedural rules and thus new methods for collecting and analysing data (such as conversation analysis) or reinvented and repopularized underused ones from an earlier period (ethnography, documentary analysis, in-depth interviews and participant observation). Hughes calls this the humanistic model of social research (a phrase also used by Berger 1963, and Bruyn 1966), and it is premised on the methodology of naturalism (this methodology is also sometimes called the interpretative or hermeneutical paradigm).

Naturalism is an orientation concerned with the study of social life in real, naturally occurring settings; the experiencing, observing, describing, understanding and analysing of the features of social life in concrete situations as they occur independently of scientific manipulation. The focus on natural situations leads to this orientation being described as 'naturalism', and it is signified by attention to what human beings feel, perceive, think and do in natural situations that are not experimentally contrived or controlled (the emphasis upon interpretation also explains why it is called the hermeneutical paradigm). These naturally occurring situations are also sometimes called 'face-to-face' situations, mundane interaction, micro-interaction or everyday life. Stress is laid on experiencing and observing what is happening naturally rather than hypothesizing about it beforehand, mostly by achieving first-hand contact with it, although researchers minimize their effect on the setting as much as possible. Stress is also laid on the analysis of people's 'meanings' from their own standpoint: the feelings, perceptions, emotions, thoughts, moods, ideas, beliefs and interpretative processes of members of society as they themselves understand and articulate them (see Box 2.2), at

---

Box 2.2

Interview with a member of Ian Paisley's Free Presbyterian Church, for research published in J. D. Brewer, *Anti-Catholicism in Northern Ireland 1600–1998* (London: Macmillan, 1998), with G. Higgins.

I believe that the Roman Catholic Church is the whore of Babylon, a system which is contrary to the word of God. I honestly have no time for the ecumenical movement. To me there can be no reconciliation between what Rome teaches and the Scriptures. I don't believe light can have any fellowship with darkness . . . I would have no problem with a united Ireland if it was under British rule. United Ireland as it means today would be a Roman Catholic dominated thing . . . The British way of life would be what I would favour.

least initially. Naturalism presents this as 'being true to the natural phenomena' (Douglas 1980: 2).

There are ontological and epistemological assumptions within this stance, which further highlight its contrast with positivism as a methodological position. Central to naturalism is the argument, going back to German philosophy in the nineteenth century (the *Geisteswissenschaften* tradition), that human beings and social behaviour are different from the behaviour of physical and inanimate objects. People are meaning-endowing, in that they have the capacity to interpret and construct their social world and setting rather than responding in a simplistic and automatic way to any particular stimuli. Moreover, people are discursive, in that they have the capacity for language and the linguistic formulation of their ideas, and possess sufficient knowledge about discourse in order to articulate their meanings. Society, thus, is seen as either wholly or partially constructed and reconstructed on the basis of these interpretative processes, and people are seen as having the ability to tell others what they mean by some behaviour, idea or remark and to offer their own explanation of it or motive for it. Society is not presented as a fixed and unchanging entity, 'out there' somewhere and external to the person, but is a shifting, changing entity that is constructed or reconstructed by people themselves. People live in material and bounded structures and locations, and these contexts shape their interpretative processes, so that we are not free to define the social world as if we existed as islands, each one inhabited by ourselves alone. All social life is partially interdependent on the concrete situations and structures in which it exists, so 'society' is not a complete invention (or reinvention) every time. But knowledge of the social world, in this methodological position, is inadequate if we do not also document, observe, describe and analyse the 'meanings' of the people who live in it. This must be the starting point of any study of society according to naturalism, although it may clearly not be the end point, in that the researcher may want to extend the analysis beyond people's own accounts, explanations and meanings. The theory of knowledge within naturalism thus sees it as essential to understand 'the freely constructed character of human actions and institutions' (Hammersley 1990: 7) in the natural settings and contexts which influence and shape people's meanings. Thus, knowledge must be inductive (the reverse of deductive), in which researchers begin with particular observations, from which empirical statements are made, which may, or may not, lead on to statements of more generality. It is discovery-based rather than hypothesis testing. The three essential tenets of naturalism are thus:

- the social world is not reducible to that which can be externally observed, but is something created or recreated, perceived and interpreted by people themselves;

- knowledge of the social world must give access to actors' own accounts of it, among other things, at least as a starting point, and sometimes as the sole point;
- people live in a bounded social context, and are best studied in, and their meanings are best revealed in, the natural settings of the real world in which they live.

Four imperatives or requirements for social research follow from this methodological position. Social researchers in the humanistic model of social research need:

- to ask people for their views, meanings and constructions;
- to ask people in such a way that they can tell them in their own words;
- to ask them in depth because these meanings are often complex, taken for granted and problematic;
- to address the social context which gives meaning and substance to their views and constructions.

The implications of these imperatives are significant and they go towards defining the attitude and approach of humanistic researchers. There are three implications. First, they predispose the humanistic researcher to study certain sorts of topics above others, ones that lend themselves readily to the study of people's views, beliefs and meanings. The reverse of this is that the researcher is cut off from studying those topics that are not appropriate to being approached in terms of people's beliefs and meanings. Second, while it is the case that most topics can be addressed in various ways, researchers with a preference for the humanistic model are predisposed to ask certain sorts of questions about that topic, approaching the topic in terms of people's meanings, attitudes, beliefs and interpretations. Let me illustrate this with the example of my research on crime in Ireland, North and South, between 1945 and 1995 (Brewer *et al.* 1997). It combined quantitative and qualitative research. In part it examined trends in crime statistics in this time period at the national level for Northern Ireland and the Irish Republic, and at city level for Dublin and Belfast, as well as trends in the official statistics for specific crimes, such as murder, robbery, theft, rape and scheduled offences under terrorism legislation. However, official statistics have profound limitations, and as a qualitative researcher first and foremost, I needed to approach the topic by asking other sorts of questions as well. An ethnographic part of the study therefore sought to supplement the quantitative analysis of crime by addressing a whole range of issues raised by crime, to permit the expression of these concerns in the actors' own terms and to capture the richness and depth of the crime problem. Thus, we also focused on two local communities in Belfast, one each in Catholic West Belfast and Protestant East Belfast, and addressed issues such as people's perceptions of the crime problem in their locality, levels of fear of crime, people's reporting behaviour, local crime management in the absence of reliance on the police, the frames of reference through which people approach crime, such as perceived levels of crime in other societies or historical comparisons with the past, and people's fears about future crime in their areas after the ceasefire by paramilitary groups. Such data captured the richness of people's experiences in their own terms, proffering a counterweight to the breadth and geographical coverage of official statistics. Actors' accounts take on added value with respect to crime statistics because of the well known limitations in official statistics on crime. Therefore, the topic itself was defined in such a way as to permit study of people's meaning-endowing capacities.

A third implication of these imperatives is that they predispose a preference for certain data collection techniques. Methods of data collection in the humanistic model of research must access people's views and meanings, and do so in depth without imposing views upon people. They must permit people to speak in their own terms and in the context of the natural settings which give meaning and substance to their views. The popular methods of data collection in qualitative research are therefore techniques such as in-depth or informal interviews, personal documents, like diaries, letters and autobiographies, participant observation and methods for the study of natural language, like conversation analysis (these data collection techniques are discussed in Chapter 3). These methods are sometimes summed up in what has here been termed 'big ethnography' or 'ethnography-understood-as-qualitative-research', or summed up in the term 'unobtrusive methods'. One of the most important is 'little ethnography', what is here called 'ethnography-understood-as-fieldwork'.

The data collected by these methods come in a particular form. Qualitative data come in the form of extracts of natural language, such as quotations obtained from in-depth interviews, notes from personal documents or records of participant observation, providing actors' own accounts. Such data capture the richness of people's experiences in their own terms. As Schwartz and Jacobs (1979: 4) write:

> quantitative sociologists assign numbers to observations. They produce data by counting and 'measuring' things. The things measured can be individual persons, groups, whole societies, speech acts and so on. Qualitative sociologists report observations in the natural language at large [see Box 2.3]. It is intrinsically important to develop ways of gaining access to the life-world of other individuals in the context of [their] daily life.

Subtitling their book 'A method to the madness', they contend that such methods are the only way for the social researcher to chart a way through the chaos and complexity of social life.

Box 2.3

Extract from J. D. Brewer, B. Lockhart and P. Rodgers, *Crime in Ireland, 1945–95* (Oxford: Clarendon Press, 1997), p. 128.

As one resident remarked after being asked whether ordinary crime was a problem in Poleglass [Catholic West Belfast] 'definitely . . . being totally honest with you, you would probably hear of most crimes. They probably wouldn't be on a big scale but you would get them – joyriding, thieving, thieving of anything; anything you leave sitting about here is going to walk, whether your name is on it or not. If it's not nailed down they'll have it'. In the Bloomfield district of East Belfast a resident recounted her experiences:

> There is a lot of crime in the area. The most common is breaking-in and vandalism. Broke into Elmgrove primary school this morning, they took what they wanted but they vandalised it as well. Last Saturday the bakery was held up and all the money taken. The day before I was in the post office and some fella was playing with the blind [collection] box, then he lifted it. I know the travel agent has been broken into. Basically all the shops around here have been broken into. I have been broken into three times. I had stuff taken from the [washing] line three or four times. The bikes have been taken umpteen times.

The methodological bases of ethnography

It is clear that the principal methodological justification for ethnography comes from naturalism and the humanistic model of social research. This gives us what we earlier called the 'humanistic' type of ethnography. It is what most people think of when they reflect on ethnography and it is what most ethnographers do when they practise fieldwork: 'getting close to the inside', 'telling it like it is', 'giving an insider's account', 'being true to the natural phenomena', giving 'thick description' and 'deeply rich' data. It is research that abandons natural science models of research practice, such as hypothesis testing, deductive analysis, description and measurement by means of assigning numbers; it abandons even the rhetoric and ambitions of natural science in favour of understanding naturally occurring behaviour in its own terms. However, the type of ethnography we called 'scientific' or 'positivist' draws on elements of both methodologies and is associated with both models of research. It does so by accepting the orthodox consensus that natural science is the standard by which research should be judged and by arguing that there is a 'real' world which it is possible to access. Yet it believes that ethnography is, perhaps, more scientific than quantitative methods because it enables researchers to get closer and better access to this 'real' world. 'Critical realist' ethnographies are like this, as was the practice of early advocates (Bruyn 1966; Blumer 1969), who argued that ethnography had a scientific character precisely because it was better suited than experimental and survey research to understanding human behaviour (see Hammersley 1990: 6).

In one important respect the two types of ethnography are identical in what they see as the proper purpose of ethnography, even though they come to this from diametrically opposed methodological positions. Both have a naive notion that there are objective truth statements that can be made about the phenomena under study, that ethnography best permits these truth statements and that these truth statements reflect the 'real' understanding of the phenomena. Both believe that it is possible to 'tell it like it is', and, further, that there is only one 'true' telling. Ethnography thus uniquely renders a problematic social world unproblematic, for it alone has the capacity to disclose the social world as it truly is. It is for this reason that Silverman (1985: 116) observed that naturalistic and positivistic types of ethnography both sought the elimination of the effects of the researcher in order better to represent the 'real' picture and the 'true' understanding of the phenomena, the former by recommending that ethnographers embrace the culture and the setting to become an 'insider', the latter by recommending the standardization of all research procedures and instruments. In this sense, both types of ethnography subscribe to what is known as 'naive realism'. Both types of 'postmodern reflexive' ethnography challenge them on this, attacking the grounds on which they claim to represent 'reality' and the criteria by which they claim legitimacy for the validity and accuracy of their data. This challenge makes ethnography 'the most hotly contested site in qualitative research today' (Denzin and Lincoln 1998: xvi); and it describes what Denzin and Lincoln (1998: 21) call the 'double crisis' of contemporary ethnography, where its representational claims are questioned by other ethnographers and the validity of its data impugned. Hence Atkinson and Hammersley (1998: 129) rightly point out that there is not a single philosophical or theoretical orientation that can lay unique claim to supply the rationale for ethnography, each endorsing a version of ethnographic work. It is to these crises that we now turn.

The double crisis of ethnography

The 'crisis of representation'

The 'crisis of representation' describes the disillusionment surrounding the ethnographer's claim to provide a privileged and special access to 'reality' by means of 'thick description'. As Dey (1993: 31) makes clear, to describe something is to recite its characteristics in either numbers or natural language. In natural science models of social research, description has low status, which is ironic, since description in the form of numbers permeates the natural science model. It is description by means of extracts of natural language that is problematic to positivism. Yet for both 'scientific' and 'humanistic' forms of ethnography, such description is central to the ethnographic enterprise, although they must be what is called 'thick' as opposed to 'thin' descriptions. 'Thick' description was a term first used by the anthropologist Clifford Geertz in 1973, and popularized in sociology by Norman Denzin, although its origins lie within the British anthropological tradition of Malinowski, where researchers were enjoined to describe phenomena from the natives' point of view. Thin description is mere gloss, a bare report of the 'facts' independent of intentions or circumstances, whereas thick description represents a thorough account (see Box 2.4), taking in the context of the phenomena described, the intentions and meanings that organize them, and their subsequent evolution or processing (see Denzin 1989: 31, 83ff). It is a form of 'subjective soaking' according to Ellen (1984), in which researchers attempt to merge with the phenomena being described. It is a 'written representation of a culture' (van Maanen 1988: 1), or what Fetterman (1998: 20) calls 'the emic perspective', where phenomena are described from the insider's perspective, which is 'instrumental to understanding and accurately describing situations and behaviours'. Fetterman (1998: 29) outlines thick description thus: 'it involves detailed description, detailed frame-by-frame analysis of events or parts of events.' Or in Denzin's own words, it:

> presents detail, context, emotion, and the webs of social relationships. Thick description invokes emotionality and self-feelings. It establishes the significance of an experience or the sequence of events. In thick description, the voices, feelings, actions, and meanings of interacting individuals are heard. It captures and records the voices of 'lived experience'.
>
> (Denzin 1989: 83)

For many 'humanistic' ethnographers, such thick description is an end in itself, since their task is solely to engage in 'cultural description' as anthropologists might say, or, as some sociologists might say, it facilitates the goal of demonstrating the reality construction done by ordinary people. If reality reconstruction is the goal, by which Schwartz and Jacobs (1979: 2) mean that 'messy, tortuous business of learning to see the world of an individual or group from the inside', then 'there is something vital that one does not know if one has no access to the inside – that is, if [we are] unable to reconstruct the world as it looks, sounds, and smells to those within it.' This is what thick description achieves, a 'realist' narrative of the social world from

Box 2.4

Extract from J. D. Brewer, *Inside the RUC* (Oxford: Clarendon Press, 1991), with K. Magee, pp. 60–2.

Another type of work which is disliked is emotionally demanding work. When they talk about work of this type, policemen stress the importance of remaining detached and emotionally cold. Young probationers are instructed to follow the 'police pattern', what Schutz would call the 'recipe knowledge'. An elderly sergeant once remarked on his experience of attending a cot death for the first time, 'You just have to say to yourself, the next time I will be better equipped to cope with this type of situation . . . There's a pattern police follow in every situation. You lay the pattern down whatever you're dealing with, and you follow it through'. If she could look at meat hanging in a butcher's, the field-worker was told when she was accompanying policemen to a post-mortem, she could look at dead bodies. The tendency to render horrific incidents of this sort into funny tales or 'atrocity stories', told ritualistically within the occupational culture of the station, is a further attempt to strip them of their emotional hold. In the midst of passing on advice to the field-worker on how to cope with her imminent attendance at a post-mortem, one policeman said, 'You get used to them. I don't mind them any more'. But after a pause he went on to add, 'Except for kids, I hate going to post-mortems for kids'. Below is an extract of conversation between two policemen who are telling a third about a cot death the two of them had recently attended.

PC. 1: Jesus, it was awful, and the worst thing about it was, when we arrived the baby was still warm, so we tried to revive it with mouth to mouth. Now the couple had expected it was dead and we gave them false hope. When we couldn't revive it, it made the whole thing worse for them. Then when the ambulance men arrived they also tried to revive it. God it was awful.

PC. 2: I always feel like saying, 'Look it's OK, I'll come back in a couple of weeks. But you never do like. You'd get the balls chewed off you if you returned without all the details.

PC. 1: But it was awful. God, the couple were really upset, it was their first baby, too.

It is not that policemen and women fail to achieve emotional detachment. Primarily what makes this type of work unpopular is the ever-present danger that work of this sort will break the veneer of coldness, exposing them as emotionally involved, which is something they dislike because it is considered unprofessional.

the inside. But 'scientific' ethnographers claim thick description to be of immense value too, for it is a form of explanation. Thick descriptions are not a preliminary to explanation, David Silverman (1985: 95) once wrote, 'but are in themselves adequate scientific explanations'. If the ambition is to achieve a positivist account of some phenomenon, to capture its 'real' features accurately and objectively, thick description can be seen as an aid to science through the achievement of 'realism'. By 1997 Silverman was parodying the ambition to 'tell it like it is' as the equivalent of the television chat show (1997a: 248–9).

In the intervening period, ethnography had become infected by what Hammersley (1990: 5; see also 1992) calls **anti-realism**. In the mid-1980s in cultural anthropology and then in sociology, ethnographers used ideas from several sources to examine critically their craft and criticized both 'humanistic' and 'scientific' ethnographers for their realist assumptions that an objective reality exists and that it is possible to represent it accurately in the ethnographic text. These assumptions are naive – hence 'naive realism'. Anthropology's critique of ethnography is longer established than sociology's, partly because ethnography is so central to anthropology, but also because of the greater demands made of the method in cultural and social anthropology. Much anthropological knowledge depends upon the capacity of the ethnographic method to represent reliably the dynamics of cultures which are strange, and some anthropologists questioned the capacity of ethnographers to represent foreign cultures objectively (Marcus 1980; Clifford 1981, 1983; Marcus and Cushman 1982; Stocking 1983; Clifford and Marcus 1986; Spencer 1989). Although drawing partly on this material to mount a challenge to ethnography in sociology, ethnographers (for example, Woolgar 1988a: 24–9; Atkinson 1990: 25–8) also draw on work in social studies of science. Naturalistic critiques of scientific knowledge (and texts) were turned upon themselves and applied to social scientific knowledge generally, and ethnography in particular (Anderson 1978; Woolgar 1988a, b). Postmodernism's rejection of the meta-narrative of science, in which the realist ambition to 'objective truth' is deconstructed to language games involving competing truth claims, was also an impulse to anti-realism.

Several issues follow from the anti-realist attack on naive realism. The first and most serious is a challenge to ethnographic representations or tellings 'of it like it is'. In naive realism, the representation of social reality is seen as unproblematic as long as the researcher follows the procedural rules and gets sufficiently close to what it is like 'on the inside'. The researcher narrates the ethnography, providing thick descriptions that give readers the impression that they are in the field along with the ethnographer. Ethnographers must thus absent themselves from the text, trying to act as a mere conduit in which the insider's account is simplistically represented in the text. As van Maanen (1988: 47) writes, 'the narrator of realist tales poses as an impersonal conduit who passes on more-or-less objective data in a measured intellectual style that is uncontaminated by personal bias, political goals or moral judgements.' Realist ethnographers thought they obtained a privileged gaze by means of their closeness and insider status, and this is what must be represented in the text via a form of ethnographic reportage which uses various rhetorical devices to construct the text as an accurate portrayal based on close association in the field and the successful development of insider status (ethnographic texts and writing are explored further in Chapter 4). The problem, according to the anti-realists, is that there is no independent and external reality, and the ethnographer's representation is not privileged; it is just as much a partial account as the insiders', and claims to realist-like objectivity, accuracy and truth are spurious. Thick descriptions, therefore, do not represent 'reality as it is' because such descriptions are selective from the various competing versions of reality that could have been produced and end up presenting a partial picture: if naive realist ethnographers see themselves as cameras, the picture is blurred because there is more than one image on the lens. 'The doctrine of immaculate perception', as van Maanen (1988: 23) termed naive realism, is undermined by the opaque nature of 'reality' and the ethnographer's selection processes. Keeping 'an open mind' is not the same as having 'an empty head' (Dey 1993: 63), and unadulterated observation is impossible. As Fielding (1993: 163) says, 'objective' observation is impossible because the observer is involved, not detached.

One of the factors that naive realist ethnographers fail to recognize as impinging on their observation is theoretical bias. Hughes's arguments within the philosophy of social research contend that their conception of ethnography in naive realist terms is itself a theoretical preference, but beyond this, naive realist ethnographers tended to present themselves as theoretically neutral, building up theories in a grounded fashion from the data themselves. Genuflection in the direction of Glaser and Strauss's (1967) explication of grounded theory was routinely made, whereby theory is supposed to be based on observation of data not deduced from prior assumptions. Anti-realists argue that ethnography's descriptions are theoretically naive and no different from those produced by ordinary people as part of their everyday life (Hammersley 1990: 60–5). They are not specialized 'theoretical' descriptions. That is, they neither adequately test nor generate theory; even the theoretical inferences made from the data are often unsubstantiated. Hammersley is particularly critical of ethnographers who do not identify the theoretical assumptions and wider values that they bring to their work, which often condition their interpretation of the data and the theoretical inferences made. Ethnographers who imply that their accounts are accurate representations of the social world 'as it is', beyond the influence of theoretical presumption or prejudice, are both ignorant of the effect of their values upon research and simplistic in suggesting that there is only one objective description which they have reliably captured.

The final criticism made by anti-realist ethnographers is that the naive realist emphasis on thick description limits the ethnographer's task to that of cultural description (as anthropologists might say) or reality reconstruction (as sociologists would say). Anti-realist ethnographers recognize both the impossibility of 'telling it like it is' (since there is more than one 'telling' and more than one 'is') and the desirability of going beyond people's words. Thus, Altheide and Johnson (1998: 297) write:

> capturing members' words alone is not enough for ethnography. If it were, ethnographies would be replaced by interviews. Good ethnographies reflect tacit knowledge, the largely unarticulated, contextual understanding that is often manifested in nods, silences, humour and naughty nuances. [And] it is necessary to give an accounting of how we know things, what we regard and treat as empirical materials – the experiences – from which we produce our second (or third) hand accounts of 'what is happening'.

Altheide and Johnson close this remark by alluding to the chief solution to the crisis of representation offered by anti-realist ethnographers, which is reflexivity.

As the postmodern ethnographer's response to the crisis of representation, 'reflexivity' is something of a buzz word in contemporary ethnography (and tiresome to a few ethnographers, for Silverman (1997a: 239–40) has written that we play the reflexivity card too often and risk being perceived as navel-gazing). The problem is that realist ethnographers (like realist social scientists generally) are unreflexive, in that they give no attention to the social processes that impinge upon and influence their data. They do not adopt a critical attitude towards their data, and even deny the influence of such factors as the location of the setting, the sensitivity of the topic or the nature of the social interaction between the researcher and researched. Thus, the strengths of the data are exaggerated and/or the weaknesses underemphasized, further undermining the reliability of ethnographic thick descriptions. Therefore, Hammersley and Atkinson (1983: 17) argue that instead of trying to eliminate the effects of the ethnographer, we should be reflexive in trying to set the data against this context (Bowden 1989 argues similarly for quantitative approaches). Although Woolgar (1988a: 21–4) means something different when he urges us to be reflexive, the injunction remains: ethnographers (like social scientists generally) must locate their data in the context of the social processes that brought them about, and recognize the limits of their representation of reality (Woolgar 1988a: 26–7). This does not mean that the ethnographer has to try to construct the relevant counterfactual by engaging in the impossible task of imagining what the data would have been like had circumstances been different. Rather, it implies that ethnographers be explicit and open about the circumstances which produced the extant data, recognizing that ethnographers (like all researchers) are within the social world they seek to analyse. Since there is no perfectly transparent or neutral way to represent the social world (or the natural one), reflexivity on the part of the researcher assists in identifying the contingencies that produced his or her portrayal of it, so we should claim no more for the account than what it is, a partial, selective and personal version (see Box 2.5). (The question of reflexivity is addressed further in Chapter 4.)

The 'crisis of representation' thus describes a situation where ethnography is unsure about the status of its descriptions and observations because its claim to privileged access to 'reality' by means of thick description is impugned. Postmodernists argue that there is no one 'reality' and ethnography captures only the version that the researcher selects. This is a general complaint about all methods, however: 'there is doubt that any discourse has a privileged place, any method or theory a universal and general claim to authoritative knowledge' (Richardson 1991: 173). Realist ethnography, like all research methods, is stripped naked under the impulse of anti-realism and postmodernism, an emperor without clothes, whose claims to authority are

---

Box 2.5

Extract from J. D. Brewer, B. Lockhart and P. Rodgers, *Crime in Ireland 1945–95* (Oxford: Clarendon Press, 1997), pp. 123–7, by permission of Oxford University Press.

Ethnographic findings can be easily misunderstood. For some, ethnography represents the only research method because it alone captures people's experiences in their own words but others denigrate it . . . However, it is necessary for ethnographers to be reflexive and identify the contingencies that helped to produce the extant data. This is our intention . . . Ethnographic research on crime in Belfast, which touches on issues such as policing and the role of paramilitary organisations in local crime management, fits the template of sensitive research. It is important to identify what bearing this sensitivity had on the research. The first was with respect to the sample. Because of the sensitivity of the topic of the research, we felt it necessary to work through local community-based agencies in order to access general members of the public; the public were not accessed by means of unsolicited knocks on front doors but through their involvement with local community groups and organisations. Initial contact with the organisations was facilitated by the network of contacts possessed by the investigators and by the snowball technique. These community organisations acted as a buffer or **gatekeeper** between the fieldworker and the public, giving each some reassurance and security when addressing controversial and deeply sensitive questions. Interviews also took place in the familiar surroundings of the organisation's premises. Fieldwork took place over twelve months between 1994 and 1995, with six months spent in each study area, and the fact that the ceasefire pertained for most of the fieldwork, and for all of that which took place in West Belfast, encouraged openness amongst respondents. People's frankness about the paramilitaries was no doubt facilitated by their thought that peace had arrived. The use of community organisations as gatekeepers also facilitated a measure of representativeness, a problem which hinders the reliability of much ethnographic research because of the small numbers of people studied. Our research design allowed us to ensure that the organisations selected were an accurate political and social representation of the locality, as well as covering a cross-section of key social groups, such as women, youth and the elderly; this social and political representativeness could not have been so readily achieved by means of unsolicited access to the general public, which can overlook members of minority groups. Some community groups, however, are often politically aligned to the mainline and fringe political groups in Northern Ireland but the wide variety of views obtained seems to show that we were not hijacked by representatives or supporters of any one political organisation . . . Our research design involved exclusively the use of indepth interviews. Interviews were arranged and conducted solely by one of the authors. In total, 115 interviews were carried out with individuals and ten with groups. They were recorded on tape and then transcribed verbatim, except where respondents objected to the interview being recorded, when notes were taken during the interview. There are ninety-two hours of tape recordings. Two areas were selected for study, one each in East and West Belfast, in order to reflect the spatial location of Belfast's communal divide. To aid comparison it was important to select closely matching sub-divisions, and ones which provided a cross-section of social classes and housing styles, large council estates, areas of inner city deprivation and suburban housing, providing a mix of community types and social classes. Fieldwork deliberately covered organisations based in most of the localities within each broad area in order to provide some geographical spread and social representativeness. Each area contained pockets where members of the other religious community live. In fieldwork we made sure that we covered organisations in these enclaves.

illusionary. The problem thereby created is how to judge good ethnography, for the postmodern condition is one that undermines all criteria by which to judge and evaluate the products of ethnographic research: all criteria are doubted, none are privileged and everything goes. This is the crisis of legitimation.

The crisis of legitimation

'Humanistic' and 'scientific' types of ethnography were both 'realist' in their different ways, in believing that there was a knowable world which the proper procedural rules, faithfully followed, could accurately tap. These procedural rules not only defined how ethnography should be practised as a data collection technique, they outlined the criteria by which the resulting data could be evaluated. Terms like 'validity', 'reliability' and 'generalizability' were suggested as the criteria. 'Validity' refers to the extent to which the data accurately reflect the phenomenon under study (also sometimes called 'internal validity'), 'reliability' to the extent to which measurements of it are consistent and 'generalizability' to the applicability of the data to other like cases (also sometimes called 'external validity'). These are terms 'owned' by positivism and appropriated enthusiastically by 'scientific' ethnography, but even 'humanistic' ethnography paid attention to the ways in which its data had validity and could be made more generally applicable (see, for example, LeCompte and Goetz 1982; Kirk and Miller 1986). 'Humanistic' ethnography's commitment to naturalism sometimes ensured that practitioners thought the sole criterion should be whether the data accurately captured the phenomenon (validity), taking solace in the notion that while ethnography had high validity but low reliability, the reverse was the case in the natural science model of social research because quantitative methods could replicate data constantly but at the expense of an accurate description of social life. Such 'validity' was achieved, Fielding (1993: 164) wrote, when the observer knew the members' rules of action sufficiently well to be able to tell others how to pass as ordinary members in the same field. But even with the stress within humanistic ethnography on validity as the sole evaluator, sampling methods were introduced into ethnography (see Chapter 3), and fields were sought where the processes being studied were most likely to occur but which were seen as single instances of more general social experiences and processes. Constant comparisons were made as the researcher was urged to develop an understanding that encompassed other instances of the process, and a focus on negative cases reiterated the intent to study the particular in order to examine the general. Thus, Denzin and Lincoln (1998: xiv) argued that any single case bore traces of the universal, and 'telling it like it is' was always associated with the idea that the 'telling' should encompass the general features of the 'it' (see Box 2.6).

The anti-realist challenge to the nature of knowledge (that there is no

---

Box 2.6

Extract from J. D. Brewer, *Inside the RUC* (Oxford: Clarendon Press, 1991), with K. Magee, pp. 30–3.

The familiar adage is that ethnographic research provides depth by sacrificing breadth, but it is possible to build an element of generality by constructing individual projects in the mould of similar ones in different settings so that comparisons can be made and a body of cumulative knowledge established. Our project was designed deliberately to follow the pattern of ethnographic studies of routine policing, so as to add to this tradition the dimension provided by studying this kind of policing in a divided society. In a strategy pioneered by the affluent-worker study in Luton, which one might call the optimal case approach, a site was chosen for the research which was not representative but was particularly germane to the topic of the investigation. 'Easton' was purposely selected because it is in an area of Belfast where routine policing is possible. If we are to establish how and to what extent routine policing is affected by Northern Ireland's divisions, it would be useless to base our research where there is only militarised political policing, for it is necessary to explore the extent to which policing in so-called 'soft' areas is contaminated by wider societal divisions. Given the nature of crime in 'Easton', the problems Northern Ireland's divisions create for routine policing are as well studied there as anywhere else . . . The social structure of the district of 'Easton' is worth noting.

---

objective and knowable 'real' world that can be accurately described) undermines the traditional criteria to evaluate ethnographic data since they are based on 'realist' assumptions. Hence the crisis of legitimation.

It is over the issue of legitimation and the criteria left to evaluate ethnographic data that postmodern, reflexive ethnographers divide. Less extreme postmodern, reflexive ethnographers accept that some criteria need to be applied or ethnographic data cannot be vouched for and evaluated. We would then be in a state of utter relativism, the epitome of the postmodern dissolution into nothingness. We would all be ethnographers then – at least we could not distinguish between good and bad ethnography – and practitioners could properly be parodied as chat show hosts or hack journalists, for the criteria to distinguish lay and professional ethnography, or good and bad ethnographic research, would be unknown or uncertain. This is precisely what extreme postmodernist ethnographers claim, but ethnographers

like Hammersley (1990) have outlined new criteria, validated by a methodology he calls 'subtle realism'. Altheide and Johnson (1998) have done likewise for a position they call 'analytical realism', and I have outlined a set of
guidelines emerging from the postmodern, reflexive critique of ethnography
to strengthen rather than undermine ethnographic practice (Brewer 1994).
The rupture of postmodernism is thus lessened to a considerable degree (see
also Lincoln and Guba 1985, for a discussion of new criteria to assess 'naturalistic' research by; for a review of what he calls 'criteriology', see Seale
1999: 32–52). This type of ethnography constitutes a kind of post postmodern kind.

Post postmodern ethnography

The type of ethnography that embraces the anti-realist critique of ethnography but reflects only the representational concerns of postmodernism is
reflexive and only loosely postmodern. This is clear from the response anti-
realist ethnographers have made to their own complaints. Whether it be
'subtle realism', 'analytical realism' or my own guidelines for the 'ethnographic imagination', this kind of anti-realist ethnography advocates the
possibility and desirability of systematic ethnography. The criticisms of
naive realism still fall short of postmodernism's abandonment of the idea of
rigorous, disciplined and systematic research practice. Thus, post postmodern ethnography remains rooted in weaker versions of realism (for an
example in cultural studies see Jenks and Neves 2000).

Subtle realism

Martyn Hammersley's (1990: 61, 73ff; 1992) account of subtle realism
makes it clear that he believes in independent truth claims which can be
judged by their correspondence to an independent reality. No knowledge is
certain, but there are phenomena that exist independent of us as researchers
or readers, and knowledge claims about them can be judged 'reasonably
accurately' in terms of their 'likely' truth (Hammersley 1990: 61). It shares
with naive realism the idea that research investigates independently knowable phenomena but breaks with it in denying that we have direct access to
these phenomena. It shares with anti-realism a recognition that all knowledge is based on assumptions and human constructions, but rejects the
notion that we have to abandon the idea of truth itself (Hammersley 1992:
52). If the idea of truth itself is not abandoned, what need to change are the
criteria by which we judge truth claims. Gone should be naive realist
notions, and in their place should be a new construct of validity, as well as
other criteria within subtle realism, such as relevance.

Validity is understood by Hammersley (1990: 61–106) to describe three processes that extend beyond mere 'accuracy': **plausibility** (whether any truth claim is likely to be true given our existing knowledge); **credibility** (whether any truth claim is likely to be accurate given the nature of the phenomenon, the circumstances of the research and the characteristics of the researcher); and evidence tests (where truth claims are not immediately plausible or credible, the evidence to substantiate them will need to be tested for its plausibility and credibility). This is a weak basis for evaluating ethnographic data compared to the idea that we can assess claims directly by their correspondence to 'reality', but this weakness must be accepted given that postmodernism makes it impossible to envisage any direct correspondence. Yet assessment of ethnographic data is not by their validity alone, for validity is joined by relevance (see Hammersley 1990: 64–70, 107–17).

Ethnographic findings must be not only valid but also relevant to issues of public concern. All 'thick descriptions' should be for some purpose beyond simply 'telling it like it is', and the descriptions can be evaluated against this agenda. As Seale (1999: 12) notes, this is a less dramatic version of the claim by extreme postmodernists that the quality of research should now be judged only by its political effects (a claim made, for example, by Lincoln and Denzin 1994). Ethnographic research could be judged on whether and how well it resolves some social problem, or achieves emancipation for some oppressed group (such as women) or release from some constraining situation or setting (such as discrimination experienced by ethnic minorities). Many feminist ethnographers are particularly concerned to ensure that their practice ends up with the emancipation of women rather than the production of valid knowledge for its own sake (Miles 1983; Harding 1987; Williams 1990). Such praxis echoes that of Marxist and critical realist ethnographers. Hammersley (1990: 107) defines two aspects of public relevance: the importance of the topic in terms of public issues, and the contributions of the findings to existing knowledge. Again this ensures that the relevance of ethnographic data is uncertain – reflecting the uncertainty of the post-modern moment – because there will be disagreement on these two dimensions, but this does not stop reasonable judgements being made.

Analytical realism

Altheide and Johnson (1998: 291–4) argue that analytical realism is based on the view that the social world is an interpreted world, not a literal one, always under symbolic construction and reconstruction by people and by the ethnographers who study them. While the ethnographer's commitment is still to obtain people's perspectives on social reality, analytical realism recognizes that most fields have multiple perspectives and voices, which means that the ethnographer must faithfully report this multivocality and show where his or her voice is located in relation to these. All knowledge is perspectival (is relative to the perspective of the knower), so the ethnographer's perspective must be specified as much as that of the subjects of the research. They call this 'validity-as-reflexive-accounting', and distinguish it from other forms of validity (validity as relevance, as culture, as ideology and as language), all of which are inadequate as the criteria to assess ethnographic data in the contemporary postmodern, reflexive moment. In this way, representation and legitimation are part of the same problem and solved in the same manner. If ethnography represents the social world faithfully, evaluating its data becomes unproblematic. This is what 'validity-as-reflexive-accounting' achieves, placing the researcher, the topic, the subjects, the field, the sense-making process and the written text at the heart of ethnography. Five processes are seen as critical for the post postmodern and reflexive ethnographer to address (Altheide and Johnson 1998: 291–2):

- the relationship between what is observed (behaviour, rituals, meanings) and the larger cultural, historical and organizational contexts within which the observations are made;
- the relationship between the observed, the observer and the setting or field;
- the issue of the perspective or point of view used to render an interpretation of ethnographic data, whether the observer's or the members';
- the role of the reader or audience in the final written product;
- the issue of the representational, rhetorical or authorial style used by the ethnographer(s) to render the description or interpretation.

Analytical realism thus calls for a particular kind of validity, which requires that ethnographers substantiate their findings with a reflexive account of themselves and the process of their research. In this way, ethnographic research is privileged, or 'disciplined' as Altheide and Johnson (1998: 293) write, compared to everyday thinking and observing, allowing ethnography to rise above the morass and meaninglessness of postmodern relativism and scepticism.

Critical realism

Critical realism is an attempt to explain the relationship of social structure and social action and is grounded in the work of Roy Bhasker. Bhasker (1989: 3–4) explains that social reality is not created by people (the error of naturalism), yet the structures that pre-exist us do not occur independent of human agency (the error of structuralism) but are reproduced and transformed by our action and everyday activities. Structures are 'real'; their effects can be demonstrated in causal connections in the material world even if such structures cannot be perceived outside of their effects. These structures also constrain agency. But they also simultaneously enable agency by providing the framework within which people act, and such agency reproduces (and occasionally transforms) the structure it occurs within. The persistence of such structures across time and space requires their continual reproduction by people in everyday activity. Critical realism is thus very similar to Giddens's structuration theory (on which see Giddens 1984), although it has a stronger empirical thrust compared to Giddens's theory. Giddens has used the critical realist ethnography of Willis, which was about young working-class school children in Birmingham, to support his theoretical claims about structuration (1984: 289–93), and it is possible to use ethnographic research to demonstrate some of the claims of structuration theory (see Box 2.7).

Likewise, Porter (1993, 1995) has used ethnography to explore the dimensions and claims of critical theory, and has appropriated critical realism to defend ethnography from its postmodern critics. He presents this critique as imposing upon aspiring ethnographers four obligations (Porter 1995: 16). These are: to make apparent the assumptions and values that underlie the investigation; particularly to identify its methodological basis; to make explicit the theoretical issues which the research is designed to illuminate; and to make explicit the ontological status that social structures are given. He contends that critical realism answers all four queries, such that the point of ethnography is not to describe small-scale social events but to examine human agency in order to shed light on the relationship between social action and social structure. The imperative for the ethnographer is to be reflexive; the agenda of the research is to focus upon 'generative structures' through close examination of human agency. While critical realist ethnography keeps to the use of ethnography-as-fieldwork as a data collection technique, it abandons the naive realism of naturalism as the methodology associated with this research practice. Understanding the actor's viewpoint may be a necessary condition for social knowledge, Porter writes (1995: 21), but it is not a sufficient one; there are more than individual interactions and interpretations that we need to know about. Davies's (1999) account of critical realist ethnography also attacks naturalism.

The ethnographic imagination

In earlier work, I have also responded to the postmodern critique of ethnography (Brewer 1994), arguing that it does not rule out the possibility of systematic and rigorous practice but instead can be used to develop a set of guidelines for good ethnographic practice in this reflexive, postmodern moment. Ethnographers need to be mindful of an important requirement if their data are to be recognized as having authority. No matter how good their practice, and irrespective of their reflexivity, ethnographers need to deploy, and encourage readers to adopt, what I call the 'ethnographic imagination'. Atkinson (1990) uses the same term to describe the artful and creative rhetorical abilities of writers of ethnographic texts, but here it is used to describe the imaginative leap necessary to recognize the authority of ethnographic data. This is not suggested as a means to ensure that readers

Box 2.7

Extract from J. D. Brewer, Micro-sociology and the 'duality of structure': former fascists 'doing' life history, in N. Fielding (ed.) *Actions and Structure* (London: Sage, 1988), pp. 152–6.

[E]x-Fascists are aware of the modern connotations of their membership. In asking the former Fascists to look back on their membership and the reasons lying behind it, they were forced to confront these typifications. In this way they became concerned to present themselves as rational beings in face of the irrationality common-sensically associated with their membership and support. This was achieved through the notion of crisis: they presented their personal biography as involving a tremendous crisis which made their membership of the BUF [British Union of Fascists] a rational pragmatic act. The connection between their support for the BUF and the perception of a crisis was mentioned by all respondents. The respondents' emphasis on crisis presents Fascism as the last chance, the only means of hope for themselves and for Britain. As knowledgeable agents the former Fascists were able to monitor reflexively their actions across time-space, to monitor reflexively the unintended consequences of past conduct by Fascists and monitor how this past agency had become transformed and reproduced into a series of pejorative common-sense typifications and idealisations [about Fascists]. The common-sense typifications of Fascists as 'killers', 'mad', 'irrational' and so on, represent the objectification of the past human agency of Fascists, and they become embodied as rules, recipes, formulae and institutional practices for the behaviour towards and assessment of Fascists. This objectification reflects and reinforces the typifications. This objectification of past agency into a series of pejorative typifications constitutes a constraint upon Fascists when they accomplish life history. They are forced to confront and challenge them. This was achieved through the notion of crisis. But simultaneously the constraints embedded in this objectification are a medium through which the accomplishment of the life history is organised. The constraints became an enablement because they provided the experiences which the former Fascists had to confront and were the principle by which the life history is organised as a practical achievement. This accomplishment of life history leads to structuration over time-space. By transforming the common sense typifications of Fascists into the theme of crisis, the former members of the BUF reproduced the very characteristics of the wider common sense world they drew on in their accomplishment, reproducing the view that Fascists really are 'mad', 'crazy' and 'irrational'.

overlook bad practice or weaknesses in data, or that they make allowances for this kind of research which they would not otherwise. Instead, it is a call to openness in people's attitudes towards ethnographic data, in which their validity, usefulness and import is not immediately dismissed out of hand.

The ethnographic imagination has three dimensions:

- The belief that fragments of recorded talk, extracts from field notes and reports of observed actions can reliably represent a social world which cannot be completely described in the restricted spatial confines of an ethnographic text, as long as the ethnographer has been reflexive and thereby established his or her integrity and the authority of the data.
- The belief that small-scale, micro events in everyday life have at least common features with the broader social world, such that general processes permeate down to and are in part reproduced at the level of people's everyday lives. Thus, microscopic events can illustrate features of broader social processes, as long as the ethnographer sets out the grounds on which these empirical generalizations are made.
- The belief that people make sense of their everyday lives, and offer descriptions and accounts thereof, involving a complex reasoning process, which must be analysed if that social world is to be understood in the round, although members' accounts should not be taken at face value.

This 'ethnographic imagination' is predicated on a set of guidelines for good practice which are integral to it. These guidelines attempt to embody the reflexive, postmodern moment which contemporary ethnography confronts, yet also to go beyond postmodernism by re-establishing the grounds for reliable, rigorous and systematic ethnographic practice. Thus, in doing and writing up ethnographic research, ethnographers should:

1 Establish the wider relevance of the setting and the topic, and clearly identify the grounds on which empirical generalizations are made, such as by establishing the representativeness of the setting, its general features or its function as a special case study with a broader bearing.
2 Identify the features of the topic that they are addressing in the study and those left unresearched, and discuss why these choices have been made and what implications follow from these decisions for the research findings.
3 Identify the theoretical framework they are operating within, and the broader values and commitments (political, religious, theoretical and so on) they bring to their work.
4 Establish their integrity as researcher and author, by outlining:
   - the grounds on which knowledge claims are being justified (length of fieldwork, the special access negotiated, discussing the extent of the trust and rapport developed with the respondents and so on);
   - their background and experiences in the setting and topic;
   - their experiences during all stages of the research, especially mentioning the constraints imposed therein;

- the strengths and weaknesses of their research design and strategy.
5 Establish the authority of the data by:
  - discussing the problems that arose during all stages of the research;
  - outlining the grounds on which they developed the categorization system used to interpret the data, identifying clearly whether this is an indigenous one used by respondents themselves or an analyst-constructed one, and, if the latter, the grounds which support this;
  - discussing rival explanations and alternative ways of organizing the data;
  - providing sufficient data extracts in the text to allow readers to evaluate the inferences drawn from them and the interpretations made of them;
  - discussing power relations within the research, between researcher(s) and subjects and within the research team, in order to establish the effects of class, gender, race and religion on the practice and writing up of the research.
6 Show the complexity of the data, avoiding the suggestion that there is a simple fit between the social world under scrutiny and the ethnographic representation of it, by:
  - discussing negative cases which fall outside the general patterns and categories employed to structure the ethnographic description, which often serve to exemplify and support positive cases;
  - showing the multiple and often contradictory descriptions proffered by the respondents themselves;
  - stressing the contextual nature of respondents' accounts and descriptions, and identifying the features which help to structure them.

Conclusion

Until very recently, ethnography was conceived of as both a method (data collection technique) and a methodology (a theoretical and philosophical framework). The philosophy of social research suggests that the two were interlocked, with methodological preferences predicting the employment of the method. For a long time, ethnographers saw this interpolation of method and methodology as unproblematic; they were fooling themselves. The ethnographic method became narrowly associated in the social sciences with one methodological stance (naturalism or naive realism), within which it was treated as a privileged technique, superior to all others. Its weaknesses as a method were thus overlooked by proponents of the methodology or set aside amid exaggerated claims for its utility. This was particularly associated with 'humanistic ethnography'. Conversely, opponents of naturalism within the natural science model of social research dismissed the method more or less out of hand. If they accorded ethnography a role at all, it was merely as a sensitizing tool for collecting the preliminary data necessary to pursue the topic quantitatively. 'Positivist-scientific ethnography' sought to accommodate itself to complaint and developed what it thought was objective scientific practice in ethnography. But ethnography has been challenged more effectively recently by ethnographers who are reflecting the anti-realism of this postmodern moment. They established a kind of 'postmodern, reflexive ethnography', which abandoned both the claim that 'reality' could be accurately represented ethnographically and the criteria by which ethnography's truth claims could be assessed. However, 'post postmodern ethnography' rescues it from the complete relativism and scepticism of postmodernism and seeks to ground good practice of the method in a surer methodological foundation than naturalism. They find this in a combination of naturalist-like realism and postmodernism, expressed differently as 'subtle realism', 'analytical realism', 'critical realism' or the 'ethnographic imagination'. All versions of post postmodern ethnography outline criteria for good practice in order to distinguish systematic ethnography from lay persons' observation. It is to the question of good practice that we now turn.

Suggested further reading

For accounts of the contested terrain in ethnography see:

Denzin, N. and Lincoln, Y. (1994) *The Handbook of Qualitative Research*. London: Sage.
Hammersley, M. (1992) *What's Wrong with Ethnography?* London: Routledge.
van Maanen, J. (1988) *Tales from the Field*. Chicago: University of Chicago Press.
Seale, C. (1999) *The Quality of Qualitative Research*. London: Sage.

3 The research process in ethnography

Introduction

The argument so far is that ethnography is a style of research that lays down the procedural rules for how to study people in naturally occurring settings or 'fields' by means that capture their social meanings and ordinary activities. While these procedural rules or methods are rooted in different methodological frameworks, differences in methodology do not alter the basic practice of ethnography as a method. What differs between these methodological positions is the status of ethnography's representations of the field and the legitimacy of the criteria to evaluate them, not the practice of the method. Most ethnographers still adhere to some form of realism and do not dissolve the practice into the methodological equivalent of postmodernism's 'anything goes', although a consequence of the postmodern critique is that practitioners also need to incorporate reflexivity into their good practice.

In turning to the nature of this good practice, the first point to stress is that ethnography cannot be broken into a series of hermetic stages but should properly be seen as a process. The 'research process' is merely the series of actions that produce the end result of the study, and in ethnography it constitutes the series of actions for producing a naturalistic study of some aspect of social behaviour and meaning. The actions that comprise this process are coordinated and planned, but they are blended together imaginatively, flexibly, often in an *ad hoc* manner as they best achieve the end result. As

Pawson (1999: 32) reminds us, there is always a difference in any type of research between the ideal and the real, and the unexpected twists and turns in ethnographic research, which happen as a result of dealing with people in their naturalistic environment, prevent ethnography being a neat series of sequential stages. It is better envisaged as a series of actions that are coordinated in a flexible manner. Another point to stress is that the research process in ethnography requires careful **research design**. This chapter is organized around the question of research design. It outlines some of the issues this involves in ethnography, such as selecting from the various data collection techniques that can be used, the use of triangulation and multiple methods, the merits of case studies and their potential for making generalizations and the dimensions involved in good practice in the research process, from negotiating access and trust to the handling of gender in the field.

Research design in ethnography

In an influential book entitled *Social Research Design*, which appeared in a prestigious series on social research in the Longman series of books on 'Aspects of Sociology', the authors implied in their Foreword that research design was only associated with quantitative research (Krausz and Miller 1974). Research design reflected the desire 'to achieve greater accuracy in the measurement of social and behavioural phenomena, and an attempt to strengthen the social sciences by means of objective research' (Krausz and Miller 1974: ix). 'This does not mean that the social scientist must become a statistician', they went on to write, 'but it does mean that he should understand statistical concepts and be numerate.' Any criticism of this quantitative view of research design, they wrote, came from 'ideologists who see the study of human behaviour as a fertile ground for the propagation of certain political viewpoints', and from an 'extreme anti-science stance which would in the end destroy the social sciences' (p. 1). Social research design, in other words, was a matter only for the natural science model of social research; everything else amounted to 'purely subjective sources of evidence'. The idea that ethnographic research could be carefully designed was fanciful, or at least did not rate any mention. However, it is worth noting that their views were written in the early 1970s when there were equally fanciful statements from some qualitative researchers who wanted to 'abandon method' itself (the title of a book at this time; see Philips 1973) or to abandon rigour and simply 'hang out', 'go with the flow' and 'do your own thing', which Ernest Gellner (1975) parodied as the 'Californian way of subjectivity'. Research design, however, is as critical for ethnographers – of whatever type – as empirical and quantitative researchers.

Research design is the strategic plan of the project that sets out the broad structure of the research. It is a necessary requirement for all research of whatever style. This does not mean that all possibilities of flexibility and impromptu decision-making in the future are ruled out, although in highly standardized quantitative research projects it means precisely that. But even in qualitative research, where later flexible amendments to the design are possible (and one of the virtues of qualitative research is that it permits these unanticipated changes of plan as problems arise or unexpected patterns emerge), careful design beforehand is still essential. Ethnographic research design is a plan that includes the following considerations:

- the outline and features of the topic or topics addressed in the work, including the aims and objectives of the research;
- the choice of research site or 'field' and the forms of sampling employed to select the field and the informants;
- the resources available for the research, including money and time, and the affects resources are likely to have on the research;
- the sampling of the time and the events to be experienced in the field;
- the method or methods of data collection, including prior commitments to the use of multiple methods;
- negotiating access to the field, including 'gatekeepers', and the negotiation of trust when in the field;
- the nature of the fieldworker role(s) that will be adopted when in the field and when interacting with informants;
- the form of analysis to be used, particularly whether qualitative computer packages are to be employed;
- withdrawal from the field and the form(s) of dissemination that will be used to report the results.

It is often worth committing this design to paper (or disk), so that the plan develops a structure in the researcher's mind and can exist as an independent record for others (postgraduate supervisors and examiners, sponsors and funders, colleagues, policy-makers or lay readers of a text). The flexibility of ethnography permits last minute adaptations to any design if needs must, and this is no major catastrophe should it happen (unlike in quantitative research designs), but planning beforehand is essential for practical and intellectual reasons. This is not inconsistent with the ethnographic thrust to discover social meanings and understand social behaviour from people's own perspectives. The sections that follow in this chapter address some of the above issues, although the order in which they appear does not suggest any sequential structure to formulating a research design or any priority in research terms.

Data collection techniques

A central feature of any research design is the formulation of the topic and the choice of methods to pursue it. Topic and method often go together within ethnography and it is easy to see why. Ethnography is not a particular method of data collection but a style of research that is distinguished by its objectives, which are to understand the social meanings and activities of people in a given 'field' or setting, and an approach, which involves close association with, and often participation in, this setting. To access social meanings, observe behaviour and work closely with informants several methods of data collection are relevant, such as participant observation, in-depth interviewing, the use of personal documents and discourse analyses of natural language. Since ethnographic research always comprises some combination of these, 'triangulation', as Denzin (1970) first termed the use of multiple methods in order to extend the range of data, is routinely a feature of ethnography.

Participant observation

Observation is fundamental to many activities, from army kit inspections to air traffic control, so one needs to distinguish between observation done to accomplish everyday life activities and that done to understand them. Here again, observation is an inherent part of many types of research; people observe the behaviour of rats in mazes and chemicals in test tubes. Social research involves observation of people in their natural social environment. Here again, there is unobtrusive observation – done by old ladies from behind net curtains and by some social researchers from behind a two-way mirror – where observers do not participate in the scene or interact with the informants. Participant observation requires such involvement. Participant observation is perhaps the data collection technique most closely associated with ethnography from its origins in classical British anthropology and the Chicago School in sociology. It involves data gathering by means of participation in the daily life of informants in their natural setting: watching, observing and talking to them in order to discover their interpretations, social meanings and activities.

The intent behind this close involvement and association is to generate data through watching and listening to what people naturally do and say, but also to add the dimension of personally experiencing and sharing the same everyday life as those under study. The researcher's own attitude changes, fears and anxieties, and social meanings when engaging in and living with the people in the field form part of the data. Data are thus not external stimuli unaffected by the intervention of participant observers, for their autobiographical experiences in the field are a central part of understanding it. This reinforces Burgess's (1982: 45) view that the main instrument of data collection in participant observation is the researcher. Thus researchers who become participant observers have to develop certain personal qualities. The primary one is to maintain the balance between 'insider' and 'outsider' status; to identify with the people under study and get close to them, but maintaining a professional distance which permits adequate observation and data collection. It is a fine balance. 'Going native' is a constant danger, wherein observers lose their critical faculties and become an ordinary member of the field; while remaining an 'outsider', cold and distant from people in the field, with professional identity preserved and no rapport, negates the method. A proper balance in the participant observer's dual role as part insider and part outsider gives them the opportunity to be inside and outside the setting, to be simultaneously member and non-member, and to participate while also reflecting critically on what is observed and gathered while doing so. Burgess (1982: 45) identifies other personal abilities: to be able to share in the lives and activities of other people; to learn their language and meanings; to remember actions and speech; and to interact with a range of individuals in different social situations.

There are two ways in which participant observation is used in the social sciences: to understand the world as it is seen by those acting within it; and to reveal the taken-for-granted, common-sense nature of that everyday world itself. The former is the traditional usage in the social sciences, where social groups or specific fields are studied from the 'inside'. But the development in the 1960s of ethnomethodology in sociology and some new forms of interactionism led to an interest in the common-sense methods and procedures by which routine activities are accomplished, such as, among many things, the organization of conversation (which has become known as 'conversation analysis'), decision making in organizational settings, even walking (Wolff 1973) and sleeping (Schwartz 1973). In the second case, participant observation was used to explore the routine grounds of everyday activities (for details of this research see Garfinkel 1967) of which everyone was capable. Professional social scientists and lay people were both ethnographers in ethnomethodology's sense, for each discovered common-sense knowledge of social structures, the former as part of their professional activity, the latter in order to manage their practical everyday affairs.

Another important distinction follows on from the above. In some cases such usage involves researchers participating in a field with which they are unfamiliar, sometimes in settings of which they are already a part. So different are the requirements and problems of using participant observation when the setting or field is either known or unknown that it is important to distinguish between 'participant observation', which involves the acquisition of a new role, and 'observant participation', which involves the utilization of an existing role, to observe aspects of either a familiar or unfamiliar setting (see Figure 3.1). What we think of as classic or traditional participant observation is the acquisition of a new role to study an unfamiliar group in a strange setting, such as my membership of Action Party to study former members of the British Union of Fascists (see Brewer 1984a, b, 1988). But this does not always come in such a pure form, for new roles can be adopted to study fields with which one is familiar but the understanding of which is extended by the

Pure participant observation	Variation of participant observation
Acquisition of a new role to research in an unfamiliar setting (e.g. Brewer 1984a).	Acquisition of a new role to research a familiar setting (e.g. Rosenhan 1973).
Pure observant participation	**Variation of observant participation**
Use of an existing role to research a familiar setting (e.g. Holdaway 1982).	Use of an existing role to research an unfamiliar setting (e.g. Cohen and Taylor 1972).

Figure 3.1

acquisition of a different role. A good example of this is Rosenhan's study (1973; reprinted in Bulmer 1982a). As a doctor familiar with aspects of medical care, he became a puesdo patient in a mental hospital in order to observe 'insanity' from the 'inside'. Likewise, classic observant participation is the use of an existing role from which to observe familiar fields, such as Holdaway (1982) using his role as a sergeant in the police to observe police occupational culture in his station. A variant of this pure form exists when an existing role is utilized to explore dimensions of a new setting or field in which the role naturally locates the observer. A good example is Cohen and Taylor's (1972) use of their role as part-time teachers in prison to study prisoners and prison life, especially prisoners' adjustment to long-term sentences. The observation can also be covert or overt in all cases, the former being where co-participants do not know they are the subject of research and the research intentions are disguised, so that the new role acquired is as a normal group member or one relevant to the setting, and the latter being where the research is known, and any new role acquired is that of researcher. (The ethical implications of covert research are addressed below.)

Participant observation has certain requirements in order to be successful. Where the role is new and the field unfamiliar, whether the role is overt or covert, the observer must win acceptance in the new role, undergo an extensive period of resocialization into the practices and values of the group, give an enormous time commitment to the field in order to experience the full range of the events and activities in the setting and, where the role is covert, show dedication, tenacity and skill in maintaining the pretence. Participant observation is thus not easy or quick. 'Smash and grab ethnographies', where observers breeze into the field and are quickly out again, are worthless, although the amount of time spent in the field can be considerably shortened, depending upon the nature of the role adopted and the diversity of the activities and social meanings in the field. With observant participation there are no problems of resocialization, acceptance or misunderstanding, since it is a familiar role and often in a familiar setting, but the observer must have a suitable role in which to observe where probing questions can be asked without appearing unusual or untypical. The role must be permanent enough to allow intensive observation over a period of time and be sufficiently broad and encompassing to permit access to a cross-section of events, activities and people in the field, and the observation must not impose impediments on the normal discharge of the responsibilities and activities of the role. While participant observation might reduce the capacity of the researcher to get 'insider' status, especially where it is overt, observant participation reduces the capacity of the researcher to achieve distance from the friendships, group ties and years of association built around the role that is being utilized for observation purposes. This returns us to the recurring theme in the literature on participant observation, which, as Burgess (1984: 47) puts it, is 'the relationship between the participant observer's outside role in society and inside role in the research setting'. As Powdermaker (1966: 9) wrote: 'to understand a strange society, the anthropologist has traditionally immersed himself in it, learning, as far as possible, to think, feel, and sometimes act as a member of its culture and at the same time as a trained anthropologist from another culture. This is the heart of the participant observation method – involvement and detachment.'

It is important not to claim more than the evidence will support. While this is true for all data collection techniques, the limits of participant observation make this especially true. The scope of a participant observer's observations is constrained by the physical limits of the role and location (see Waddington 1992: 27). From an unknown universe of events, the observer records only a small selection; that rereading field notes evokes memories of things not recorded at the time shows that selection occurs (Seale 1999: 150). The basis of this selection is often non-random and influenced by various conditions, although reflexive participant observers can indicate the basis on which some events were recorded and others not. Lone observers are bound to be selective because of the impossibility of taking everything in, which is why multiple observers can sometimes be used. Lone observers are particularly susceptible to focusing on the abnormal, aberrant and exceptional. There is also the problem of personal perspective. Participant observation can only be a partial portrait of a way of life compiled from selective records, and is thus highly autobiographical, 'the observations of a single individual selectively recorded' (Waddington 1992: 30). It is partial because it is one person's personalized view (or several people's personalized views), and because it is a vignette whose representativeness is unsure. However, as we shall see below, generalizations can be made if the research is designed properly and a reflexive observer can identify the grounds on which generalizations are permissible. Postmodern ethnographers recognize that the participant observer's view is *a* view, and a view is sometimes better than no view, and there are occasions when there is no alternative to a period of participant observation, but it should never stand alone as a research method for these sorts of reasons.

Interviewing

Some important distinctions need to be drawn before we discuss interviews as a method of data collection in ethnography. All interviews of whatever type use a verbal stimulus (the question) to elicit a verbal response (the answer) from a respondent (or set of respondents where groups are interviewed by means of focus group interviews). Some of these stimuli come in the form of 'closed questions' that shape the response, in which respondents are asked merely to select from a set of mutually exclusive answers determined beforehand (see Box 3.1). The stimulus can also come in the form of 'open questions' where the respondent has the latitude to respond freely. A questionnaire is a written device for securing written answers to closed questions by using a form that respondents fill in themselves, and is not a type of interview at all, although the questionnaire form is sometimes confused with a formal interview schedule. An interview schedule is a set of written questions to be asked of respondents in an interview; the interview itself is a face-to-face encounter between researcher and respondent in which a subject responds to the questions posed by another. Some interview schedules are formal documents with closed questions that the interviewer fills in on behalf of the respondent; some merely constitute a list or guide of open questions, the answers to which are recorded on tape or by means of notes. Highly structured interview schedules are associated with what is called structured or formal interviews, and the looser form with unstructured interviews. Semi-structured interviews may have some combination of the two, with some closed questions in the form of a structured interview schedule recorded on the schedule itself (mostly requesting fairly factual and unambiguous information of a socio-demographic kind), and other open questions written beforehand as guides and recorded on tape or by notes.

The essential feature of interviews is that a verbal stimulus is used to elicit a verbal response (whether recorded on tape or written down at the time as notes or on the interview schedule itself). However, the 'answer' is rarely itself the main object of the research but is usually taken as an index of something else that is unseen in the interview and that is the real purpose of the research. Interviews collect verbal reports of behaviour, meanings, attitudes and feelings that are never directly observed in the face-to-face encounter of the interview but that are the data the question is supposed to reveal. This means that interviewing is based on two assumptions that are critical to the technique, namely that respondents' verbal descriptions are a reliable indicator of their behaviour, meanings, attitudes and feelings, and that the stimuli (the questions) are a reliable indicator of the subject of the research.

Box 3.1

Taken from the Northern Ireland Social Attitude Survey 1994, reprinted in R. Breen, P. Devine and L. Dowds (eds) *Social Attitudes in Northern Ireland: the Fifth Report* (Belfast: Appletree Press, 1996), pp. 230–1.

Q268
How would you describe yourself?
As very prejudiced against people of other religions?
A little prejudiced?
Not prejudiced at all?
Don't know
Refuse to answer

Q272
What about relations between Catholics and Protestants?
Would you say they are better than they were five years ago?
Worse?
About the same as now?
Don't know
Other
Refuse to answer

Q289
What about the Fair Employment Commission – how does it treat Catholics and Protestants?
Catholics treated much better
Catholics treated a bit better
Both treated equally
Protestants treated much better
Protestants treated a bit better
It depends/can't say
Don't know
Refuse to answer

Proponents of other forms of data collection which go beyond verbal reports to the actual behaviour and social meanings themselves, like unsolicited personal documents, conversation analysis and, above all, participant observation, query whether these assumptions can be made.

The extent to which the questions reflect the subject of the research is a technical problem of question setting, but it is essential that they elicit what the researcher intends. Careful question setting goes hand in hand with pilot testing the questions beforehand. Ambiguous questions may result in respondents interpreting the question in different ways from each other, so that answers are not comparable, and in a way that the researcher does not intend, so that it does not reveal what the researcher thinks it does (which means that it is often beneficial to seek the same information in a number of ways by asking different questions on the same thing). Ambiguous concepts and theoretical ideas can also be difficult to operationalize in questions simple enough for people to understand while still reflecting what the researcher intends. Pilot testing various formulations is important.

With respect to the other assumption, people sometimes lie, they can be inconsistent by not doing that they say they do, they can seek 'social approval' and say things in interviews that are socially accepted and approved rather than what they actually believe, feel or do. This has the effect of minimizing the articulation of extreme opinions and behaviour and exaggerating the centre, and communication can be distorted by what is known as the 'interviewer effect'. The interview is a face-to-face encounter between people, and the socio-demographic characteristics of the people involved can influence the course of the interaction and the responses given. The interviewer thus creates the reality of the interview encounter by drawing the participants together and therefore produces situated understandings that are tied to the specific interactional episode of the encounter. For example, respondents may worry about the purpose of the research, why they themselves have been chosen and what use the data will be put to, and these anxieties can affect honesty and openness. The social cues of the interviewer, in terms of gender, age, religion, ethnicity, social class, educational background and so on, can interact with anxieties within the interviewee to distort the replies. Respondents may be reluctant to admit to something or express an opinion depending upon what they think about the person asking the questions, although this reactive effect occurs in all forms of overt research where people know they are research subjects, including participant observation.

The interviewer effect, however, can be moderated to a degree. Some forms of unstructured interviews can be so informal that they almost take the form of natural conversations, and skilful interviewers can manage and manipulate the topic choice to an extent that it constitutes an interview. It is also possible to have one person do all the interviews so that respondents are at least subject to a constant interviewer effect; to randomize the effect by picking a random set of interviewers; to minimize the inequalities between interviewer and respondent by matching them in socio-demographic terms; and to institute controls and supervision to monitor the extent of the interviewer effect. Reflexivity by researchers is also important to ensure that they are aware of the situated understandings that interview data represent and that they convey this to readers when writing up.

Advocates of interviews as a data collection technique – and it is one of the most popular techniques used in qualitative and survey research – have been forced to take these criticisms on board. A number of different types of interview encounter, with varying procedures, have been developed in order to try to counteract these flaws and ensure that respondents' replies are truthful and unswayed by extraneous factors. Interviews are normally classified according to their degree of standardization. One solution to these difficulties is to standardize and try to eliminate all known sources of bias. The structured or formal type uses an interview schedule with closed questions, with explicit instructions to interviewers about when to prompt and what to say in order to ensure that the stimuli (the questions) take the same form for everyone. Clear guidelines exist to ensure standardization of this kind of interview (see Box 2.1). Since the stimulus takes the same form, differences in the response are assumed to be real differences rather than variations provoked by differences in the way questions were asked. At the other pole are unstructured interviews. The solution here is to avoid structure so that exploration of respondents' meanings is untrammelled by formality. In this type of interview there may be some questions worked out beforehand, or a guide to topics that need to be addressed, but open questions are used and there is a relative absence of structure. Researchers give themselves the latitude to ask whatever they want, in the form and order they determine, and to prompt, probe and ask supplementary questions as the occasion or respondent warrants. It takes the form of a natural conversation that is skilfully guided or focused by the researcher. The rationale behind this type is that the absence of formal structure gives greater freedom for respondents to answer accurately and in depth. Semi-structured interviews fall in between.

Each type is best suited to dealing with particular kinds of research problem. The humanistic or qualitative researcher values the unstructured or semi-structured type because it gives access to people's meaning-endowing capacities and produces rich, deep data that come in the form of extracts of natural language. Unstructured interviews require great interviewer skills; the interviewer needs to be able to sustain and control conversation, to know when to probe, prompt and when to listen and remain silent, and to read the social cues from respondents and know when to stop pushing a line of questioning. They also depend upon a good relationship between interviewer and respondent, especially where the information being sought is controversial, sensitive and emotional. This sometimes comes from prefacing the interview with a period of ice-breaking but can involve more extensive preparatory meetings before the interview takes place; which is why it is often used in conjunction with participant observation. Non-threatening questions are also best asked first and sensitive topics addressed only after a rapport has been established. Positivist or quantitative researchers sometimes use the unstructured type in pilot testing as a preliminary to a more structured type (especially in order to determine the 'answers' from which respondents are later asked to select in closed questions), but mostly they value the structured type. This is because it allows people to be interviewed quickly over a vast geographical area using relatively untrained interviewees (since the format is worked out beforehand and the nature of the interaction in the interview is pre-programmed, interview skills can be negligible). It collects data that can be rendered easily into numerate form and be characterized as 'hard' and 'objective'.

Ethnographers thus clearly tend towards the use of unstructured or indepth interviews, although positivist ethnography may have limited use for structured interviews and closed questions. Burgess (1984: 102) calls this type of interview 'conversations with a purpose'. This highlights its central feature: to engage in as informal a face-to-face encounter as possible so that it appears almost like a natural conversation between people with an established relationship. It is often used in combination with participant observation and other techniques that access social meanings, although it can be used in isolation. Humanistic and positivist ethnographers alike consider the unstructured, in-depth interview as an important means to access life on the 'inside' and to represent it accurately. By following various rules for 'how to do' unstructured interviewing, they see problems as surmountable, especially by developing close relationships with the respondent beforehand and by combining the method with observation (see Box 3.2).

In contrast, postmodern ethnographers have looked critically at interviewing (see especially Douglas 1985; Krieger 1983). Since interviewers are human beings acting in a face-to-face encounter that forms a piece of social interaction, they query the role played by the interviewer, whom they see as 'creating' or 'producing' the data (see Fontana and Frey 1998: 62). Interview data are thus 'situated' and context bound to the interviewer (much like the participant observer). They are also bound to the situation in which they were collected. Since unstructured interviews are largely situational encounters in everyday life, the advice given in textbooks on 'how to do' interviewing they see as largely irrelevant. In Douglas's (1985) account of what he calls 'creative interviewing', researchers using unstructured interviews must be creative, forget 'how-to' rules and adapt themselves to the ever-changing situations they face in interview encounters, thus allowing their subjects to express themselves more freely. The thrust of the postmodern in-depth interview is to try to allow subjects a greater voice and to minimize the influence of the interviewer, and Krieger's (1983) 'polyphonic interviewing' and Denzin's (1989) 'interpretative interactionism' are alternative modes of unstructured interviewing in which subjects are supposedly allowed a greater voice, although what they really describe is alternative ways of presenting interview data in the text rather than differences in the nature of the face-to-face encounter.

'Feminist interviews' are much the same in redrawing the power relationship between respondent and researcher in order to get better access to the subject's voice. This involves a critique of conventional interviewing,

Box 3.2

In making a case for the unstructured interview in qualitative sociology, H. Schwartz and J. Jacobs, *Qualitative Sociology* (New York: Free Press, 1979), pp. 41–2, argue:

> In any kind of interviewing there is a possibility that there will be discrepancy between what people say and what they mean. If it is true that people do not always say what they mean or mean what they say, then it can be argued that the researcher in a face-to-face informal interview may be as easily deceived as the survey researcher employing structured interviews or questionnaires ... The informal interviewer has a greater degree of feedback [which] can be used as a way of evaluating the status of the respondents' accounts. In addition, the social organisation of this kind of interview situation allows it to alter its own ongoing course [and] the interviewer is free to alter his line of questioning accordingly ... Exactly how does face-to-face unstructured interviewing provide a stronger basis for assessing the goals, intentions, purposes and behaviour of another than structured interviewing and/or questionnaires? The respondent, knowing his own life history, the ins and outs of the cultural milieu of which he is a part, and his own self-concept and practical purposes of the interview, has an 'ethnographic context' in which he decides both what to say to the interviewer and the precise meaning and significance of what he is saying. Unless provision is made for it, the interviewer does not have such an ethnographic context within which to interpret what the respondent means. In this connection a respondent [should] be asked a series of detailed ethnographic questions about the main issues covered in the interview. In this way, the interviewer may acquire this elusive 'ethnographic context' and be better able to interpret the significance of a respondent's remarks. Obviously it is better to be familiar with this ethnographic context before the interview starts through some kind of prior observation of (and participation in) the subject's life-world.

whether informal or standardized, as masculine. Conventional interviews are masculine in the language used, the power imbalance between respondent and researcher, the exploitation of subjects for opportunistic reasons of research and the gloss given to women's experiences and lives. Thus, stress is laid on capturing women's narratives, stories and biographical experiences by means of natural conversations in a personalized manner where interviewer and subject are partners. Feminist-based interviews require openness, emotional engagement and the development of potentially long-term relationships based on trust and emotional reciprocity. In the process of collecting data from subjects (normally women), the researcher seeks to empower them in their particular setting, enabling them to deal better with the problems they experience as women. The feminist ethic of commitment and egalitarianism contrasts markedly with the positivist ethic of detachment and role distance (for a selection of writers who argue thus see Oakley 1981; Roberts 1981; Smith 1987; Reinharz 1992). Thus, feminist interviewing redefines the nature of the face-to-face encounter, so that researcher and subject become co-equals; people are not 'respondents' but 'participants', not 'objects' but 'subjects'. It is this that makes 'feminist methodology' distinct (on feminist epistemology see Stanley and Wise 1990; Fonow and Cook 1992; for an account of a feminist ethnography see Harvey 1994), although as Luff (1999) has shown, these ideals tend not to work when the subjects of the research are powerful women hostile to feminism.

As well as a certain style of interviewing, feminist interviews are also characterised by a focus on certain sorts of topics, although the two things go together. Women's lives and experiences are revealed and disclosed in their own words and in their own way in an interview situation in which they are empowered and not made to feel subordinate. This means that normally women researchers do feminist interviewing to avoid 'patronizing', 'paternalistic attitudes' that misunderstand and misrepresent women's experiences and to ensure that the gender of the interviewer affects the situated meanings disclosed in the encounter in such a way as better to elicit the female subject's voice. Fontana and Frey (1998: 66) have alluded to the similarity between feminist-based interviewing and humanistic models of social research because of the commitment to maintain the integrity of the subject's experience in their own terms, and also to postmodern ethnography because of the realization that there cannot be an 'objective' interview, in that the sex (in this case) of the interviewer and respondent makes a difference. But feminist interviewing is distinguished by its heightened moral concern for the subject, the attempt to redress the patriarchal power struggle through the empowerment of subjects and the discrediting of male researchers interviewing female subjects (the same applies to white women researchers interviewing black women or middle-class ones interviewing working-class women).

Feminist interviewing is focused on narratives which capture women's lives, and is very similar to the life history and oral history interviews, techniques which go back to ethnography's origins. Anthropologists often focused on the life of one or two key individuals as informants, and life histories were used in Thomas and Znaniecki's famous study of the Polish peasant (see Burgess 1984: 125–6), which was one of the early classics of the Chicago School. Life history interviews focus on the autobiography of a key actor because they are interesting in their own right or because they are representative of a group. Oral history interviews (see Box 3.3) take a backward look too, but the aim

---

Box 3.3

Extract from J. D. Brewer, *The Royal Irish Constabulary: an Oral History* (Belfast: Institute of Irish Studies, 1990), pp. 14–19.

Oral history is not a subject area of history but a data collection technique which can be applied to any topic within the living memory of people. It offers a view from below. By looking at events from the vantage point of those at the bottom of society, it charts the history of the unknown people, people who do not figure in documents and records – the soldiers rather than generals, the followers rather than leaders, the citizens rather than monarch . . . The complaints made against oral history are several. First it is supposed to be marginal because it is restricted to the modern sphere. A more important criticism is the claim that it is trivial because it ignores all those broader processes and issues which do not penetrate people's minds and of which they are ignorant. The implication of this is that analysts are interested only in broader structural processes and the ordinary features of life are of little import . . . In another sense, the criticism assumes significance only if the method is not augmented by other data sources . . . The most damning criticism levelled against oral history is that the data is methodologically suspect. These include poor memory, systematic evasion, untruthfulness, *ex-post facto* glorification or idealisations of the past. None are unique to oral history . . . This is true of all sources that rely on people's self reports but can be overcome. Oral historians should search for internal consistency in the narrative, cross check details, weigh evidence, and develop an innately critical attitude toward their data . . . Most of the supposed weaknesses of oral sources, therefore, are not insurmountable. There are positive qualities to this form of data. Speech is a less restricted social skill than literacy and is not so affected by advancing age. Oral history allows people the opportunity to offer interpretations of the past . . . It is also applicable where there is difficulty in obtaining ready access to a large number of people for reasons of sensitivity, which is why the oral-history-as-life-history approach has been used most frequently to study deviants.

---

is to reconstruct the past, or versions of the past, by means of personal historical information rather than reconstructing a key person's biography (on oral history see Thompson 1988), although the two can merge. Oral history interviews mostly focus on groups excluded from official historical sources, and are thus very popular with feminist researchers, among others.

With respect to life histories, Fetterman (1998: 51) explained that key actors, whether male or female, 'often provide ethnographers with rich, detailed autobiographical descriptions'. These life histories are very personal, and told by people who are sometimes not representative of any group, but their personal story reveals much about the fabric of social life across time. But as well as revealing the actor's autobiography and perspective, the life history interview can be used to collect family tree data that give an account of social changes across time, place and the generations in numerate form (see Miller 2000). It is important to see the life histories that people disclose as situated in the present, and thus they can be subject to distortions, attentional modifications, as Schutz calls them, and memory loss. But how an actor constructs a biographical account or life history from the vantage point of the present can itself become the object of the research, as it was with Garfinkel's (1967: 116–85) study of Agnes the transsexual or my study (Brewer, 1984a, b, 1988) of former fascists looking back on their membership (see Box 3.4).

Box 3.4

Extract from John D. Brewer, Micro-sociology and the 'duality of structure', in N. Fielding (ed.) *Actions and Structure: Research Methods and Social Theory* (London: Sage, 1988), pp. 150, 154.

Between 1973 and 1976, the author undertook a series of interviews over several meetings with fifteen former members of the BUF [British Union of Fascists]. The data have been used to explore many issues about Sir Oswald Mosley's peculiar brand of Fascism. The interviews were partly designed to elicit the respondents' accounts of why they joined the movement. In this respect, the former Fascists were doing life history as an ordinary practical accomplishment. All such biographical accounts are retrospective and influenced by the passage of time. The life histories of the former Fascists are unusual because they are more retrospective than most and more indexically conditioned by the time-space differences between their membership and the occasions of their account. The awareness among the former Fascists of this difference, and the change in meaning which being a Fascist has undergone as a result of it, is a fundamental feature of the accomplishment of a life history . . . To offer an account of one's actions is both to explicate the reasons for them and to supply the normative grounds whereby they may be justified. This was what the former Fascists were doing in emphasising the theme of crisis in the account of their life history.

Personal documents

Records are kept about us by schools, doctors, tax offices, banks, hire purchase companies, credit card companies, mobile phone companies, universities, various government departments, perhaps even the police and the courts. Many of these records contain personal information, others are used as the basis of various sorts of official statistics. All these documents and written records provide data for the aspiring researcher. Their use carries certain advantages. Most already exist prior to the research (however, some researchers ask informants to keep diaries during fieldwork, and even interview them on the contents; see Burgess 1984: 128–30), so they are unsolicited; the documents are normally compiled under natural conditions as a routine part of the operation of society, so they are not contrived; they have been compiled for a very long time and some may provide longitudinal data; they often exist independently of the person about whom they contain material, so permission may not be necessary, although this is not the case with some data sources covered by the Data Protection Act and certain personal documents; and, perhaps above all, they are non-reactive in that they were complied without the respondents' knowledge that they were going to be used for research purposes.

There are several dimensions on which it is possible to classify types of documents. The first is whether they are primary or secondary. Primary documents are original sets of data compiled by the writer, like a letter, tape recording of conversation or transcript of a court trial. Secondary documents contain data obtained at second hand from someone else's primary document, like a newspaper report of a court trial, an edited transcript of someone's letters or an edited transcript of a conversation. A second dimension is whether the documents are contemporary, compiled as a document at the time and containing a record of data as it happens, or retrospective, produced as a documentary record after the event. Not all historical documents are retrospective. Parish records, old manuscripts, minutes of meetings and other archival material may well have been recorded at the time of the events or behaviour they describe. Likewise, not all diaries, for example, are contemporary, for they can contain recollections recorded well after the event. This dimension, therefore, does not refer to the age of the document, but the length of time it took for the information on the document to be recorded after it happened. The third dimension by which to classify documents is whether or not they are personal or official. Personal (or 'informal') documents are those which provide the individual's own account, like diaries (for a study which involved informants keeping a diary see Finch 1983), letters (for a report on a study using letters see Burgess 1984: 135–7), suicide notes (for a study using suicide notes see Jacobs 1979) and autobiographies (on which see Stanley 1993). Official (or 'formal') documents are produced by a person about someone else, mostly for institutional or organizational purposes, like clinic records, parish records and death certificates, Hansard (the verbatim record of parliament) or the census. This gives us a typology reflected in Figure 3.2.

Generalizations from documents are problematic if there are only a few of them, and may be impossible if they are personal documents pertaining to one individual (unless that person is somehow typical or representative of a group), although some personal documents, such as letters or suicide notes, can be obtained with such frequency that sampling can be undertaken and generalizations drawn. Often, however, access to documents depends upon availability, and few may be found. The authenticity of the document should be investigated (the well known 'Hitler diaries', for example, turned out to be a spoof), and their contents should be examined for deliberate deception as well as distortion, exaggeration and misrepresentation. The dogs that do not bark, as followers of Sherlock Holmes will know, are important and researchers should address the significant omissions from personal documents.

CONTEMPORARY PRIMARY Compiled by the writer at the time		CONTEMPORARY SECONDARY Transcribed from primary sources at the time	
Personal	**Official**	**Personal**	**Official**
Letter. Tape of talk. Suicide note.	Court record. Hansard. Census. Minutes of meeting.	'Ghosted' autobiography. Edited transcript of talk, letters etc.	Research using the census.
RETROSPECTIVE PRIMARY Compiled by the writer after the event		**RETROSPECTIVE SECONDARY** Transcribed from primary sources after the event	
Personal	**Official**	**Personal**	**Official**
Diary. Autobiography. Life history. Oral history.	Novels. Historical archives. Film archives.	Research using diaries. Biography using the subject's autobiography.	Medical records Parish records. Newspaper reports.

Figure 3.2

Studies of natural language

Language is ubiquitous, but mostly studied for the content of the talk. An area of study called 'pragmatics' or 'discourse analysis' examines the structure of the talk itself. Sometimes language is studied in this way because the organization of talk is itself the topic, but often because it reveals something about the social situation in which the talk takes place. In this latter regard, studies of natural language are a data collection technique (as argued by Wooffitt 1993). Pragmatics studies natural language in naturally occurring settings, and it is relevant as a data collection technique for three reasons: language is a form of social interaction; it presupposes shared knowledge; and is inseparable from its social setting. Data can be collected on all these things. Language and setting are so closely tied, for example, that it is sometimes possible to reconstruct from a fragment of conversation the whole social world that produced it. The single word 'nagging', for example, conjures a whole universe of gender relations and social stereotypes.

Three types of discourse analysis are relevant to the study of social behaviour. The first is the analysis of the discrete discourse styles that relate to particular social settings, or what Goffman (1981) calls 'forms of talk', such as the types of discourse associated with, say, teaching, the court room, and radio announcing. The second is what Hymes (1962) calls the 'ethnography of communication', where the analysis is devoted to the functions of language in particular settings, such as the function of humour in drawing moral boundaries (Davies 1982), doctor–patient communication in establishing professional distance or what Emmison (1988) calls 'defeat talk' among sports people, by which they adjust to defeat without losing faith in their ability. The third is known as 'conversation analysis', associated with Harvey Sacks and ethnomethodology, which explores how conversations are organized and structured into the turn-taking format (for a programmatic statement of this in the context of research methods see Heritage 1997; ten Have 1998). A great deal of the early work in this field concentrated on explicating the organization of conversation as a form of social interaction and the common-sense procedures and devices which structured it. With this clearly understood, conversation analysis has been employed more recently as a form of data collection to study an array of social settings and behaviours, including stigma among adults with learning difficulties (Yearley and Brewer 1989; Brewer *et al.* 1991), politeness (Brown and Levinson 1987), gender differences (Zimmerman and West 1975) and court room behaviour (Atkinson and Drew 1979; a review of some of this research can be found in Boden and Zimmerman 1991).

Vignettes

In the context of data collection, a **vignette** is a technique that involves hypothetical or real scenarios being put to respondents for their comments. Finch

(1987) identified their use in the context of survey research, where they were used as short stories featuring social circumstances or scenarios that interviewees were asked to respond to. They are more commonly used in qualitative research (Hughes 1998; Barter and Renold 1999). In qualitative research, respondents are usually asked to respond to a particular situation – real or hypothetical – by stating how they would respond, what they would do or how they imagine a third party behaving. The vignettes offered for response invariably involve some moral or ethical dilemma. It is thus often used to explore sensitive topics, like drug injecting and HIV risk (Hughes 1998) or sexual and physical abuse of the elderly (Rahman, 1996), or with sensitive groups like children, among which it has been used to explore the effects of divorce and sexual abuse (for a review see Hill 1997).

In outlining its possible usages in qualitative research, Barter and Renold (1999) suggested that it could be used as an ice-breaker at the beginning of an interview or a closure at the end, and as part of a multi-method approach to enhance existing methods (for an example with relation to child abuse see MacAuley 1996) or to generate data untapped by other methods. They give the following advice. The stories in the vignettes must appear plausible and real, should not depict eccentric and extraordinary events, should refer in some way to the respondent's personal experience and should describe events and circumstances they can understand.

Triangulation

Ethnography-understood-as-fieldwork may include observational work alongside informal (and occasionally formal) interviews, life histories and personal documents. Rarely is one data collection technique used without others, and while all can be used outside the context of ethnography, what marks their deployment in ethnography is the development of 'relationships between the researcher and those researched' (Burgess 1984: 5) in which there is close involvement in the setting, and sometimes direct participation in the activities under study. The use of multiple methods, or triangulation, is a routine injunction to researchers (Denzin 1970), yet ethnography does this as a matter of routine. Denzin argued that triangulation should involve not just multiple methods (data triangulation), but also multiple investigators (investigator triangulation) and multiple methodological and theoretical frameworks (theoretical and methodological triangulation). Combined operations like this are feasible in ethnography, and one of the central features of ethnography is the range of data collected from different sources.

Triangulation was traditionally associated with humanist, positivist and post postmodern notions of ethnography as a procedure for improving the correspondence between the analysis and the 'reality' it sought to represent faithfully. Silverman (1993) doubts whether it has relevance to postmodern ethnographers who have lost the ambition to represent accurately the social world. But even in this type of ethnography, practitioners recognize that all methods impose perspectives on reality by the type of data that they collect, and each tends to reveal something slightly different about the same symbolic 'reality'. Thus, data triangulation is essential in this type of ethnography, not as a form of validity (which is seen by them as a spurious 'scientific' notion) but as an alternative to validation (Denzin and Lincoln 1998: 4). Hence Denzin and Lincoln's (1998: 3–4) remark that ethnographers, like qualitative researchers generally, are *bricoleurs*, or jacks-of-all-trades, professional do-it-yourself people who collect data from all sources and in all ways as best fits the purpose. This 'methodological pragmatism' (Burgess 1982: 163) or 'kitchen sink' approach to data (Miller 1997: 24) is recommended in all types of ethnography, however, ensuring a more rounded picture of the one symbolic reality because various sources of data are used to explore it.

Case studies and generalizations

Two other closely related features of research design are the selection of the case or cases to be studied and planning for the possibility of generalizations from the research. In his critique of ethnography, Hammersley (1992: 183ff) rightly reminds us that there is nothing intrinsic to 'case studies' that makes them qualitative and ethnographic. A 'case' as such can be defined as any phenomenon located in time and space about which data are collected and analysed (Hammersley, 1992: 184), and can comprise single individuals or a group, particular events or situations, a specific organization, social institution, neighbourhood, national society or global process. Case studies can address the micro situation of a single person in everyday life or the macro situation of a nation state in the global world. Case studies are defined by the focus on the instance of the phenomenon, not by the method used to study it. As Robert Stake remarked, 'case study is not a methodological choice but a choice of object to be studied' (Stake 1998: 86). There is no necessary association between 'the case study approach' and data collection via ethnography, participant observation or qualitative methods generally, nor any natural link with the objective to explore people's social meanings and reality-constituting processes. Some case studies can be quantitative and highly statistical.

Nor does it follow that case studies focus on the particular at the expense of the general. Generalizability of the findings is possible with a case study, although attention needs to be given to the grounds on which generalizations are made. Stake (1998: 88–9) identified three different types of case study. The *intrinsic* case is the study of one particular instance (or perhaps the only instance) of the phenomenon because it is interesting in its own right; the *instrumental* case is studied because it facilitates understanding of something else, whether it be a theoretical debate or a social problem; and the *collective* case studies several instances of the same phenomenon to identify common characteristics. Collective cases permit empirical generalizations, while instrumental ones permit theoretical inference (among other things), both of which Hammersley (1992: 86) identifies as forms of generalization.

While not all case studies are qualitative, all ethnographic research involves case study. Ethnographic case study is distinguished by exploration of the case or cases as they present themselves naturally in the field and by the researcher's direct involvement and participation in them. It shares the weaknesses of all case study, namely the problems associated with small sample size and concerns over the feasibility of studying the general by means of the particular. These weaknesses are related. By studying small samples, it is said, ethnographers produce findings that cannot be generalized. Ethnographers responded to this criticism by arguing that their trade-off merely reversed that of survey researchers, where depth was sacrificed for breadth. Collecting very detailed, 'rich' and 'deep' data is time consuming and demanding, and ethnographers are not able to devote themselves to more than one or two fields, and although this may involve many cases depending upon the number that naturally present themselves in the field, the restriction to only one or two fields can also limit generalizations. It is essential not to exaggerate the generalizability of findings obtained from one or two fields, as Fielding (1993: 169) warned, but this does not mean that generalizations from ethnographic research are impossible.

As Dey (1993: 261; also Hammersley 1992: 86) explains, generalization involves theoretical inference from data to develop concepts and connections, and empirical application of the data to a wider population. In the first instance we infer a general statement about the data; in the second we apply that statement beyond the data on which it is based. Because it involves a limited number of cases, or just a single case, in a restricted field or setting, ethnographic research is better at making theoretical inferences than at applying them to a wider population; but this is still a form of generalization (ethnography and theory building are discussed in Chapter 5). However, empirical generalizations to a wider population are feasible, despite the limited number of cases, if the cases permit comparisons and have been selected by a sampling procedure. The comparative method is normally associated with multivariate statistical techniques to study social processes across nation states, but this variable-oriented form of comparative method is only one type. The other is case-oriented comparisons (see Ragin 1987), which involves holistic comparison of cases. There are two ways this can be done (see Finch 1986). First, it is possible to design the individual project in the mould of similar ones in different fields so that comparisons can be made across them (see Box 3.5) and a body of cumulative knowledge can be built up that is longitudinal, historical and comparative. The second is to design the project as a series of parallel ethnographic studies with different cases or with the same case in different fields (see Box 3.6), perhaps even using multiple

Box 3.5

Extract from J. D. Brewer, *Inside the RUC: Routine Policing in a Divided Society* (Oxford: The Clarendon Press, 1991), with K. Magee, p. 31.

Our project was deliberately designed to follow the pattern of ethnographic studies of routine policing, so as to add to this tradition the dimension provided of studying this kind of policing in a divided society. In a strategy pioneered by the affluent-worker study in Luton [Goldthorpe *et al.* 1968], which one might call the optimal-case approach, a site was chosen for the research [which] was particularly germane to the topic [because] routine policing is possible as a result of the virtual absence of political violence in the locale. If we are to establish how and to what extent routine policing is affected by Northern Ireland's divisions, it would be useless to base our research where there is only militarised political policing.

Box 3.6

Extract from J. D. Brewer, B. Lockhart and P. Rodgers, *Crime in Ireland 1945–95* (Oxford: The Clarendon Press, 1997), pp. 123, 127.

The rationale behind the ethnographic study of crime in Belfast is to use the benefits of the ethnographic method to supplement the quantitative approach to crime trends. The data are drawn from two closely matched police sub-divisions in Belfast, Castlereagh in East Belfast and Woodburn in West Belfast, the former largely Protestant and the latter largely Catholic, thus reproducing the city's communal divide . . . To aid comparison, it was important to select closely matching sub-divisions, and ones which provided a cross-section of social classes and housing styles. While the sub-divisions largely reflect Belfast's 'religious geography', each contain pockets where members of the other religious community live. In fieldwork we made sure that we covered organisations in these enclaves.

researchers. In Miller's (1997) ethnographic study of the effects of modernity on Trinidadians, he selected one case study area that was typical of these social changes, and within that concentrated on four different communities or fieldwork sites with the intention of making some broad generalizations about the way modernity is experienced ethnographically by people. As another example, Willis's (1977) remarks about class and cultural reproduction in capitalist society were based on how working-class kids 'learnt to labour' and thus ended up in the same kinds of jobs as their parents (an ethnography enthusiastically appropriated by Giddens as an illustration of structuration theory; see Giddens 1984: 289–309). It was based on fieldwork in one poor district of Birmingham but within this field involved systematic comparison between six different cases and fieldwork sites (see Willis 1977: 4–7).

The key to making empirical generalizations from case-oriented comparisons is effective sampling of cases. Sampling is traditionally associated with quantitative research, but it is important to qualitative research as well. To **sample** means to select the case or cases for study from the basic unit of study where it is impossible to cover all instances of that unit. In some rare examples, where the unit is small or unusual, it is possible to include a universal study of the unit, but mostly it is impossible to have complete coverage. In these circumstances, a sample is drawn from the universe of units. In quantitative research, a distinction is made between probability and non-probability sampling. In the former, each instance of the unit has the same probability of being included in the sample; in the latter, there is no way of estimating this probability, nor even any certainty that every instance has some chance. This is relevant to sampling in ethnographic research in two ways. Probability sampling can be used when surveys of the population are used as a form of triangulation to accompany more qualitative methods, most frequently in community studies where the universe of units (the people who live there) is clearly identifiable and accessible (a good example is Miller 1997: 30). Mostly, however, ethnographers use non-probability sampling to select cases from a wider universe. Such sampling can be made of the fields in which to site the research (selecting the location of the case or cases) and of the units of study within them (such as selecting informants from the universe of people in the field who exemplify the case).

Because the prefix 'non' implies that probability sampling is the standard, those ethnographers who reject the natural science model of social research and its associated forms of sampling procedure prefer other terminology with which to describe their sampling practice. Thus Denzin (1970), for example, prefers the nomenclature of 'interactive' and 'non-interactive' sampling, in which the former becomes the standard to analyse 'natural' interaction. Glaser and Strauss (1967) use the term **'theoretical sampling'** to describe the inductive approach of the ethnographer (more on which in Chapter 5). These semantics, however, do not alter the basic procedures used to obtain non-statistical samples. These are the snowball technique (obtaining units, such as informants, from other units), quota sampling (selecting units on the basis of their presence in the universe, proportional or not), judgemental sampling (the researcher selecting the most appropriate instances of the unit for the topic at hand) and, as sometimes happens, sheer accident and good fortune.

Through these sampling strategies, ethnographers must sample the research case and site, the time frame spent there and the events and people to be studied. This provides two benefits: first, it ensures the representativeness of the findings as instances that make up the case; second, it facilitates generalizations to other cases or fields. The first is important irrespective of an ambition to engage in empirical generalizations in order to avoid focusing on the unusual and abnormal, but ethnographers who seek to generalize must design their sampling in order to maximize this opportunity. If this is the intent (and it need not be), researchers should sample field sites in such a way that they have multiple fields around which they can move easily and thus make comparisons, as represented in the examples of Miller (1997) and Willis (1977) (see also Box 3.7). On the selection of field site, Burgess (1984: 61; also see Spradley 1980) identified five criteria, although he warned that few sites permit them all and compromises have to be made:

- simplicity (selecting a site that offers the opportunity to move from simple to more complex situations and sub-sites);
- accessibility (selecting a site that permits access and entry);
- unobtrusiveness (selecting a site that permits the researcher to be low profile;
- permissibleness (selecting a site in which the research is permissible and the researcher has free entry);
- participation (selecting a site in which the researcher is able to participate in the ongoing activities).

The activities that occur in the field vary with time. This presents the researcher with two choices. The first concerns the length of time devoted to fieldwork, which must be long enough to experience the full range of routines and behaviours contained in the case and to develop a proper understanding of them. If the ethnographer is not in the field permanently during fieldwork (as some social anthropologists and community study researchers are), the second choice is the sampling of the time spent in the field collecting data. Visits to the field must be frequent enough and be at times which provide a representative sample of the events and activities that occur there. A form of 'time sampling' can be adopted in which ethnographers record all the activities that take place in a 12- or 24-hour period in order to gauge the range of activities (for an example of such an approach see Burgess 1984: 61–71). Similar results are obtained by asking informants to complete time budget diaries. Sampling of events is related to that of time, given that it is impossible to record details on everything that occurs. Ethnographers need to sample the events they encounter in the field, and distinguish frequent routine activities, irregular events that are special but typical and events that

Box 3.7

Extract from J. D. Brewer, *Inside the RUC: Routine Policing in a Divided Society* (Oxford: The Clarendon Press, 1991), with K. Magee, p. 19.

The fieldworker's contact in the field was restricted at the beginning to a few hours a shift once a week, gradually being built up to a full shift, including nights, twice a week. Time was initially divided between two sections [groups of police officers] within the station in order to broaden the range of contacts, and visits were made to other stations. As the time devoted to data collection lengthened and data collection itself became more intensive, the focus narrowed to one section. However, other constables were encountered regularly in the canteen, on guard duty, and in the neighbourhood and community policing units, and the personnel in the section periodically changed as a result of transfers. We were provided, therefore, with as broad a range of contacts as is possible within one station, while still becoming close to one section, as is necessary in ethnographic research. Fieldwork took place over a twelve-month period.

are abnormal and unusual. These kinds of events need to be selectively sampled over a given time period and comparisons made.

The sampling of people is also critical. In some ethnographic research, the people to be studied are identifiable because of the field selected as the research site (a police station, hospital, local neighbourhood), although even here selection may be involved in identifying informants, while some people (such as members of deviant groups or cultures) may be harder to identify. In the latter circumstance, snowball sampling may help to locate people. Key informants can be usual in providing ethnographers with contacts to other group members, and different individuals can be selected in this way so as to provide access to different sites or open up difficult corners of access in one site. The more individuals who act in this capacity the better, since no person has full knowledge and it avoids being misled by one informant. Key informants are thus usually selected for their ability to portray and make accessible aspects of the field, which involves judgemental sampling on the part of the ethnographer as they select various key informants on the basis of race, class, age, status, role and even appearance, as best fits the field and topic. As Burgess (1984: 75) explains:

The selection of individuals in field studies is a different procedure from the selection procedures associated with statistical sampling. In field research informants are selected for their knowledge of a particular setting which may complement the researcher's observations and point towards further investigation.

Sometimes, however, key informants appear by sheer luck and fortune. Whyte's account of how he came across 'Doc' in his ethnography of American-Italian street gangs in the 1950s (Whyte 1955) shows how opportunism can end up making the key informant almost as famous as the ethnographer. Ken Pryce's (1979) study of the St Paul's district of Bristol, an inner city area with a large Afro-Caribbean community, is also revealing on the issue of luck in meeting 'Segie', his 'Doc'. As a West Indian himself, Pryce (1979: 280) wrote:

> when I started my research, not only the coloured community but the entire city of Bristol was totally unfamiliar to me. Getting to know the St Paul's area was especially difficult . . . As I was boarding a No. 11 bus going into the St Paul's district, a very friendly and garrulous Jamaican saw me and asked me if I was new in Bristol . . . When we parted that night, we agreed to meet again.

Other issues of good practice

There are several other issues that need to be thought about carefully in an ethnographic research design and that are equally fundamental to the research process. These include negotiating access, developing and maintaining a role in the field, establishing trust, recording data unobtrusively, ethical practice in the field, the question of gender and other identities that have to be handled in the field and the exit strategy from the field. We can consider these remaining issues now; that they have been left to last does not demean their importance.

Access

Without access to the field, the research could not be done (for a discussion of access see Hornsby-Smith 1993). Ethnographers gain entry to the field in a variety of different ways, which vary from case to case, meaning that practitioners must remain flexible. Sometimes access is by means of an introduction by a member, and the closer the ties the member has to the group the greater their ability to vouch for the researcher. Where no such intermediary exists, entry can be effected by performing some non-threatening role in the field, such as going along to church services, volunteering time in a school or visiting local cafes and neighbourhood stores (see Fetterman 1998: 33–4). Careful planning is thus advisable in order to be prepared. Berg (1998: 130) recommends that a period be spent in the library attempting to locate as much information about the field as possible (the people, groups, location and the circumstances and problems which affect them). Entry to the field is affected by whether the research is overt or covert: if the former, access must be negotiated and permission obtained; if the latter, while permission is not needed since the research is disguised, entry must still be thought about in order to establish the most suitable role from which to research covertly (it must be a role that warrants one's presence in the field and permits features of the inquiry, such as asking questions and taking notes).

With overt research, thought needs to be given to what is sensitive about the field and the issues that are likely to be controversial (on sensitive research see Renzetti and Lee 1993; Lee 1994). These sensitivities may well affect how you approach the issue of access with the gatekeeper (see Box 3.8). Gatekeepers are those individuals that have the power to grant access to the field, such as gang leaders, tribal chiefs and heads of organizations and bureaucracies like headteachers and police chiefs. These are formal gate-keepers and they can impose what Douglas calls 'retrenchment from the front'. However, at lower levels in the organization or group there are usu-ally a number of informal gatekeepers who can affect access, sometimes positively (being more open and forthcoming than the formal gatekeeper), sometimes negatively (by objecting to the permission given on their behalf by someone else and trying to limit what is seen and heard). These 'limits from below' are equally important. With respect to police organizations, Fox and Lundman (1974) identify two 'gates' through which researchers must pass: winning the support of senior managers and that of the rank-and-file members. Dingwall (1977) discusses similar problems with respect to his research on health visitors, as I do in the RUC (Brewer 1990, 1991a: 28). It is for this reason that we should distinguish between 'open' and 'closed' access, the latter involving fields where controls are likely to be imposed and barriers erected to research (see Hornsby-Smith 1993: 53).

Access within overt research therefore requires skilful negotiation and renegotiation, often requiring 'research bargains' or compromises with either the gatekeeper who holds the key to entry or the subjects in the field; and the more sensitive the research, the greater are these compromises likely to be (for the example of the RUC see Brewer 1990: 592). This is what Pawson (1999) means by the contrast between the ideal and the real in research practice. Burgess (1984: 45) explains that obtaining access to undertake research in various schools required him to negotiate with several people at different levels within the field, and that so doing influenced the kind of investigation that could be done and imposed constraints later on when informants were being selected and observation undertaken.

The fieldworker role

The ethnographer has a choice of various roles when in the field, sometimes using different ones for different locations or groups depending upon the multiplicity of fields being studied. The best typology of these roles remains

---

Box 3.8

Extract from J. D. Brewer, Sensitivity as a problem in field research, *American Behavioral Scientist*, vol. 33, 1990, pp. 581–5.

The Chief Constable's permission for the research was necessary if the researchers were not to be morally responsible for getting those police officers who talked to us privately sacked because they had done so without the Chief Constable's permission . . . A major problem was presenting the research in such a way that permission would be given, something which the Chief Constable had never done. On the assumption that the Chief Constable considered certain topics too sensitive, the researchers needed to be careful in how they presented the research. The key to this undoubtedly lay in the attraction to the RUC of the idea of research on how routine policing is affected by Northern Ireland's security situation. This topic had less attraction for ordinary police officers who ran the risk associated with answering someone's questions and from being observed while doing their job . . . But this strategy of carefully presenting the research with the central gatekeeper's permission in mind constituted an important compromise. The interests of a gatekeeper were allowed to affect some of the conduct of the researchers: a topic was chosen which we thought the Chief Constable would give permission to undertake . . . The permission of the Chief Constable was a disadvantage in the field because it raised doubts among respondents about the purposes of the researcher's questions . . . Concern about our motives in doing the research was combined with a feeling that it would do those participating in it little good, but would certainly benefit those in the police management and outside who wanted to do them harm.

Gold's account (Gold 1958), which essentially describes four levels of participation in the field: complete participant (participating as a normal group member and concealing the research); participant-as-observer (researching the field while participating fully in it); observer-as-participant (participation in the field is limited and the role of researcher is to the fore); and complete observer (no participation in the field). Most ethnographic research involves the first two roles (Burgess 1984: 80) because they involve the most participation. The first involves covert research, the second overt.

These distinctions are best seen as ideal types, for in practice the overt–covert distinction is a continuum with different degrees of openness, and the roles developed in the field vary with time and location. Permission may well have been negotiated with some people in the field but not all, requiring different degrees of openness in the extent to which details of the research are revealed to everyone. Moreover, gatekeepers may have given permission on other people's behalf but people in the field are unaware of the full details. This will require ethnographers to slip between the roles of researcher and group member as the occasion determines, developing roles that approach both complete participant and participant-as-observer simultaneously (see Pryce 1979: 282, for some of the interactional difficulties in maintaining different pretences). Roles also change with time spent in the field, because fieldwork roles go through phases. People see the ethnographer differently as a relationship is built up and trust developed, and even ethnographers who have the complete researcher role can establish rapport with members in the field and become accepted in that role, allowing them to develop something more like a participant role.

Developing a role and establishing trust

Ethnographers need to trust the people they are working with and vice versa. Only then has the ethnographer a chance of getting close to the multiple realities in the field. This bond of trust must be premised on the same qualities people bring to all their social relationships: honesty, communication, friendliness, openness and confidence-building. It is based on verbal and non-verbal behaviour. Non-verbally, Fetterman (1998: 141) explains, the ethnographer must be careful about self-presentation and demeanour, have an open physical posture and be profuse with handshakes and other cues for friendliness. Yet actions speak louder than words and the ethnographer's behaviour in the field must cement relationships with the people whose natural environment it is. The social skills the ethnographer employs for this in their own life should be put to the service of the research; taciturn, uncommunicative people make bad ethnographers. The ethnographer must also quickly learn the special meanings given to specific forms of behaviour in the setting if they are different from his or her own (by hours spent in the library beforehand if necessary). Ethnographers earn people's trust by showing a willingness to learn their language and their ways, to eat like they eat, speak like they speak and do as they do. (Ethical dilemmas are thereby created if this involves the ethnographer engaging in deviant behaviour, or, more likely, becoming aware of deviant behaviour. People need to feel they can trust the ethnographer, so deviant behaviour cannot be exposed. Thought should be given in the planning phase to the likelihood of this occurring and whether it will be morally problematic. These sorts of boundaries may need to be discussed when negotiating access.)

Trust is rarely instantaneous and is usually like any friendship in being a slow, steady process. The time spent in the field can even be restricted at the beginning in order for people to get used to the presence of the ethnographer slowly, although thereafter it needs to be intensive. Nor is trust a one-shot agreement, which, once won, need never be addressed again. Trust has to be continually worked at, negotiated and renegotiated, confirmed and thereafter repeatedly reaffirmed. Ethnographers should be aware that people in the field may continually seek reassurance, even setting tests of their trustworthiness, and winning trust can be hard work and emotionally draining, especially where the research is sensitive. The experience of Kathleen Magee, the young Catholic research assistant employed on my ESRC-funded project into routine policing in the overwhelmingly male and Protestant RUC, is instructive. Over a 12-month period in the field, a fieldworker's persistent inquisitiveness is bound to become something of an irritant, and van Maanen (1982: 111) warns that ethnographers cannot be expected to be liked by everyone. But leaving aside moments of irritation, most informants in the station became confident enough of her presence to express what were widely held fears about the research, sometimes by humour (there were running jokes about spelling people's names correctly in Sinn Fein's *Republican News*), and once by anger. Towards the end of a long and tiring night shift, when news was coming through of the murder of another member of the RUC, one policeman in particular decided to put the fieldworker through a gruelling test of trust that was something like a rite of passage (Brewer 1991a: 21–4).

PC1:   Look, just hold on a minute. What gives you the right to come here and start asking these personal questions about our families and that . . . You're not going to learn anything about the police while you're here. They're not going to tell you anything . . . And you know why? Because you're always walking around with that bloody notebook writing everything down, and you're not getting anywhere near the truth . . . Like, what use is this research you're doing anyway? Is it going to do me or my mates any good? What are you doing it for? 'Cos, let me tell you, the only people who are going to be interested in your bloody research are the authorities.

WPC: Can't you see that? They're just using you . . .

PC1:   And I'll tell you another thing, you're too much of a liability. See, when I go out, I'm looking out for me and my mate, I don't want some researcher in the back who's just a liability . . . How do I know I can trust you? What religion are you? How do I know I can trust you if I don't know what religion you are?

Res: I'm a Catholic.

PC1:   Are you ashamed of it? Then what are you crying about? Like, I'm just asking things everybody wanted to know . . . Has anyone spoken to you like this since you've been here? Do you know, it makes it a lot easier for us to work with you if we find out these things about you. See this research, as far as I'm concerned you'll learn nothing. It's a waste of time. To be honest, I couldn't give a monkey's fart about your research. If you really wanted to learn something you should have started at the top. It's them you need to be looking at. They don't care about the family man getting shot, they don't care about the families. The guy shot tonight will be forgotten about in another few weeks. It's them you should be talking to. The so-called big men at the top don't care about us.

WPC: But it's us who are getting shot and blown up.

PC1: Like, you're apologising for crying. Nothing wrong in that, but if you want to learn anything about us we have to feel we can trust you. I didn't speak to you before because I didn't know you . . . Like, I've seen my name written down about five times on that last page. If the authorities read that they'd put me on the next bus to [name of border area] and keep me there.

PC2: I'll tell you this. See when I come in here on a night, it's not the IRA I'm worried about, it's them upstairs.

PC1: I don't care what you're writing down, just as long as I don't see it in *Republican News*. Maybe the police has made me this way, but don't you see that if you're going to come in here asking questions about my family, if you're going to want to know all these things, I've got to be able to trust you? Like after this night, I'd let you come out in a vehicle with me.

This extract is useful to illustrate how the fieldworker, on the one policeman's admission, needed to be tested for her trustworthiness (and note by his admission that she was successful in passing the test). These trials are common in fieldwork (Douglas 1972; van Maanen 1982) because they are part of building the bond of trust.

Recording data

This extract also highlights the problems of recording data when in the field. The ethnographer's conventional notepad can be obtrusive, yet when the time in the field is extensive it is impossible to do without this aid. To recall events in detail in the evening or when in private is difficult and will result in general impressions rather than 'thick description'. Sometimes a tape recorder or video camera can be used to record data but these are even more obtrusive. If note taking is the main form of recording data, one way of allaying fears is by taking notes as unobtrusively as possible. This can be achieved by reducing the visibility of the pad and the physical activity of note taking, occasionally forgoing it when the situation seems appropriate, and by emphasizing that the notebooks are not secret. In my RUC research, the fieldworker was instructed to consider certain spaces in the station as private (the recreation and television rooms), where note taking was not done *at the time* (but left to later), and to leave the notebook around the station so that people could read it and thus know it was not secret. We occasionally reiterated this point by showing respondents extracts of the data (discussed in Brewer 1990: 29).

Irrespective of the occasion on which the ethnographer decides to record the data, writing up the field notes from the notebook in a more legible form is essential. The sooner this is done after the data were recorded the better. This typing may be done using software that permits the use later of computers to organize and analyse the data, as discussed in the next chapter. If this software is not used, the typing should involve an indexing system that allows the data to be ordered to assist later analysis (for the data will be numerous). With respect to the ethnography on the RUC, I always insisted that writing up of notes be done before the next venture into the field so that points of clarification at the next visit could be identified and new issues addressed. As Fetterman (1998: 114) reminds us, 'ethnographic work is exhausting and the fieldworker will be tempted to postpone typing the day's hieroglyphics each night. Memory fades quickly however, and unrecorded information will soon be overshadowed by subsequent events. Too long a delay sacrifices the rich immediacy of concurrent notes.'

Further points are worth remembering about note taking. While notes are a running description of events, people and conversations (Fielding 1993: 162), ethnographers should always make a note of the time, date, location, identities of the people involved and other exigencies and circumstances involved in any instance that is recorded (Burgess 1982: 192 calls these 'methodological field notes'). Where conversation is recorded, a record needs to be made of whether it is verbatim or a precis. Do not confuse observation and interpretation; record what is seen and heard (called 'substantive field notes') and keep this separate from one's interpretation of it (called 'analytic field notes'). Ethnographers should always record these initial tentative interpretations, because data analysis occurs simultaneously with data collection, but they should not be confused with literal data. It is also worth keeping a diary separate from the field notes in which the ethnographer records their impressions, feelings, and emotions, reflecting on such things as the developing relationships in the field, the emotional costs and problems in the field and other exigencies that are affecting the research. This will be the basis of the later reflexivity which ethnographers use to contextualize the research. Finally, make duplicate copies of the notes once they have been written up and keep them in different places for security reasons.

Ethics

Ethical considerations affect all kinds of scientific activity, from medical experiments like cloning and other forms of genetic engineering to euthanasia.

Many things that are possible scientifically are not necessarily thought desirable ethically, so that ethics limits the pursuit or application of scientific knowledge. So it is with the poor cousin of the natural sciences, the social sciences. Ethics affected social science in North America well before Britain because of the greater role of the social sciences in public life in North America, and much of the debate in British social science has revolved around the desirability of covert methods of data collection, almost exclusively that of covert observation (for Britain see the debate in Bulmer 1982a). The focus on ethnography is unfortunate because it suggests that other areas are free of ethical problems. This is not so. An increasing problem is that of sponsorship in research, which grows along with the increasing role of public and private bodies in funding research (for a general discussion of this see Barnes 1979). It is reflected in the limits sponsors can impose on research, not merely by censoring findings or preventing publication (for an example see Miller 1988), but by fixing the research agenda by failing to fund research on certain topics (for an example see Moore 1978) or not funding research which uses particular methods. Ethnographers particularly feel that they lose out in competition for funding because of the obsession with the natural science model of research (see Ditton and Williams 1981), and complain that the use of expensive profit-making market research companies to undertake surveys on behalf of academics uses up a disproportionate amount of scarce research money (Payne 1979).

Ethical issues are thus pervasive. If we focus on ethical practice by ethnographers as the most relevant dimension, there are several questions worth addressing, from the ethics of covert methods, through the standards of behaviour in the field to the dissemination of the results. Ethnographers are perhaps unique among social researchers in sharing the lives of the people they study. This means that they cannot, as Fetterman (1998: 129) writes, work as if in a vacuum – they pry into people's innermost secrets, witness their failures and participate in their lives – which means they must operate a code of ethics that respects their informants. Many go further, by arguing that this ethical code should respect the integrity of the discipline and the interests of future researchers who may wish to enter the same field. Nor is this solely a personal code of ethics, reflecting the ethnographer's individual values, for many professional associations have developed ethical statements which members should follow (going beyond ethnographic practice to describe general research conduct). When such associations are themselves gatekeepers, in providing either financial sponsorship or access, researchers must formally sign up to the code. Anyone wishing to undertake ethnographic research in a hospital setting anywhere in Northern Ireland, for example, must submit a proposal to the Research Ethics Committee of The Queen's University of Belfast and obtain permission for the research from them as well as the hospital concerned. Institutional review boards are common in North American universities, and it was estimated that they spend three-quarters of their time

Box 3.9

Extract from the British Sociological Association's statement of ethics. Reproduced with permission and available from web site http: //www. britsoc. org.uk/ethgu2.htm

BSA Statement of Ethical Practice
The British Sociological Association gratefully acknowledges the use made of the ethical codes produced by the American Sociological Association, the Association of Social Anthropologists of the Commonwealth and the Social Research Association. Styles of sociological work are diverse and subject to change, not least because sociologists work within a wide variety of settings. Sociologists, in carrying out their work, inevitably face ethical, and sometimes legal, dilemmas which arise out of competing obligations and conflicts of interest. The following statement aims to alert the members of the Association to issues that raise ethical concerns and to indicate potential problems and conflicts of interest that might arise in the course of their professional activities.

While they are not exhaustive, the statement points to a set of obligations to which members should normally adhere as principles for guiding their conduct. Departures from the principles should be the result of deliberation and not ignorance. The strength of this statement and its binding force rest ultimately on active discussion, reflection, and continued use by sociologists. In addition, the statement will help to communicate the professional position of sociologists to others, especially those involved in or affected by the activities of sociologists. The statement is meant, primarily, to inform members' ethical judgements rather than to impose on them an external set of standards. The purpose is to make members aware of the ethical issues that may arise in their work, and to encourage them to educate themselves and their colleagues to behave ethically. The statement does not, therefore, provide a set of recipes for resolving ethical choices or dilemmas, but recognises that often it will be necessary to make such choices on the basis of principles and values, and the (often conflicting) interests of those involved.

Professional integrity
Members should strive to maintain the integrity of sociological enquiry as a discipline, the freedom to research and study, and to publish and promote the results of sociological research. Members have a responsibility both to safeguard the proper interests of those involved in or affected by their work, and to report their findings accurately and truthfully. They need to consider the effects of their involvements and the consequences

of their work or its misuse for those they study and other interested parties. While recognising that training and skill are necessary to the conduct of social research, members should themselves recognise the boundaries of their professional competence. They should not accept work of a kind that they are not qualified to carry out. Members should satisfy themselves that the research they undertake is worthwhile and that the techniques proposed are appropriate. They should be clear about the limits of their detachment from and involvement in their areas of study.

Members should be careful not to claim an expertise in areas outside those that would be recognised academically as their true fields of expertise. Particularly in their relations with the media, members should have regard for the reputation of the discipline and refrain from offering expert commentaries in a form that would appear to give credence to material which, as researchers, they would regard as comprising inadequate or tendentious evidence.

Relations with and responsibilities towards research participants
Sociologists, when they carry out research, enter into personal and moral relationships with those they study, be they individuals, households, social groups or corporate entities. Although sociologists, like other researchers are committed to the advancement of knowledge, that goal does not, of itself, provide an entitlement to override the rights of others. Members must satisfy themselves that a study is necessary for the furtherance of knowledge before embarking upon it. Members should be aware that they have some responsibility for the use to which their research may be put. Discharging that responsibility may on occasion be difficult, especially in situations of social conflict, competing social interests or where there is unanticipated misuse of the research by third parties.

I Relationships with research participants
  • Sociologists have a responsibility to ensure that the physical, social and psychological well-being of research participants is not adversely affected by the research. They should strive to protect the rights of those they study, their interests, sensitivities and privacy, while recognising the difficulty of balancing potentially conflicting interests. Because sociologists study the relatively powerless as well as those more powerful than themselves, research relationships are frequently characterised by disparities of power and status. Despite this, research relationships should be characterised, whenever possible, by trust. In some cases, where the public interest dictates otherwise and particularly where power is being abused, obligations of trust and protection

may weigh less heavily. Nevertheless, these obligations should not be discarded lightly.

- As far as possible sociological research should be based on the freely given informed consent of those studied. This implies a responsibility on the sociologist to explain as fully as possible, and in terms meaningful to participants, what the research is about, who is undertaking and financing it, why it is being undertaken, and how it is to be promoted.
- Research participants should be made aware of their right to refuse participation whenever and for whatever reason they wish.
- Research participants should understand how far they will be afforded anonymity and confidentiality and should be able to reject the use of data-gathering devices such as tape recorders and video cameras. Sociologists should be careful, on the one hand, not to give unrealistic guarantees of confidentiality and, on the other, not to permit communication of research films or records to audiences other than those to which the research participants have agreed.
- Where there is a likelihood that data may be shared with other researchers, the potential uses to which the data might be put may need to be discussed with research participants.
- When making notes, filming or recording for research purposes, sociologists should make clear to research participants the purpose of the notes, filming or recording, and, as precisely as possible, to whom it will be communicated.
- It should also be borne in mind that in some research contexts, especially those involving field research, it may be necessary for the obtaining of consent to be regarded, not as a once-and-for-all prior event, but as a process, subject to renegotiation over time. In addition, particular care may need to be taken during periods of prolonged fieldwork where it is easy for research participants to forget that they are being studied.
- In some situations access to a research setting is gained via a 'gatekeeper'. In these situations members should adhere to the principle of obtaining informed consent directly from the research participants to whom access is required, while at the same time taking account of the gatekeepers' interest. Since the relationship between the research participant and the gatekeeper may continue long after the sociologist has left the research setting, care should be taken not to disturb that relationship unduly.
- It is incumbent upon members to be aware of the possible consequences of their work. Wherever possible they should attempt to anticipate, and to guard against, consequences for research participants which can be predicted to be harmful. Members are not

- absolved from this responsibility by the consent given by research participants.
- In many of its guises, social research intrudes into the lives of those studied. While some participants in sociological research may find the experience a positive and welcome one, for others, the experience may be disturbing. Even if not exposed to harm, those studied may feel wronged by aspects of the research process. This can be particularly so if they perceive apparent intrusions into their private and personal worlds, or where research gives rise to false hopes, uncalled for self-knowledge, or unnecessary anxiety. Members should consider carefully the possibility that the research experience may be a disturbing one and, normally, should attempt to minimise disturbance to those participating in research. It should be borne in mind that decisions made on the basis of research may have effects on individuals as members of a group, even if individual research participants are protected by confidentiality and anonymity.
- Special care should be taken where research participants are particularly vulnerable by virtue of factors such as age, social status and powerlessness. Where research participants are ill or too young or too old to participate, proxies may need to be used in order to gather data. In these situations care should be taken not to intrude on the personal space of the person to whom the data ultimately refer, or to disturb the relationship between this person and the proxy. Where it can be inferred that the person about whom data are sought would object to supplying certain kinds of information, that material should not be sought from the proxy.

2 Covert research
There are serious ethical dangers in the use of covert research but covert methods may avoid certain problems. For instance, difficulties arise when research participants change their behaviour because they know they are being studied. Researchers may also face problems when access to spheres of social life is closed to social scientists by powerful or secretive interests. However, covert methods violate the principles of informed consent and may invade the privacy of those being studied. Participant or non-participant observation in non-public spaces or experimental manipulation of research participants without their knowledge should be resorted to only where it is impossible to use other methods to obtain essential data. In such studies it is important to safeguard the anonymity of research participants. Ideally, where informed consent has not been obtained prior to the research it should be obtained post-hoc.

3 Anonymity, privacy and confidentiality
  i The anonymity and privacy of those who participate in the research
    process should be respected. Personal information concerning
    research participants should be kept confidential. In some cases it may
    be necessary to decide whether it is proper or appropriate even to
    record certain kinds of sensitive information.
  ii Where possible, threats to the confidentiality and anonymity of
    research data should be anticipated by researchers. The identities and
    research records of those participating in research should be kept
    confidential whether or not an explicit pledge of confidentiality has
    been given. Appropriate measures should be taken to store research
    data in a secure manner. Members should have regard to their obli-
    gations under the Data Protection Act. Where appropriate and prac-
    ticable, methods for preserving the privacy of data should be used.
    These may include the removal of identifiers, the use of pseudonyms
    and other technical means for breaking the link between data and
    identifiable individuals such as 'broadbanding' or micro-aggregation.
    Members should also take care to prevent data being published or
    released in a form which would permit the actual or potential identifi-
    cation of research participants. Potential informants and research par-
    ticipants, especially those possessing a combination of attributes
    which make them readily identifiable, may need to be reminded that
    it can be difficult to disguise their identity without introducing an
    unacceptably large measure of distortion into the data.
  iii Guarantees of confidentiality and anonymity given to research par-
    ticipants must be honoured, unless there are clear and overriding
    reasons to do otherwise. Other people, such as colleagues, research
    staff or others, given access to the data must also be made aware of
    their obligations in this respect. By the same token, sociologists
    should respect the efforts taken by other researchers to maintain
    anonymity. Research data given in confidence do not enjoy legal privi-
    lege, that is they may be liable to subpoena by a court. Research par-
    ticipants may also need to be made aware that it may not be possible
    to avoid legal threats to the privacy of the data.
  iv There may be less compelling grounds for extending guarantees of
    privacy or confidentiality to public organisations, collectivities,
    governments, officials or agencies than to individuals or small groups.
    Nevertheless, where guarantees have been given they should be hon-
    oured, unless there are clear and compelling reasons not to do so.

4 Reputation of the discipline
During their research members should avoid, where they can, actions

which may have deleterious consequences for sociologists who come after them or which might undermine the reputation of sociology as a discipline.

Relations with and responsibilities towards sponsors and/or funders

A common interest exists between sponsor, funder and sociologist as long as the aim of the social inquiry is to advance knowledge, although such knowledge may only be of limited benefit to the sponsor and the funder. That relationship is best served if the atmosphere is conducive to high professional standards. Members should attempt to ensure that sponsors and/or funders appreciate the obligations that sociologists have not only to them, but also to society at large, research participants and professional colleagues and the sociological community. The relationship between sponsors or funders and social researchers should be such as to enable social inquiry to be undertaken as objectively as possible. Research should be undertaken with a view to providing information or explanation rather than being constrained to reach particular conclusions or prescribe particular courses of action.

1 Clarifying obligations, roles and rights
   • Members should clarify in advance the respective obligations of funders and researchers where possible in the form of a written contract. They should refer the sponsor or funder to the relevant parts of the professional code to which they adhere. Members should also be careful not to promise or imply acceptance of conditions which are contrary to their professional ethics or competing commitments. Where some or all of those involved in the research are also acting as sponsors and/or funders of research the potential for conflict between the different roles and interests should also be made clear to them.
   • Members should also recognise their own general or specific obligations to the sponsors whether contractually defined or only the subject of informal and often unwritten agreements. They should be honest and candid about their qualifications and expertise, the limitations, advantages and disadvantages of the various methods of analysis and data, and acknowledge the necessity for discretion with confidential information obtained from sponsors. They should also try not to conceal factors which are likely to affect satisfactory conditions or the completion of a proposed research project or contract.
2 Pre-empting outcomes and negotiations about research
   • Members should not accept contractual conditions that are contingent upon a particular outcome or set of findings from a proposed inquiry. A conflict of obligations may also occur if the funder requires particular methods to be used.

- Members should try to clarify, before signing the contract, that they are entitled to be able to disclose the source of their funds, its personnel, the aims of the institution, and the purposes of the project.
- Members should also try to clarify their right to publish and spread the results of their research.
- Members have an obligation to ensure sponsors grasp the implications of the choice between alternative research methods.

3 Guarding privileged information and negotiating problematic sponsorship
- Members are frequently furnished with information by the funder who may legitimately require it to be kept confidential. Methods and procedures that have been utilised to produce published data should not, however, be kept confidential unless otherwise agreed.
- When negotiating sponsorships members should be aware of the requirements of the law with respect to the ownership of and rights of access to data.
- In some political, social and cultural contexts some sources of funding and sponsorship may be contentious. Candour and frankness about the source of funding may create problems of access or co-operation for the social researcher but concealment may have serious consequences for colleagues, the discipline and research participants. The emphasis should be on maximum openness.
- Where sponsors and funders also act directly or indirectly as gatekeepers and control access to participants, researchers should not devolve their responsibility to protect the participants' interests onto the gatekeeper. Members should be wary of inadvertently disturbing the relationship between participants and gatekeepers since that will continue long after the researcher has left.

4 Obligations to sponsors and/or Funders During the Research Process
- Members have a responsibility to notify the sponsor and/or funder of any proposed departure from the terms of reference of the proposed change in the nature of the contracted research.
- A research study should not be undertaken on the basis of resources known from the start to be inadequate, whether the work is of a sociological or inter-disciplinary kind.
- When financial support or sponsorship has been accepted, members must make every reasonable effort to complete the proposed research on schedule, including reports to the funding source.
- Members should be prepared to take comments from sponsors or funders or research participants.
- Members should, wherever possible, spread their research findings.
- Members should normally avoid restrictions on their freedom to publish or otherwise broadcast research findings.

At its meeting in July 1994, the BSA Executive Committee approved a set of Rules for the Conduct of Enquiries into Complaints against BSA members under the auspices of this Statement, and also under the auspices of the BSA Guidelines on Professional Conduct. If you would like more details about the Rules, you should contact the BSA Office at the address/phone number given at the end of this statement.

British Sociological Association, Units 3F/G, Mountjoy Research Centre, Stockton Road, DURHAM, DH1 3UR [UK]. Tel.: [+44](0)191–383–0839; fax: [+44](0)191 383 0782; e-mail: enquiries@britsoc.org.uk

dealing with the issue of informed consent (Homan 1991: 16). British and American professional associations in anthropology and sociology have similar ethical codes (see Box 3.9), although do not themselves act as gatekeepers.

The standards of behaviour indicated in these codes include respect for human dignity, both the ethnographer's and those of his or her subjects, respect for privacy and confidentiality, and the avoidance of deception and lying – where complete candour is difficult, general statements which are not in themselves lies should be used. On one occasion, when I wanted to interview conservative evangelicals about their anti-Catholic views, I surmised that they would be reluctant to give consent knowing this intent, so I presented the interview as one about the problems facing the modern church and conducted it as such. Only later in the course of the interview did I start to turn the topic around to that of the Catholic Church. Rather than lie or deceive, I conducted an interview that was about what I said it was, and only used about half of the material. Compare this with Pryce (1979: 285), who as an atheist was baptized as a Pentecostal believer in order to study West Indian Christians, or myself in my youth, when I was bold and foolish enough to join the Action Party to study former fascists. (On the whole, postgraduates – which is what Pryce and I were when we did our covert observation – are more likely to engage in this sort of research, although less likely than they once were. Warren (1988: 66) notes that ageing ethnographers tend to retreat to interview research.) Burgess (1984: 201) considers that truthful statements are always preferable to lies except under very special circumstances, such as protecting colleagues, clients or sources, and maintaining confidentiality. However, harmless 'white lies' can sometimes be employed where they assist in data collection or in establishing a fieldwork role (Burgess 1984: 201–2), although discovery of the deceit by informants can still be problematic (for example, see Pryce, 1979: 283). However, Fetterman (1998: 140) considers any deception as inappropriate in the context of the sort of long-term relationships normally built up in ethnography.

Many of these issues come to a head in the debate around covert versus overt observational methods. This began in the United States, with an exchange between Erikson (1967, 1968, 1982) and Denzin (1968, 1982), represented in Britain by the debate between Homan (1980, 1982, 1991) and Bulmer (1980, 1982a). Erikson's original argument was that ethnographers, like all researchers, have responsibilities to their subjects, which covert methods infringe because they involve misrepresentation and failure to obtain informed consent, and to their colleagues, who can be jeopardized by covert methods that damage their professional reputation. This caused stress to the researcher in keeping up the pretence, something borne by those least capable because they were, on the whole, graduate students. Erikson also said that it was bad science. Denzin queried whether there was a tight distinction between private and public spheres anymore and whether covert methods were alone in breaching privacy or failing to obtain informed consent (consent is anyway often given by a gatekeeper on others' behalf, who themselves do not get the opportunity to give permission). He also doubted that covert methods were damaging, disruptive or threatening. Postgraduates can find coping with harassed and insecure interviewees just as problematic as maintaining a double role in covert observation. However, there is something deeper behind Denzin's response, reflected best perhaps in Jack Douglas's view that the primary task of social science is truth and tortured moral judgements should not impede its search, especially when studying the centres of power, which themselves operate deceit, secrecy and misrepresentation. Denzin believed that researchers have the right to make observations on anyone in any setting to the extent that it is done with scientific purpose. However, lines have to be drawn somewhere, or ethnographers become like spies or private investigators, and Bulmer argues that the rights of our informants and their dignity override those of science.

Covert methods can be too readily used, and should be restricted to those instances where there is no alternative: Homan's chief defence was that there was no other way to study his informants (old time Pentecostalists); likewise my former fascists. That is, covert methods are defensible where access is likely to be closed and the gatekeepers impose impossible barriers or controls on research. Thus, the decision to employ covert methods ought to be a pragmatic as well as a moral one (on morality and covert methods see Reynolds 1982). Categorical moral statements are of little value when a researcher is unable to develop a relationship of trust, or obtain informed consent and access. But, pragmatically, it is often unnecessary to use covert methods since permission can be granted or other roles utilized. Bulmer (1982a: 239) distinguishes four possible fieldworker roles, similar to the types of observation identified in Figure 3.1: overt outsider (the researcher looking in); covert insider (the researcher as covert participant); covert outsider (the researcher does not disclose the observation but does not pretend to be an insider either); and overt insider (the researcher adopts a new insider role and discloses the fact of the research, such as training to become a policeman in order to study the police). How practical the last is compared to that of covert insider is worth thinking about before embarking on a new career. Overt research for Bulmer thus remains the best choice, but the degree to which these different roles involve openness varies, which illustrates that the distinction between overt and covert research should be seen as a continuum. Informed consent, for example, associated with overt methods, is often ambiguous or given on someone else's behalf, and the implications of the research are rarely fully explicated when consent is being sought. Overt research can be invasive and intrude on privacy, and involve varying degrees of truth. Thus, morality is not necessarily always on the side of overt researcher (for some examples of ethnographers who reflect on the ethics of their research practice see: Dingwall 1980; Homan, 1980; Fielding 1982; Holdaway 1982; Hammersley 1990: 135; for a feminist ethnographer see Harvey 1994: 156–65).

Handling identity in the field

If informants are people and have rights that affect ethical practice, ethnographers are also human and have identities that affect research practice. Most attention has focused on the issue of gender, but other features of identity can affect research practice, such as age, social class, race and ethnicity, and religion. It fits the postmodern drift in ethnography to admit that it is a personal method in which data are highly conditioned by the biography and experiences of the ethnographer. The myth that ethnographers are people without personal identity, historical location and personality, and would all produce the same findings in the same setting, is the mistake of naive realism. Because gender is perhaps the primary identity, feminist ethnographers were among the first to deconstruct ethnographic practice and identify the ways in which identity influenced fieldwork relations (for an excellent overview see Warren 1988). Within this, attention has been given to the special problems of female ethnographers in obtaining entrée, the problems around establishing rapport and trust, and sexual politics in the field.

In cultures where the institutions of marriage and the family are pervasive, the childless, single woman in the field can find it difficult to establish entrée and a field role (unless, perhaps, she is elderly: see Wax 1979) or develop access to men and male behaviour. This is why in some anthropological research women work in husband and wife teams. In urban settings this is more unusual and lone ethnographers – including lone female ethnographers – are more common. This reinforces the importance of handling identity. Van Maanen (1981: 480) once argued that researchers on the police, for example, had to be male in order to be able to participate fully in the masculine occupational culture of the police, although maleness alone does not ensure access to all male worlds, including the police (for the difficulties of a male researcher in establishing rapport in the police see Warren and Rasmussen 1977: 358). Moreover, female ethnographers have discussed how they have been treated as sex objects in masculine occupational cultures. However, on the positive side, this ensured they were seen as a light relief from the demands of the job and as less threatening than males might have been, which facilitates rapport (Hunt 1984), and treated as 'acceptable incompetents' (Lofland 1971: 100), resulting in informants giving them more time and taking more care to explain (for example, see Easterday *et al.* 1977; Hunt 1984; for Kathleen Magee's experiences see Brewer 1990: 585). Warren's (1988: 18) experience in some of her ethnographic research is that men sometimes talk to her more than other women. The downside is that young female ethnographers can be subject to sexual hustling, fraternity and paternalistic attitudes from male respondents, and treated as gofers, mascots or surrogate daughters. Although some of these roles may be useful in establishing rapport with men (some female ethnographers have explained that rapport was enhanced by taking a lover from within the field; see Davis 1986), women ethnographers can receive the unwanted sexual attention of male informants (for examples of ethnographers to whom this happened see Warren 1988: 33; male ethnographers rarely write about their sexual experiences in the field). Kathleen Magee, the young female research assistant on my ESRC-funded project on routine policing by the RUC, was a part-time model, and was asked for a date by several policemen, and it was only after some time spent in the field, when her presence became routine, that we were sure she was being talked to as a person rather than a sex object. The veracity of what informants said was treated with more confidence at that point. None the less, female ethnographers should not risk over-personalized interaction and should be on guard for the sexual hustle disguised as research cooperation.

A distinct advantage of female ethnographers is that they push the research agenda towards certain issues glossed by male counterparts, which include gender issues. A benefit of Kathleen Magee's identity in the context of studying the RUC was that it immediately raised the profile of gender as an issue in this masculine occupational culture (for a discussion of which see Brewer 1991a: 239–46; Brewer 1991b). The same was true of her religion as a Catholic in an overwhelmingly Protestant occupational culture. This illustrates the fact that, in some settings, gender is not the primary identity, although there is very little discussion in the methodological literature on other features of the ethnographer's biography. The primary identity may be race or ethnicity when studying, for example, lifestyles among West Indians in inner-city Britain (see Pryce 1979), where it may be an advantage to minimize identity differences because of the problems of being white. Suttles (1968) records his difficulties in developing relationships with informants from ethnic minority groups in a Chicago slum area because of his ethnicity, and even where white researchers become friends with black informants, they are usually allocated outsider roles and sensitivities to colour difference remain (see, for example, Liebow 1967: 248–9). The primary identity marker might be age when one is studying, for example, youth gangs (Patrick

1973; Parker 1974), or where unbounded energy, daring and danger are needed in the field (for an example see Moore 1977; for a general discussion of dangerous fieldwork see Lee 1995), or where heavy drinking or drug use is required to be an 'insider' (for an example see Burns 1980). The primary identity could be religion when studying, for example, the Protestant-dominated RUC, where attitudes towards Catholics are affected by the experience of policing civil unrest. Magee's religion was thus assumed by us to be problematic and we first tried to conceal it, which reflected our naivety in underestimating the skill the Northern Irish have in telling identity from various subtle cues (for a discussion of how we managed the effect of her religion on fieldwork see Brewer 1991a: 24–7). Instances like this reinforce the importance of ethnographers being reflexive when writing up the results but also of ensuring that fieldwork is sufficiently prolonged and intensive that relationships of trust can be built up in the field.

Withdrawal from the field

An exit strategy is an important part of any research design and thought needs to be given at the beginning to how withdrawal from the field will be managed. This means two things in ethnographic research (Berg 1998: 153): physical removal from the field and emotional disengagement from the relationships established there. The former can be mechanical and simple, the latter more difficult. Where the research is overt, ethnographers need to prepare the community (and themselves) for removal from the setting, and sometimes it is best to leave in stages with a gradual withdrawal. Efforts should be made to avoid distress to the informants, and some ethnographers have had to remain emotionally engaged with their respondents long after the research was completed – this is seen as one of the virtues of feminist ethnography. The possibility of this long-term commitment should be recognized at the planning stage. Withdrawal is harder to manage when the research has been covert, where quick exits are best, because informants then become aware of the intruder in their lives and can feel hurt at the deception. Interaction is terminated, although there may be ongoing engagements of a different kind. I received abusive letters from the leadership of the Action Party once my deceit was revealed, and had they not been old men by that stage, the former fascists may well have expressed their hurt in more physically threatening ways (Fielding's study of the National Front wisely used overt methods, see Fielding 1981, 1982). Wallis's experience with the Scientologists is salutary for covert ethnographers, for they threatened legal action, sent anonymous letters to his wife alleging adultery and otherwise made life unpleasant for him and his family (see Wallis 1977). However, Punch's (1989) experience with the Amsterdam police after doing overt research on corruption shows that informed consent does not prevent informants feeling angry once results are published.

The writing up of results is addressed further in the next chapter, but it is necessary to consider publication of findings in the context of withdrawal from the field. Publication of results is perhaps more problematic in ethnography because of the emotional engagement it involves and because, occasionally, it reveals publicly to respondents that they have been duped. The effects of both these circumstances are the same: ethics should constrain the form and content of data dissemination and publication. Ethical practice involves ethnographers writing up their findings in ways that protect their informants' identity (in the case of the RUC even their personal security). This involves being mindful of the use and misuse people make of the findings, especially where the research is sensitive or political (for an example see Rainwater and Pittman 1966), and recognizing that people's bigotry may be inflamed by what they read and that the results can be interpreted by members of the public with various slants. Agonizing over prose is also necessary to avoid revealing information that might be used to threaten the physical safety of informants, or that might threaten the continued enjoyment of their life and behaviour, or impinge on their freedom from inquisitive outsiders, even in some cases the police, or prevent damage to their way of life or community. Publication of Ditton's ethnography on fiddling and pilfering among bread roundsmen (Ditton 1977) could have involved his former colleagues, who were unaware of his research, being prosecuted or having wages cut in lieu of these 'perks'. He was aware that he probably lost many of his earlier friends in the bakery in consequence (Ditton 1977: vii). Similar ethical considerations affected Leonard's ethnography on the informal economy in West Belfast (Leonard 1994a), which risked exposing some informants as social security cheats. She managed this by letting it bear heavily on her practice in withdrawing from the field and in the use of prose when publishing the results, in her respect for confidentiality and anonymity, and in her protection of the secrecy of her sources (Leonard 1994b), although this duplicity in the deviancy of others is itself an ethical issue and its effects on the researcher need to be borne in mind at the beginning when designing the research. The use of pseudonyms and the modification of identities, events and location is common practice, but ethnographers should also bear in mind that sometimes the reassurances they give informants cannot be guaranteed over inquisitive investigative journalists or legal disclosures (for an example see Morgan 1972). Very occasionally, the informants themselves change their behaviour in reaction to reading the findings.

Conclusion

Modern methodology has moved away from the idea of research as a series of hermetic stages, with set operations and set techniques performed in sequence. Research is conceived now as a process. It does not follow a neat pattern but is a messy interaction between the research problem, the design of the research and data collection and analysis. The complexity of the research process and the lack of sequence does not threaten good practice in the conduct of the research. Ethnographic research, which is perhaps the most chaotic style of research, is thus not impugned by its flexibility, but has an advantage in enabling the researcher to make adjustments. However, careful design is still necessary so that the complexities are expected and planned for, and last-minute alternatives are anticipated and known. Flexibility or not, modern ethnographers should not be taken unawares.

It follows from the conceptualization of research as a process that data analysis and interpretation are not discrete stages, tagged on after data collection is complete and before writing up, but done from the beginning and interacting with earlier procedures in the research process. The next chapter considers data analysis and interpretation.

Suggested further reading

For general textbooks covering data collection and others aspects of research practice see:

Berg, B. (1998) *Qualitative Research Methods*, 3rd edn. Boston: Allyn and Bacon.
Gilbert, N. (1993) *Researching Social Life*. London: Sage.
Silverman, D. (1997) *Qualitative Research: Theory, Method and Practice*. London: Sage.

4 The analysis, interpretation and presentation of ethnographic data

Introduction

There are many issues surrounding the analysis, interpretation and presentation of ethnographic data of a technical kind and of deeper theoretical concern. Before these are considered, it is first worth reminding ourselves of some of the qualities of ethnographic data, since these have a bearing on the topic of this chapter:

- data come in the form of extracts of natural language;
- they are personal to the researcher;
- they can be generalized although they are limited in scope;
- they tend to be voluminous in scale.

Although ethnographers can collect and make use of numerate data, ethnographic data take the form of extracts of natural language, such as long quotations from in-depth interviews, entries from diaries and other personal documents, extracts from observation field notes and transcripts of conversations. Such data are parodied as unsystematic and unrigorous, and while this common-sense image is false, ethnographic data are personal to the researcher in a way that numerate data are not. There are at least four reasons for this: the ethnographer is often participating in, and always heavily involved with, the setting and people under study, rather than detached and aloof; the understandings that ethnographers develop are based partly on introspection – auto-observation – where their own experiences, attitude changes and feelings when in the field become data; ethnographers have to select from an infinite series of events on the basis of their personal interests; and the socio-biographical characteristics of the ethnographer compared to the people in the field can affect what is seen and recorded and how it is interpreted. Ethnographic data are thus autobiographical data: the observation of a single individual or several separate individuals, selectively recorded, provide a portrait from one person's vantage point.

Ethnographic data are also limited in value because of small sample size. The scope of the data can be extended by careful research design in order to furnish theoretical inferences and empirical generalizations, but this is never as easy as in quantitative research. If ethnographic data are short on scope, they compensate in the sheer scale and complexity of the data. A lot of ethnographic data are talk-based, especially when collected with in-depth interviews, participant observation and conversation or discourse analysis. They are thus premised on simply watching and listening attentively. What ethnographers want to listen to and watch is influenced by whatever it is they want to find out. Sometimes ethnographers have a clear sense of what this is before entering the field, sometimes not, or their interest changes once in the setting. If they are unsure, as yet, about what interests them, they go into the field with a broad trawl, collecting data on many things, the significance or value of which is uncertain for the moment. Sometimes people refrain from conversation with the researcher. If in some setting people are reluctant to talk (for examples of which in police research see Westley 1970; Brewer 1991a: 29), in which private one-to-one contact with the ethnographer is avoided in preference for public encounters using non-intimate discourse, ethnographers must hang around long enough to force people to talk (Westley 1970: viii) or use those naturally occurring moments when sensitive topics come up in conversation casually or can be artfully manufactured to appear as if casual by using props (see Box 4.1). Be reassured, however, that the biggest problem is not trying to get people to talk, but stopping them. Talk-based ethnographic data are voluminous. I collected over three thousand pages of typed field notes in the study of routine policing by the RUC, contained in over half-a-dozen large box files, and over 92 hours of tape recordings in the ethnography of crime, plus other field notes and material. Bulk and complexity thus both characterize ethnographic data (Bryman and Burgess 1994: 216).

All these qualities reinforce the importance of proper analysis, interpretation and presentation of ethnographic data. 'Analysis' can be defined as the process of bringing order to the data, organizing what is there into patterns, categories and descriptive units, and looking for relationships between them; 'interpretation' involves attaching meaning and significance to the analysis, explaining the patterns, categories and relationships; while 'presentation' constitutes the act of writing up the data in textual form. Skilful analysis is needed to work a way through the sheer volume of data in order

Box 4.1

Extract from J. D. Brewer, Sensitivity as a problem in field research: a study of routine policing in Northern Ireland, *American Behavioral Scientist*, vol. 33, 1990, p. 589.

A study of policing in Northern Ireland is aided by the fact that conversation and social context are so interrelated. Sensitive and controversial topics often occur naturally in the conversation, or can be introduced in what appears a casual manner, because the social context encourages this. Events seen on the television the night before, read about in the day's newspaper, or relayed as they happen in police stations throughout the province, facilitate natural talk on sensitive topics or can be used as contextually related props to achieve the same end.

to bring order and structure, so that the patterns, categories and relationships can be discovered. Interpretation is important so that the correct meaning can be attached to the data by the researcher in a way that does justice to the complexity of the meanings of the people in the field. And careful writing and text is required so that the analysis and interpretation can be supported with sufficient extracts of natural language from the field, but no more – or no less – is claimed for the data than the scope of the ethnographer's personal vantage point permits.

Analysis, interpretation and presentation are partly a matter of practical and technical know-how, but some theoretical issues need to be addressed for each as well. At one time, minimum attention was devoted to data analysis in ethnography (see Fielding and Lee 1998: 2; Huberman and Miles 1998: 179), but it is now recognized as central and addressed in several texts (see Dey 1993; Bryman and Burgess 1994; Miles and Huberman 1994; Coffey and Atkinson 1996; Huberman and Miles 1998; for an early text see Lofland 1971). The focus on analysis has been reinforced by the arrival of computer-assisted qualitative data analysis and management. Some of these texts are autobiographical, where leading ethnographers describe how they engaged in analysis (Lofland 1974; Bryman and Burgess 1994), but most are codifications of good practice and provide an exegesis of the theoretical debate surrounding the process.

Analysis

An ethnographer once wrote that analysis is not an exact science (Berg 1998: 151). Perhaps not, but it can be systematic and rigorous, and involves some general principles. The first thing to note about analysis is that it is a continuous process. Given that ethnography is best perceived as a process rather than a sequence of discrete stages (like all research), data analysis is simultaneous with data collection. Huberman and Miles (1998: 180) define data analysis as involving three sub-processes: data reduction (selecting units of the data from the total universe of data); data display (assembling the information in some format); and conclusion drawing (interpretation of the findings). This last sub-process has been separated here from analysis. They stress, however, that these sub-processes occur before data collection (during research design), during data collection (as interim analyses are carried out) and after data collection (developing the finished analysis). Most ethnographers would baulk at suggesting that analysis begins before data collection and, for most, analysis usually begins when the field notes are read and typed before the next visit to the field, when categories, descriptive units and links between the data appear. It is necessary to keep these initial analytical ideas (called analytic field notes) separate from the data themselves (substantive field notes), and not to be bound rigidly by them. Bogden and Biklen (1982) distinguish between analysis in the field and analysis after data collection, the latter being more general in the codes and categories it develops.

Another point to note is that the analytical process varies slightly in the different types of ethnography. Data analysis within positivist ethnography remedies the weaknesses of ethnographic compared to numerate data by constructing objective indicators of insiders' understandings and expressing them in a formal language, almost as a kind of measurement, such as the development of codes, diagrams and other categories which map the insider's cultural world as a series of variables between which there are supposedly causal links (a good example of which is Huberman and Miles 1998). The analysis is devoted to developing the variables that capture social meanings rather than necessarily 'telling it like it is'. With a focus on the objective indicators rather than the subjective meaning, it is believed that such studies can be replicated (that is, they are 'reliable' in the technical sense of the word) and the 'validity' (in its technical sense meaning accuracy) of the objective indicators can be tested against the objective world they seek to analyse. Humanistic ethnography also seeks to reconstruct the 'reality' of the insider's world and construct accurate descriptions of this as if from 'the inside'. However, analysis in this kind of ethnography is devoted to capturing 'the inside' in the terms which insiders themselves employ, avoiding formalistic language and dubious 'indicators' of meaning that are divorced from the people in the field. This sort of data analysis allows the humanistic ethnographer to believe it is possible to convey with accuracy (that is 'validity') the meanings of people in the field under study by remaining true to the meanings themselves, by 'telling it like it is' in members' own terms. In this way, 'reality' is captured more objectively by means of greater attention to the subjective meanings of people.

Postmodernist and post postmodernist ethnography denies that there is an objective reality that can be captured accurately by either distancing the analysis from social meanings (in the form of external indicators) or immersing the analysis in them (by 'telling it like it is'). For this kind of ethnography, there are competing versions of reality and multiple perspectives that the analysis must address. Moreover, the data are seen as created in and through the interactions that occur between the researcher and people in the field, and analysis must therefore illustrate the situated or context-bound nature of the multivocal meanings disclosed in the research. Reflexivity is thus a critical part of the analysis in these types of ethnography, in which the ethnographer constructs the sense-assembly procedures through which the data were created, locating them, and therefore the analysis, in the processes that brought them about. Analysis in these kinds of ethnography thus directs itself to the social phenomenon being analysed, but also looks inward: inward to the sort of relationships developed in the field and the social characteristics and gender of the researcher and how these related to those of the people in the field; inward to the time, setting and circumstances in which the research was carried out, to the methodology and fieldwork practice used, the sensitivities and dangers surrounding the topic and location, and even the broad socio-economic and political situation at the time of the research.

Despite these variations in how analysis is conceived in the different types of ethnography, there is common ground. As indicated, analysis can be defined as the process of bringing order to the data (what Huberman and Miles call data reduction), organizing what is there into patterns, categories and descriptive units, and looking for relationships between them (data display), and ethnographers of all type share this intent. There is also a shared commitment to analytic induction and grounded theory as general strategies for analysis, although not necessarily in pure form and often just as lip service. Although analytical induction and grounded theory began in positivist ethnography, in weaker form they have proved useful to ethnographers generally. Induction begins with the particular observations, and empirical generalizations and theory building are bottom-up, moving from the data themselves. In pure form, however, analytic induction involves a process where hypotheses are examined against the observations and reformulated as counter cases are found (see Seale 1999: 83, for an outline of the stages of analytic induction). As Bryman and Burgess (1994: 4) note, analytic induction properly followed is very demanding because the appearance of a single counter case necessitates further revision of the hypothesis and a return to the field. For these reasons, ethnography is generally committed to induction only as lip service. Lip service is also given to grounded theory (on which see Glaser and Strauss 1967; Strauss 1987; Strauss and Corbin 1990, 1998), a similar analytical approach which involves the discovery of theory from the bottom up, building generalizations and inferences from the data themselves (this is discussed in greater detail in the next chapter). This is done through a complicated set of procedures for memo writing as an initial form of analysis, developing codes, categories and other concepts, and for 'saturating' them by testing them against the data. Again, Bryman and Burgess (1994: 5) note that there are very few genuine cases of grounded theory, but it is evoked frequently as 'an approving bumper sticker' (Richards and Richards 1991: 43) to describe the qualitative approach to data analysis. The stickers are proudly displayed, however, because both epitomize and evoke the principle that runs through much ethnographic data analysis, which is 'being true to the data themselves', although the postmodern turn makes these notions seem out of place. Seale (1999: 85) values the lip service, however, as reminders to ethnographers to be systematic.

Having discussed some of the general issues surrounding data analysis, it is necessary to turn to the complex task of describing how it is done. Desperate ethnographers are known to cry: 'How do I begin? Where do I begin?' These queries always arise when ethnographers survey the wondrous volume of data they have collected. The things that begin to focus the analysis are:

• the original questions that were generated in the planning stage and prompted the research in the first place;
• the insights about analysis that occurred during data collection.

Further analytical insights come once analysis proper begins after data collection. They do not come without effort. It is best to consider analysis as a series of processes or steps, which are time consuming and laborious but end up with an exhaustive and comprehensive analysis. The steps are:

• data management (organizing the data into manageable units);
• coding (indexing the data into categories and themes);
• content analysis;
• qualitative description (identifying the key events, people, behaviour, providing vignettes and appropriate forms of counting);
• establishing patterns in the data (looking for recurring themes, relationships between the data);
• developing a classification system of 'open codes' (looking for typologies, taxonomies and classification schemata which order and explain the data);
• examining negative case (explaining the exceptions and the things that do not fit the analysis).

It is worth noting that some steps may be inappropriate to one or more type of ethnography. Even extreme postmodern ethnographers still engage in analysis; the difference is that they do not impose a strong presence for the author by suggesting that there is a single 'true' analysis. The above steps should not be read as reintroducing the strong authorial presence and the single narrative analysis, but whether one analysis or several, the process of analysis needs to be done along lines suggested by them. The steps are also described here as if unassisted by qualitative computer packages. Computer-assisted data analysis is addressed separately afterwards.

Steps in ethnographic data analysis

All analysis begins with data management; that is, organizing the data into manageable units so that they do not appear as an amorphous mass. This begins with 'index coding'. The data are read and reread in order to code or index the material. Some ethnographers dislike the word 'code' because it has different connotations in quantitative research and to adopt it flatters that style of research, although others use it precisely because of this. Two sorts of 'codes' exist: the first are merely index categories for organizing and retrieving segments of the data; the second are known as 'open codes' and are developed at a later stage of the analysis. The former does not necess-arily fix meaning on the data; this should be left to later stages of coding. Indexing coding is the simplest and first procedure, and should be done in conjunction with a content analysis of the data. One reads through the data and asks oneself what it is that people in the field (or various field sites) are saying and doing. For example, the themes that emerged among people in West Belfast in our ethnography of crime (Brewer *et al.* 1997) included such things as drugs, joyriding, the paramilitaries and police–public relations. These things emerged from what people themselves said, and we could match to this how they acted (say, in dealing with joyriding or in reporting crime to the police compared to the paramilitaries; for an analysis of this see Brewer *et al.* 1997). And we could compare these across our two field sites, one in largely Catholic West Belfast, one in largely Protestant East Belfast. The data thus begin to be ordered into topics, which are labelled and classi-fied under 'index codes'. Note needs to be taken of the locations in the data of every extract that constitutes the code. By this means the ethnographer knows where every reference is to an index category or code (say, 'sectari-anism', 'drugs', 'joyriding' or whatever).

Data management is not a form of analysis – it merely assists in organiz-ing one's way through the volume of data. Yet it can assist the subsequent steps, such as qualitative description, the identification of patterns and the formulation of a classification system of 'open codes' to explain the data. One way it does this is by enabling all segments of data for a code or sub-code to be drawn together by means of scissors and paste or, if on disk, by means of a word processor word search. (Hence the importance of multiple copies of the data to permit them to be cut and pasted; word processing, of course, requires multiple copies for security reasons only.) Computers will now also do this task. Drawing together segments of data for a code facili-tates analysis because it allows codes to become more sophisticated by being broken into sub-codes: 'sectarianism', for example, could be broken into 'at work', 'on the streets', 'experiences by victims' and so on, with each sub-code broken down further, say 'sectarianism – experience by victims – young people'. Codes can be cross-referenced, so that, say, the sub-code 'joyriding – reaction of paramilitaries' can be cross-referenced to the code 'punishment beatings' and to the sub-code 'paramilitaries – policing methods', with the same location noted for each. In the past ethnographers would use old-fashioned index cards for each code and sub-code and record every reference to it in the data, with appropriate cross-references, although computer software packages will now do this. In this way, there is a gradual shift from indexing to analysis proper.

After index coding and content analysis come harder steps in analysis, yet qualitative description is probably the easiest and it is best to begin there. One of the premier advocates of humanistic ethnography, Lofland (1971: 7), argued that the field researcher's central task was to describe and explain that which had been observed, and six areas in the field were identified for description: acts, activities, meanings, participation, relationships and setting. Alternatively, to focus the qualitative description first address the index codes that have emerged in the content analysis. Read through the data and find good descriptions of the behaviour and talk that the codes represent. Discover which bit of the data, for example, is a good description of how policemen and women deal with drunks who are perceived as non-trouble-makers compared to other drunks (for an example of such analysis see Box 4.2). This bit is a good description of what the paramilitaries do to persistent joyriders, that bit a good example of what a joyrider says about the IRA. This is not necessarily 'thick description'. Thick description needs to take in the context of the phenomena described, the intentions and meanings that organize it and its subsequent evolution or processing; not all data will be sufficiently recorded to provide 'thick descriptions'. But qualitative description as a step in the analysis can highlight those special parts of the data where 'thick descriptions' are possible.

As another focus for the qualitative description it is useful to pick out the key events in the field which were 'focal events' for the people under study, about which comprehensive descriptions should be developed. Key events are of many kinds: festivals and celebrations, life events like birth, marriage or death, moments of special significance to the group or noteworthy activities. Special times in the calendar may be important as a measure of the activities and social meanings of people in the field. For example, it was especially important for me to see how the overwhelmingly Protestant RUC did police work on the night of 11 July, when Protestants generally hold bonfires (even on the public highway) to celebrate their culture, which in hard-line Loyalist areas usually results at best in considerable rowdiness, drunkenness and damage, and at worst in sectarian violence and murder (the three Quinn brothers were burnt alive in their beds on 11 July 1998 after

---

Box 4.2

Extract from J. D. Brewer, *Inside the RUC: Routine Policing in a Divided Society* (Oxford: Clarendon Press, 1991), with K. Magee, pp. 77–8.

Easton's section police have two sets of primary typifications: one for categorising trouble-makers, the other the abnormal. Criminals and other trouble-makers are widely referred to as 'gougers'. The term is flexible in that it refers to known criminals as well as others who look or act as if they have a potential for crime . . . Local knowledge is one important influence on the application of the typification . . . But it is not the only influence. Middle class notions of respectability enable policemen and women 'to tell just by looking at someone whether there's something suspicious about them' and 'to be able to recognise the decent member of the public' (Field notes, 20/6/87, p. 20). For example, a drunken woman was brought into the station one night after assaulting a policewoman and for using very abusive language, but she was allowed home uncharged after spending a night in the cells: she was even allowed to leave early enough in the morning to avoid all but the milkman from seeing her arrive home in a police vehicle. Talking about the woman, a policewoman said, 'she was a clean person wasn't she? She wasn't the usual gouger element type. She was probably just seeking attention.' The injured policewoman added 'she just needed someone to talk to I think' (Field notes, 25/9/87, p. 24). Through remarks like these the police were normalising the behaviour to distinguish it from that which can be expected from gougers.

---

thugs decided to harass Catholics on a mixed housing estate). Key people may also warrant special attention for qualitative description, and the data should be analysed to identify the key players in the group or setting. Portraits of the characters can then be used as part of the qualitative description. These key people may be selected because they are leaders or important to the group for some other reason, or ordinary members chosen simply because they exemplify some relevant point.

This description can go beyond key players. Case analyses can be provided of almost anything in the data. Some particular teacher, class or school may be worth picking out for fuller qualitative description in some ethnography on education; or some particular church or congregation in an ethnography of the new church movement. These act like case analyses and can be written up for special description as vignettes (the word is used not in the sense of giving people real or hypothetical stories to generate data but as micro analyses of some feature of the data). Thus, it is worth looking through the data to see if there are any special cases of the phenomena that can provide an interesting vignette for more detailed qualitative description. The case analysis could be a single person, group, critical event or community that in some way exemplifies or illustrates the phenomena under study. For example, in building an analysis of ordinary crime in a society torn by civil unrest and terrorism, it was important to pull out from the data vignettes of specific crimes which demonstrate Belfast to be like anywhere else, despite its history of sectarian violence (domestic violence, theft and so on), and those crimes that pointed to differences (joyriding, the relative absence of drug-related crime). We also pulled out processes for qualitative description that were unique to Belfast (the involvement of paramilitaries in crime or their policing role in crime management) and those that occur everywhere (reporting behaviour, fear of crime and so on).

It is worth recalling that qualitative description can be facilitated by assigning numbers to the data and engaging in elementary forms of counting. Not all events, behaviours or forms of talk are countable – those that are tend to be unambiguous, well defined and often trivial. But numbers can enhance analysis by avoiding anecdotalism (Silverman 1993: 163) and, where possible, simple counting techniques should be used to enumerate the frequency of examples, cases or whatever, although this will not have the power of full statistical analysis. However, numerical data collected by other methods than fieldwork, such as a survey, in a triangulation of techniques, can be incorporated in the analysis.

Qualitative description is not the end result of the analysis. Within the humanist tradition of ethnography, to describe was often to explain, and to describe meant to reproduce 'the structure, order and patterns found among a set of participants' (Lofland 1971: 7): telling it like it was. The positivist ethnographer wanted more; the postmodern one denies that this is possible. But for all ethnographers, analysis requires searching for the patterns within the data and explaining the relationships between segments of data. It is the status these patterns have and whose patterns they are that postmodern, reflexive ethnographers query (they see the patterns as situated by the relationship between researcher and researched and as having the status of only one telling among several possible ones). The positivist-scientific ethnographer usually went further and built on top a complicated classification system that 'told it like it was', but in the language of the analyst not the participant, and that rendered members' subjective meanings into an analyst's objective model. But searching for patterns is common ground (Bryman and Burgess 1994: 6, refer to this obsession with patterns as the 'pattern model' of analysis). Fetterman (1998: 92) describes this step of analysis as searching for patterns of thought and action repeated in various situations and with various players, comparing, contrasting and sorting categories and minutiae until a discernible pattern of thought or behaviour becomes identifiable. Connections between the data emerge as one looks for regularities and variations in the data and between the categories used to code them. Correlations between the categories can thereby be identified, extending the data analysis. There will be patterns of several things within the data, and several patterns to identify – the postmodern ethnographer would argue there are several competing patterns of the same thing – so that patterns may have to be compared and perhaps placed within a broader matrix of an overarching pattern. This is why Dey (1993: 47) likens patterns to building blocks, which are assembled and reassembled in different ways until the finished product is complete, although note that postmodern ethnographers contend that the finished product is never the definitive version. Advocates of computer-assisted analysis use the analogy of a tree to describe the same process.

From these patterns comes the classification system the analyst uses to conceptualize (and perhaps theorize) the data. Initially this is little more than an extension of codes, although more abstract conceptualizations are possible at a later stage. Sometimes these concepts are new and original; mostly ethnographers relate their data to pre-existing notions (Bryman and Burgess 1994: 7). The development of typologies and taxonomies is a more common result of ethnographic data analysis than theory generation. Within taxonomies sub-groups are delineated within a general category or different categories are related under a general classification schema. Ken Pryce's ethnography of West Indian life in the St Paul's district of Bristol in the 1970s offers a good example. He argued that West Indians faced a structural circumstance in terms of socio-economic position and racial discrimination (referred to graphically as 'slave labour' and 'shit work'), which led to two responses or 'life orientations', which he called the 'expressive-disreputable' and the 'stable-law abiding' orientations (for a summary see Pryce 1979: 267–78). The first essentially rejected these circumstances; the second accommodated itself to them. Within each life orientation, however, there were different lifestyles, representing the different ways of living and adaptations of West Indians in the area. Within the expressive-disreputable orientation Pryce identified 'hustlers' (who thieved, pimped off prostitutes and engaged in hedonistic criminal behaviour) and 'teenyboppers' (who absorbed anti-authority black Rastafarian culture). The stable law-abiding orientation had 'proletarian respectables' (God-fearing, working-class people who wanted to 'get on'), 'saints' (Pentecostal and absorbed in religion), 'mainliners' (middle class, semi-professional and white-collar workers who were 'getting on') and 'in-betweeners' (conscious of being black but essentially young middle class who would 'get on'). This was a complicated taxonomy, but even simpler classifications can be useful for organizing material, developing categories and variations within them and establishing linkages between categories. Such classification systems can be used to assist explanation and build theory.

I confess to a penchant for taxonomies and typologies. In the course of my observational study of routine policing by the RUC, I was interested in understanding the problems faced by policewomen as women in the highly masculine environment of a police station in Northern Ireland. I developed a classification system that categorized two types of policewomen, each handling their femininity differently, and having different patterns of behaviour and responses to masculine police occupational culture. I later elaborated the types by using the metaphor of Hercules's ninth labour and referred to the types as the Amazons and Hippolytes (see Brewer 1991b). More recently, based on in-depth interview research and documentary analysis, I developed a classification system for understanding linkages and variations in the phenomena of anti-Catholicism in Northern Ireland (see Brewer 1998; Brewer and Higgins 1999). Anti-Catholicism is a general cultural motif in Northern Ireland, with strong historical roots and many contemporary cultural representations. It is part of the sectarian culture of the place, and like many cultural symbols it can be imbibed unreflectively, without thought or systematic formulation, and reproduced unthinkingly in language with no malicious or discriminatory intent. Where anti-Catholicism is unsystematic at the level of ideas and not reflected in behaviour I described it as 'passive anti-Catholicism' – the kind that some Protestants have transmitted to them as part of their social learning but which remains as a cultural backdrop, rarely articulated or enacted. 'Active anti-Catholicism' is something different and represents a fully formulated structure of ideas, language and behaviour. I developed a taxonomy of three modes of active anti-Catholicism, called the covenantal, secular and Pharisaic modes. I plotted them on two axes or continuums: theological content (high to low) and political content (high to low). This representation of the various modes of anti-Catholicism neatly captured the paradox of the process, in that it can be grounded in an interpretation of Scripture (covenantal and Pharisaic modes), which may (covenantal mode) or may not (Pharisaic mode) have political expression, and also be relatively devoid of theology and highly political (secular mode), emphasizing an approach to politics much like one of the more theological modes (the covenantal). Each mode had a common structure, with its own set of foundational ideas on which it was premised, using a characteristic form of rhetoric by which to express anti-Catholicism, emphasizing different things in the articulation of anti-Catholicism, appealing to a different primary constituency and having different implications for relationships with Catholics. Not only did this classification scheme assist in describing the phenomenon, it helped to explain the process by identifying variations and linkages.

Classification is a conceptual process (Dey 1993: 44–5) and is clearly part of the process of interpretation by which meaning is brought to the data by the analyst. To classify is to break down the data into bits that relate together as classes that comprise concepts. This may involve a novel ordering or an existing classification system used by someone else, but it is always classification for a purpose. Classification schemes are not neutral (Dey 1993: 46), for the ethnographer is guided by the purpose at hand, the research objectives and personal whims. Postmodern ethnographers would consider such schemata as personal to the researcher anyway and context-bound to the circumstance of the research, although this would not prevent postmodern ethnographers developing them as long as their status was understood. The other types of ethnography are much keener on classification systems. Positivist ethnographers enthusiastically endorse such schemata as a way of objectifying social meanings, but humanistic ethnographers would wish to ensure that the classification system did not inhibit the faithful representation of people's meanings and understandings. Thus, it is important to distinguish between indigenous classification schemes, used by the participants themselves and incorporating their terminology, and researcher-led schematas that are developed by the analyst and use terminology that is not native to the participants. Humanistic ethnographers might develop a researcher-led classification scheme but would still ground it in the social reality they see it faithfully capturing. Positivist type ethnographers, however, would rarely stay with indigenous systems of classification.

Indigenous classification schematas are a normal part of the data and analysts may or may not want to remain with this system. In his account of social phenomenology, Alfred Schutz (1967) claimed that people in everyday life routinely developed classification schemes in order to cope with its complexity and ambiguity. Thus, members in the field can be expected to have developed their own common-sense categories and classificatory schemata to comprehend the world. My RUC research offers a good example. Policemen and women are members of a close-knit occupational world with a discrete culture and also face a world which has great variability and confusion, and considerable attention has been focused on the indigenous classificatory schemata, typologies and taxonomies they use to accomplish police work. It has been one of the central preoccupations of ethnographic police research. These idealizations are referred to by Holdaway (1983: 63–4) as their 'mental map'; Kathleen Magee and I referred to it as their 'cognitive map' (Brewer 1991a: 75–82). The classificatory schemata of the policemen and women we studied include typologies for categorizing people, distinguishing between 'gougers' (trouble-makers and criminals) and 'ordinary decent people', which was applied to the people they encountered and particularly to Catholics in order to determine those Catholics who could be trusted. These constituted what we called 'primary' classifications, that formed major categories in their map, but there was an array of 'secondary' ones for classifying people they encountered less rarely. There were also schemata to contrast types of police work, different kinds of police station and different kinds of managers. We felt we could not improve on these schemata, or their vocabulary, and used them wholesale.

The final step in analysis is searching for negative cases, what Becker (1998: 207) calls deviant cases. This is a fundamental part of analytical induction, and even though the commitment to this analytical procedure is of the bumper-sticker variety, inductive analysis of any kind should seek out and account for negative cases. It takes the form of what Becker (1998: 307) calls a kind of 'not-so-rigorous analytic induction' (for an account of how Becker himself used deviant cases see Becker 1970: 53). It is never enough, Coffey and Atkinson (1996: 191) write, to illustrate good ideas with supportive examples: there must be systematic scrutiny of all the evidence. Sometimes the negative cases result in the modification of the original formulation, but they often strengthen the analysis by illustrating the complexity of the phenomenon and the researcher's reluctance to engage in an easy gloss over difficult evidence (for an account of deviant cases in conversation analysis see Perakyla 1997). There are always exceptions to the rule in everyday life, and classification systems will always leave things that do not fit. To the postmodern ethnographer this is a virtue because all researchers offer partial explanations of a reality that cannot be captured in a single account, although to call them 'negative' or 'deviant' invests one of the analyses with an authority they would dispute. Hammersley and Gomm (1997), for example, while recognizing in postmodern fashion that all research is a construct, argue that examining negative cases can guard against error and personal bias. Negative cases are also a virtue to other kinds of ethnography because confronting them improves the correspondence of the analysis to the reality it seeks to represent.

Computer-assisted data analysis

It was confidently asserted in 1993 that the days of scissors and paste were over because of the arrival of computers (Dey 1993: xi). Others query the value of computers to substitute for the ethnographer's imagination and insight (Okely 1994), and they are only as good as the data that are entered by the ethnographer. Fetterman, himself an exponent of computers and the Internet, writes that computers 'still require the eyes and the ears of the ethnographer to determine what to collect and how to record it as well as how to interpret the data' (Fetterman 1998: 84). They have tremendous value, however, although the claim that computers assist theory and concept generation is exaggerated, or, at least, they do these things only indirectly by improved data management.

Exponents of computer-assisted qualitative analysis (see Fielding and Lee 1991, 1998; Richards and Richards 1994, 1998; Kelle 1995) argue that the move from filing cabinets, photocopiers, scissors and pots of paste to computers improves three things: data management; concept and theory generation; and the emulation of the natural science model of social research. Data management in ethnography is problematic because of the volume of data collected and their different sources, which include transcripts, field notes, extracts from personal documents, diaries and video or audio recordings, much of which is redundant or will become non-relevant for the purpose at hand. Manual procedures to index this data are slow and laborious; the computer offers speed, efficiency and comprehensiveness. The code and retrieve process in computer software packages allows the researcher to label passages of data, collate identically labelled passages and retrieve the collation at the press of a button.

Computers, it is argued, also offer greater effectiveness than manual procedures in data management because the enhanced code and retrieve process improves concept and theory generation. Two well known advocates recently wrote that computers assisted in the discovery of unrecognized ideas and concepts, in the construction and exploration of explanatory links between the data and in overall understanding (Richards and Richards 1998: 213; see also Kelle 1997). Theory *construction* is a creative enterprise, not a mechanical one, but theory *emergence* is not. Given that theory emerges from the interweaving of ideas, categories and concepts into yet further abstractions, computer-assisted code and retrieve procedures facilitate the handling of codes and the exploration of links which later creativity on the part of the researcher can construct into theories. As Fielding and Lee (1998: 58) stress, this stretches the capabilities of qualitative research in a way that mechanical analytical methods cannot match. The analytical procedures behind some theory or conceptual account can be trailed or logged by a subsequent person, thus allowing, for the first time, qualitative research to be replicated. Team analysis is also more feasible with the use of computers. Therefore, they assert, qualitative research has its acceptability and credibility enhanced by the use of computers, making it appear more scientific and thus allowing practitioners more leverage with policy-makers and funders (Fielding and Lee 1998: 58–9). Dey (1993: 4) believes that the rapprochement between qualitative and quantitative research styles is easier with the use of computer-assisted qualitative data analysis packages.

The arrival of word processors for inputting and retrieving text marked the beginnings of computers in qualitative research. There are now nearly twenty dedicated qualitative analysis programs, many in several versions, and exponents have an umbrella group, CAQDA (Computer Assisted Qualitative Data Analysis), to lobby and evangelize. Some programs are little better than word search facilities on word processors and require, as Fielding (1993) put it, 'a very light touch' by the analyst, being confined to simple, albeit rapid, text retrieval (such as *SONAR*). But other packages, notably *NUDIST* and *The ETHNOGRAPH*, are said to transform qualitative data analysis. Weitzman and Miles (1995) distinguish three kinds of software: code and retrieve packages; code-based theory building programs; and concept network builders (the latter making more advanced claims for data linkages). *The ETHNOGRAPH* was probably the first dedicated qualitative analysis package, and was developed in the early 1980s. It is a code and retrieve package, substituting for cutting and pasting, but it does not allow simultaneous access to data files by multiple users and is not suited to complex forms of analysis. *NUDIST* is probably the best known. Developed by the husband and wife team of Thomas and Lyn Richards in Australia, *NUDIST* has overtaken other programs, like *HyperRESEARCH, HyperSoft, Kwalitan* and *Textbase Alpha* (Fielding and Lee 1998: 15). Each has its adherents, although *Atlas-ti* is closest to *NUDIST* in function and popularity. *NUDIST* is specifically designed for multi-access use, provides audit trails of coding and retrieving for subsequent replication and testing, links to the SPSSX quantitative analysis program and, above all, assists in the emergence of concepts and theories through its rather daunting 'tree structures' (or hierarchies) that build codes up into greater levels of abstraction. It permits the manipulation of very large segments of data (ideal for long field notes) and allows for the handling of much more data, but is very difficult to learn. (CAQDAS provides training in some packages, especially *NUDIST*.) A thorough discussion of the relative merits and capabilities of each package is provided by Fielding and Lee (1991: Resources Appendix), Barry (1998) and, more briefly, Fielding (1993). Fetterman (1998: 82) provides an excellent profile, which is reproduced as Table 4.1.

The process of data analysis and subsequent theory building in programs like *NUDIST* and *HyperRESEARCH* works as follows. Data like field notes, extracts from personal documents, transcripts of interviews and so on are converted into text (or ASCII files if transporting text from another document). Data can then be retrieved by searching for key words or strings of words, or by labelling segments of data by a code based on their meaning and then searching for the code. Documents can thereafter be created of all

Table 4.1 Computer-assisted qualitative data analysis packages

Program	Operation
Word processors, *Metamorph, Orbis, Sonar, The Text Collector, Word-Cruncher, ZyINDEX*	Text retrieval via word or phrase search
AskSam, Folio VIEWS, Tabletop, MAX	Organizing and sorting text
HyperQal2, Kwalitan, QUALPRO, Martin, The ETHNOGRAPH	Find and display coded data, retrieve coded data
AQAD, HyperRESEARCH, NUDIST	Theory generation
Atlas-ti, MECA, SemNet	Theory testing

Source: Fetterman (1998: 82).

material under the code or string of words. The document can be manipulated by developing further codes that identify variations in the root code or parallels with other codes. Code refinement follows in tandem with further levels of data analysis as categories, sub-categories, typologies and taxonomies emerge to classify the data. The coding system can be modified during the analysis, new codes inserted to describe overlapping coded segments and changes made to the boundaries of the text segments as code refinement occurs. The data can be manipulated on screen to form a hierarchical tree structure to enable researchers to visualize how the pieces fit together. This sets the possibility for patterns to be identified, for data to be sorted and compared, and for patterns and models to emerge at a glance: the things ethnographers used to do in their heads they can now see on screen (Fetterman 1998: 98). The parallel between this and grounded theory (at least, in its pure form) is noted by several commentators (Lonkila 1995; Coffey *et al.* 1996).

Critics remain unconvinced however. At best, many packages are computer-based storage and retrieval systems rather than forms of analysis as such (see Coffey *et al.* 1996: 6–7; in response see Richards 1999). Coding is not a form of analysis, and coding and computing carry the danger of imposing a spurious scientific gloss to qualitative research. Coffey *et al.* (1996) give several warnings. Computer-assisted analysis risks becoming the new orthodoxy, with ethnographers uncritically adopting a set of strategies that become taken for granted. Coding can be overemphasized. It is not the only way to manage and manipulate data and it excludes a more 'fine grained hermeneutic analysis' (Lonkila 1995: 49) wherein meanings emerge in a less mechanistic and more interpretative fashion. This is something Richards (1999: 13) denies, arguing that better access is provided to the data by the software's ability to manipulate masses of data, ensuring none are left unattended. But critics contend that computers risk losing the ethnographer's 'feel' for the data and thus threaten the humanistic intent to capture the phenomenon in its own terms. 'In our view', Coffey *et al.* (1996: 7) write, 'qualitative research is not enhanced by poor imitations of other research styles. Analytic procedures which appear rooted in standardised, often mechanistic procedures are no substitute for genuinely "grounded" engagement with the data.' The analytical 'gold standard' provided by computers also runs counter to the postmodern trends which stress the multiple voices and perspectives that exist in the data and thus both the plurality of analyses that are possible and the different modes of textual presentation. The modernist tendency which computer-assisted qualitative data analysis represents thus offends postmodern sensibilities. For this reason, Coffey *et al.* (1996) advocate computing strategies that are not code and retrieve procedures but that experiment with the textual presentation of data through hypertext and hypermedia programs. In essence, they write, the underlying ideas of hypertext are simple. The reader's relationship to a given text need not be restricted to a linear reading in a predetermined sequence. Computers facilitate experimentation by allowing readers to become authors of their own reading as they create pathways through the data by browsing, cross-references and other interactive procedures (discussed below).

The chief complaint of the critics of CAQDAS is not Luddite fear of new technology (something which Richards 1999: 11–12 claims), but that its use is mainly restricted to coding and retrieval (and whatever analytical task is dependent on coding and retrieval). There is much besides. Not only can computers be used to experiment with the presentation of text, they give us access to the Internet. The net's relevance is not so much to analysis, although Fetterman (1998: 72) describes it as the most powerful resource available to ethnographers. There are several tasks in the research process which the Internet can facilitate, such as searches for topics when undertaking a preliminary bibliographical search, by using either one of the various 'search engines' (a collection of specified web sites and resources) or a special bibliographical holding like BIDS; it is even possible to enter library catalogues and encyclopaedias. There is a special bibliographical site for social scientists maintained by the Economic and Social Research Council (ESRC) in the United Kingdom at <http://www.regard.ac.uk>. The various 'chat' services (found under any search engine) and discussion lists (a list of e-mail addresses for exchange of messages) can be used to conduct interviews or share notes or preliminary ideas; some users will be random members of the public, but discussion lists can be specialized and may be used as data sources or as sounding boards among colleagues. Locating discussion lists can be problematic, but some among serious academics and researchers may be found at the Directory of Scholarly and Professional E-Conferences: <http: //www.n2h2.com/KOVACS/>. Some sites will contain useful data. Many government and official documents are now accessible on the web, mostly for free, and on-line electronic journals can be accessed, such as *Sociological Research Online*, <http://www.socresonline.org.uk/socresonline/>. An American equivalent is *The Qualitative Report*, at <http://www.nova.edu/sss/QR/>. Many public bodies have their own web sites with useful material about themselves, including, for example, annual reports. Census material and official statistics are easy to locate for most countries. There are also several data archives on the web. The ESRC in the UK has a data archive at <http://155.245.254.47>, which stores the largest collection of computer readable data in the social sciences in the United Kingdom. An American equivalent is the University of California's Social Science Data Extraction site, at <http://sun3.lib.uci.edu/~dtsang/ext.htm>. Even more relevant to ethnography is the Qualitative Data Archive at the University of Essex <http://www.essex.ac.uk/qualidata>, which preserves primary qualitative data that can be used for secondary research (see Box 4.3 for an illustration of what the web home page looks like for the ESRC qualitative data archive). In planning ethnographic research, it is wise to carry out a search of its holdings just to see what has been done. What is more, all these resources can be accessed from the field while in location as long as the researcher has a laptop computer with modem and access to a telephone line. Fetterman (1998: 74) is an advocate of using the Internet in ethnographic research and has a special web site for ethnographers with information, resources and links to other relevant sites. The address is <http://www.stanford.edu/~davidf/ethnography.html>. But perhaps the best resource is Stuart Stein's recent book (Stein 1999), which not only explains how the Internet can be used in learning, teaching and research, but also contains a host of web sites in the social sciences and humanities from across the globe, and is essential reading for any social researcher.

Interpretation

A postmodern ethnographer once declared that 'in the social sciences there is only interpretation', for nothing speaks for itself (Denzin 1998: 313). Interpretation is the process whereby the ethnographer attaches meaning to the data. In realist versions, ethnographers disclose their understanding and explanation of the phenomenon using the single, authoritative author's voice. In postmodern terms, ethnographers disclose the multiple meanings and voices surrounding the phenomenon. There is very little to be said about interpretation, since it is a creative enterprise that depends on the insight and imagination of the ethnographer. It is not mechanical but requires skill, imagination and creativity. It does not occur separately from analysis but is simultaneous with post-indexing stages in the analytical process. This is why advocates of computer-assisted ethnographic data analysis contend that their software assists in interpretation as well, because 'the exploration of meanings in the data demands data management methods that support insight and discovery, encourage recognition and development of categories' (Richards and Richards 1998: 214). Post-index forms of coding are thus part of the interpretative process. Luddites or other critics, especially those postmodernists who resist the positivist thrust behind computer-assisted data analysis, prefer to see interpretation as an art rather than a mechanical process (see Denzin 1998: 314). But even postmodernist ethnographers have to engage in interpretation and to 'construct' a reading or readings of an event. They suggest only that the interpretation is but one of several possible tales or readings, including the members' own narratives; interpretations are stories, there is no single interpretative truth.

However, some things are less true than others. Anti-realist ethnographers like Hammersley accept the postmodern moment that ethnography finds itself in, but do not wish to abandon the search for truth statements. All but the most radical postmodern ethnographers are committed to establishing truthful knowledge claims. As Hammersley (1990: 60) puts it, 'no knowledge is certain, but knowledge claims can be judged reasonably accurately in terms of their likely truth.' But likely truth can be judged

Box 4.3

E S R C QUALITATIVE DATA
ARCHIVAL RESOURCE CENTRE
(Qualidata)

Welcome to the WWW site for QUALIDATA. This site provides information relating to the work of QUALIDATA and also provides links to other social science research resources.

Highlight an option from the menu below:

About Qualidata
Guidelines for Archiving Qualitative Data
Confidentiality and informed consent and Copyright
Applying for ESRC grants (Research and Programmes)
List of Deposits by Discipline
Search QUALIDATA's On-line Catalogue – QUALICAT
What's Happening: Activities
Complete our Researchers' Survey
Other useful social science links
Links to National libraries and repositories
References to records of interest for social scientists
QUALIDATA staff
Who to contact at Qualidata

STUDY PACKS available from Qualidata

SLIDE SHOW : Overview of Qualidata

Contacting Qualidata

Qualidata
Department of Sociology
University of Essex
Wivenhoe Park
Colchester CO4 3SQ
United Kingdom
Telephone/Fax: 01206 873058
International: +44 1206 873058

If you have any suggestions about the information at this site please let us know, either by e-mailing QUALIDATA, or by completing this comments form.

© Qualidata Last modified by Louise Corti QUALIDATA, Jan 1999

Reproduced with permission.

against many standards (which is the postmodernist's point). Two in particular are important: the ethnographer's understanding and the members in the field. This requires ethnographers to do five things when interpreting findings:

- check their interpretations with members to ensure people in the field find them truthful (since even a postmodernist 'reading' needs to correspond to something outside the ethnographer's head);
- in developing this interpretation, ethnographers none the less adopt a critical attitude towards what members say (since people may deliberately try to deceive);
- look for and seek alternative explanations, even if only to dismiss them, since this shows how deeply the material has been thought about;
- keep methods and data in context, since interpretations are tied to the methods used;
- represent the polyphony of voices in the field (since there will be many versions of truth among members, even if the ethnographer has developed their own).

The first four requirements are associated with positivist and humanistic types of ethnography, and have a long tradition of endorsement lying in the naive realist intent to provide a convincing interpretation. In Bruyn's (1966) humanistic approach to ethnography, one index of the subjective adequacy of the researcher's interpretation was 'social consensus', in which group members checked the findings. Hughes (1976) understood verifiability of findings to be achieved when the ethnographer could communicate members' knowledge to them and pass as an ordinary member. Member validation forms a significant part of Seale's (1999: 61–72) discussion of research practice, where he identifies three main kinds: checking interpretations by their power to predict members' future behaviour; the researcher trying out the interpretations by engaging in behaviour that passes as that of a member of the setting; and asking members to judge the adequacy of the interpretations, either by their evaluation of the final report or by getting them to comment on the interpretations. The origins of this go further back to Schutz (1964: 64) and his 'postulate of adequacy' (for an account of the postulate see Carroll 1982). The problem for Schutz was to ensure that the researcher's interpretations (what he called 'second order constructs') were true to the members' common-sense interpretations (what he called 'first order constructs'). This was achieved by relating the researcher's conceptualization back to the data it attempts to explain and describe. Carroll (1982) suggested that this postulate was satisfied when researchers referred their interpretation – their models, taxonomies, typologies and explanatory categories – back to the subjects to achieve a negotiated account. Wallis and Bruce (1983) argued that this should be a general process for researchers who wish to 'account for action', and Bruce (1992) put it into practice in his ethnographic study of the Loyalist paramilitary group known as the Ulster Defence Association, when he checked facts and interpretations with the gunmen, partly to protect himself, partly to protect accuracy. I did the same with my analysis of former members of the British Union of Fascists when I went back to the informants (see Box 4.4). I had developed an interpretation of their membership based around the theme of crisis, which I felt made their membership to them a rational sequence of means–ends, and I gave them the opportunity to respond to this interpretation. Not only did this supply further data, it enabled me to meet the 'postulate of adequacy' (discussed in Brewer 1984b: 755–7).

The case of the former fascists illustrates well, however, that despite the injunction to engage in member validation, researchers should not take what members say at face value or uncritically, for they can deceive, misrepresent or simply be plain wrong-headed. Moreover, people's accounts are often full of contradictions and inconsistencies that need to be represented and explored. This is not to support the realist notion that there is

---

Box 4.4

Extract from an interview with a former member of the British Union of Fascists in which I discussed with him my interpretation of people's membership, dated 17 October 1974. His remarks both confirmed my interpretation as one true to his 'first-order constructs' and supplied additional useful illustrative material.

> Yes, my support was connected with a crisis, which I perceived and which I summed up in 1939 as 'all is finished'. The relationship between crisis and the BUF was that the BUF came into being in a social and artificial economic crisis. It emerged through the decay of the old order as all other good and bad revolutions emerge.

In an interview on 28 November 1974, I asked him to clarify his earlier expression 'all is finished'. He said:

> Clearly the old order, the character of the people, society and outlook generally had gone. The 1914–18 war was the end of constructive living, the 1939 war the end of intelligent living. From the declaration of war in 1939 the old order changed, never to return . . . it was replaced by world chaos, infamy and despair. Famine and pestilence is prevalent. In savagery and debasement, wars beget wars . . . Those who brought sanity, prosperity in a real sense, and true happiness, have been discredited, abused, maligned, mentally tortured or liquidated. Indeed, all is finished.

a single interpretative truth. There are multiple interpretations in the field that need to be captured in the ethnographer's representation of the polyphony of voices, but sometimes people are wrong in the truth they hold or try to conceal the truth they hold by saying something else. The postmodernist commitment to multivocality still requires that an assessment be made of the veracity of what a voice says when it conflicts with other voices. This is what Hammersley (1990: 73) means when he says that, even within his anti-realist approach (called subtle realism), ethnographers remain obliged to make reasonable judgements about the likely validity of any member's claim, as manifested in their plausibility and credibility. Ethnography should not just be a celebration of the knowledge of members on the basis that they are insiders, or remain content merely to map members' competing accounts in a polyphony of different readings. Douglas (1976) suggests that ethnographers should test members' accounts against reliable evidence and check them against both what other people say and what can be experienced and observed. This is something Hammersley (1990: 61–3) considers essential to the methodological position he calls subtle realism, where interpretations must be assessed by their plausibility and credibility, among other things. Fielding (1993: 165) urges that an ethnographer's interpretations should maintain the fine balance between appreciation and being conned.

It is also important to keep methods and data in context when interpreting the findings. Data are contextually tied to the methods used to collect them, the location of the study and the context in which the research was done, so that interpretations are limited by these factors. While this is true of all styles of research, the restricted vision of ethnographers requires that they should avoid claiming too much for their data. Realist and postmodern ethnographers would agree on this. A qualitative study of crime in East and West Belfast does not enable the ethnographer to interpret crime in Downpatrick or Delhi, unless the grounds for this are clearly established beforehand. An issue such as this highlights the importance of reflexivity on the part of ethnographers when interpreting the results and writing them up.

Reflexivity

Reflexivity and the writing-up process are inseparable; so much so that Hertz's (1997) collection examined 'reflexivity' and 'voice', with reflexivity being described as a concern with how the selves and identities of the researcher and researched affect the research process (see also Davies 1999), and voice being the textual representation of the multiplicity of perspectives of subjects in the field. But then, so are reflexivity and interpretation integrally bound together, since the attribution of meaning to the data needs to be done reflexively. Reflexivity thus acts as a bridge between interpretation and the process by which it is conveyed in text, and is discussed here before the final section on presentation and writing up results.

Reflexivity involves reflection by ethnographers on the social processes that impinge upon and influence data. It requires a critical attitude towards data, and recognition of the influence on the research of such factors as the location of the setting, the sensitivity of the topic, power relations in the field and the nature of the social interaction between the researcher and researched, all of which influence how the data are interpreted and conveyed in writing up the results. Reflexivity thus affects both writing up the data (called representation) and the data's status, standing and authority (called legitimation). It is associated with the idea that ethnographic representations of reality are partial, partisan and selective, and thus with anti-realist and postmodernist denials that there is a perfectly transparent or neutral way to represent the social world (or the natural one). It is, therefore, a fundamental part of the postmodern, post-positivist type of ethnography. However, ethnographers disagree as to whether reflexivity threatens the quality of ethnographic data, or improves it; whether it is the problem or the solution.

We now live in what is known as the 'reflexive turn' within ethnography. Critics who wish to reassert some of the old certainties in ethnography contend that this is a card 'now being played too regularly in the social sciences' (Silverman 1997a: 239). While reflexivity is a much-used word, it is also much abused (on its meanings see Babcock 1980; May 1998, 1999). The variety of its usage owes a lot to the diverse origins of the term, for it is associated with the 1960s radical critique of sociology, feminist critiques of research methodology, social studies of scientific knowledge and only more recently with anti-realism and postmodernism in anthropology and sociology (May 1998: 8–9 links it to fundamental theoretical debates about the nature of action and structure). However, as Altheide and Johnson (1998: 285) remark, the main meaning of reflexivity is that the scientific observer is part and parcel of the setting, context and culture he or she is trying to understand and represent (see also Davies 1999: 7). But the implications of this vary for different aspects of the research process. A review of these antecedents shows two implications as giving the most concern: the authority that can be claimed of the data (the problem of legitimation) and its effects on the writing-up process (the problem of representation). Reflexivity to some ethnographers is thus the problem: as part of the social world under study, ethnographers produce situated knowledge that is partial, threatening the legitimation of the data and their representation. To others, reflexivity is also the solution: by making explicit the partial nature of the data and the contingencies into which any representation must be located, the legitimation and representation of the data can be improved.

The emergence of reflexivity as an issue

There were three sorts of radical critique in sociology in the 1960s into which reflexivity fits (for a different analysis of these origins see May 1998). The one began with Garfinkel and ethnomethodology, in which reflexivity was understood to describe the situated nature of all social knowledge (Garfinkel 1967: 7–9), and was meant as an attack on abstract, general theorizing. A sociologist's descriptions of the social world were within and part of the world they describe, so that they reflect something of the social situation in which they are situated. This reflection or reflexivity could be of the social relationships behind the description, the moral evaluations embedded in them or the political, moral or social consequences they contain (Schwartz and Jacobs 1979: 51). An entirely different radical critique of sociology emerged at roughly the same time in the work of Gouldner (1970, 1973), where practitioners of sociology were told to cast a cold eye on their own doings (Gouldner 1970: 488–90) and come to view their own beliefs with the same critical attitude as they do those held by others. Gouldner (1973: 77) came later to write that a reflexive sociology required us to establish the relationship in our work between our identity as sociologist and as person, which was meant as an attack on the notion of objectivity and the belief that there can be uncontaminated research. He was attacking the myth of value-free research. Rather than value freedom, Gouldner (1973: 78) argues, 'knowledge is moulded by a man's technical skills and by his intelligence, moulded by all that he is and wants, by his passion no less than by his objectivity. Reflexive sociology attributes importance to the theorist's infrastructure – his domain assumptions, his sentiments, the things that are real to him and the way these things shape his theory.' Reflexivity in the sense of Garfinkel and Gouldner was associated with a critical attitude towards data and anxiety over the authority, status and standpoint the data possess (the concern over legitimation).

The use of male pronouns in Gouldner's work highlights the need for the other critique that was to emerge in sociology at this time, that of feminism. Yet, strangely, this critique was more embedded in Gouldner than in Garfinkel. It was not just that feminist methodology required a 'reflexive concern with gender', as Cook and Fonow (1986) put it, by means of which there was a conscious-raising with respect to women's issues and position built on the notion of reflexivity (see also Fonow and Cook 1992). Reflexivity in feminism went further, for feminist theory and praxis questioned the privileged position accorded to the sociologist's observations against those of the voiceless (female) subjects, and encouraged a self-critical approach on the part of the researcher. Reflexivity in feminist praxis, therefore, merged legitimation and representation (a point stressed by Wolf 1992). This was a concern with representation to ensure that female subjects were not rendered voiceless in the writing-up of the text, and with legitimation to ensure that feminist researchers identified the procedures by which evaluations, interpretations and conclusions were reached (a point stressed by Stanley 1993: 44).

A development which owed more to Garfinkel than Gouldner was the contribution that 'relativist-constructionist' social studies of science made to reflexivity (although the tradition of social studies of science lies in orthodox areas and began as a realist preoccupation). The point these relativist-constructionist studies made was that even natural science produces socially situated knowledge. The reflexive turn these studies later took (represented well by Woolgar 1988b) amounted to a recognition that the studies which demonstrate science to be a social product are themselves social products, contingent on various social processes into which their data must be located to affect their authority and status (see Woolgar and Ashmore 1988: 1–2). This required experimentation with textual forms in order to demonstrate both the multivocal character of any analysis and interpretation, and the fallacy that there is a single reading (see Woolgar 1998b). This approach reinforced the association of reflexivity with both representation and legitimation.

Anti-realism and postmodernism cemented the reflexive turn in ethnography. Postmodern cultural anthropologists (Marcus 1980; Clifford 1981, 1983; Marcus and Cushman 1982; Stocking 1983; Clifford and Marcus 1986; Spencer 1989) deconstructed the practice of ethnography and the ethnographic text and reduced the data to one narrative among many (the crisis of legitimation) and the text to telling a story (the crisis of representation). So it was, too, in sociology (in the United States see van Maanen 1988; in the United Kingdom see Hammersley and Atkinson 1983; Atkinson 1990, 1992). Probably the first ethnographers in Britain to expound the implications of reflexivity were Hammersley and Atkinson (1983: 14–23). Social research, they wrote, had a reflexive character (p. 14), by which they meant that researchers are part of the social world they study. The implication of reflexivity for the practice of social research made it futile to eliminate the effects of the researcher; rather, we should set about understanding them (p. 17). This was seen primarily in the context of the problems it created for the authority, standing and status of the data, although Atkinson came later to focus on the problems posed for textual representation. The upshot now is that we are encouraged to be reflexive in our account of the research process, the data collected and the way we write up, because reflexivity shows the partial nature of our representation of reality and the multiplicity of competing versions of reality.

Reflexivity tended not to be a feature of traditional ethnography – positivist or humanistic – since neither believed there to be any complication in the ethnographer's ability to capture reality faithfully and accurately as it is on the inside given good research practice. Yet such ethnographers are finding it increasingly difficult to avoid the force of the attack on realism, and even here reflexivity is now being presented as part of good practice. Thus, Fetterman (1998: 22) hints at the need for reflexivity when he writes: 'ethnographers must attempt to view another culture without making value judgements, but ethnographers cannot be completely neutral. We are all products of our culture. We have personal beliefs, biases, and individual tastes. Socialization runs deep. The ethnographer can guard against the more obvious biases by making them explicit.' Anti-realists who are not extreme postmodernists and who offer quasi-realist methodologies to ground good ethnographic practice, while taking on board much of the thrust of postmodern critiques of research practice, such as Hammersley's 'subtle realism' or Altheide and Johnson's 'analytical realism', also stress the importance of reflexivity. Thus, post postmodern ethnographers like Altheide and Johnson (1998: 292) write: 'the ethnographic ethic calls for ethnographers to substantiate their interpretations and findings with a reflexive account of themselves and the process of their research.' Reflexivity in this view is a way to *improve* legitimation of the data – 'validity-as-reflexive accounting' as Denzin and Lincoln (1998: 278) put it – although Denzin himself, as a more radical postmodernist ethnographer, sees reflexivity as an alternative to the traditional criteria by which ethnographic data are normally judged. In either view, however, reflexivity is now part of good practice.

Being reflexive

Stanley (1996) usefully distinguished between 'descriptive' and 'analytical' reflexivity (for another typology, see May 1998). The former involves reflectiveness on the impact that various contingencies had on the outcome of the research, such as a description of the social location of the research, the preconceptions of the researcher, power relations in the field and the nature of the interaction between the researcher and subjects. It requires the development of a critical attitude towards the data. Ethnographers who seek to rescue their craft from the extremes of postmodernist deconstruction and retain some form of realism normally end their reflexivity with this type. Descriptive reflexivity can be used to provide a secure realist-like foundation to the research, but it can also be used as part of the postmodern project. If the latter, it is normally done in conjunction with 'analytical reflexivity'. 'Analytical reflexivity' is a much tougher requirement. It deals with epistemological matters and knowledge claims, and requires a form of intellectual autobiography in which researchers explicate the processes by which understanding and interpretation was reached and how any changed understanding from prior preconceptions came about.

Being reflexive in the descriptive sense requires that ethnographers ask themselves a series of questions and reflect on how the answers impinged upon and helped to situate and shape the data and their analysis and interpretation of it. With respect to analysis and interpretation, Lofland (1974: 308) listed a number of questions, which he put to a group of influential ethnographers:

- In what manner did you keep field notes?
- What was the rate of data accumulation or waves of accumulation?
- How did you record data?
- How did you file, code or otherwise sort material?
- How did the leading ideas evolve?
- What kinds of models or images are you aware of employing to organize the material and what was their source?
- To what extent did you organize your analysis before writing it out in text?
- What were the important difficulties experienced in analysis and writing up?
- How would you have modified your practices?

Descriptive reflexivity requires attention to other features of the research process as well, and questions need to be asked about social relations in the field and the bearing these had on data collection and interpretation. Altheide and Johnson (1998: 295) identify the importance of reflecting on this issue:

> Reflexive ethnographers [should] illustrate that each and every setting, without exception, is socially stratified. The stratified hierarchies vary from one setting to another, and the stratification has different consequences in one setting compared with others, but all settings are stratified in some manner, and commonly on the basis of gender, age, race and/or ethnicity, or social class/education/occupation. The personal qualities of a given ethnographer will 'fit' or 'not fit' somewhere in this schema. The quality and validity of the information thus obtained will be related to how a given observer met and resolved these issues for the particular setting studied. Claims of full membership or 'becoming the phenomenon' do not adequately resolve this dilemma.

Reflexive ethnographers should thus account for themselves and their social relations, as well as the substantive findings and construction of the text.

Analytical reflexivity requires yet more difficult reflection. In this sense ethnographers should ask themselves questions about the theoretical framework and methodology they are working within, the broader values, commitments and preconceptions they bring to their work, the ontological assumptions they have about the nature of society and social reality, and what Stanley (1996: 48) calls the 'felt necessities' the researcher has about the topic and the approach to it that resonates with them passionately. This rejects the notion of the detached, aloof and objective researcher who produces knowledge claims as if in a vacuum, in favour of one who not only engages with their subjects but also reflects upon the processes by which conclusions were reached and displays these argumentative procedures in ways that readers can reconstruct.

In sum, ethnographers who seek to be reflexive in both descriptive and analytical senses should reflect on the following issues as part of good practice (adopted from Brewer 1994: 235–6, and from Chapter 2 above):

1 The wider relevance of the setting and the topic, and the grounds on which empirical generalizations are made, if any, such as establishing the representativeness of the setting, its general features or its function as a special case study with a broader bearing.

2 The features of the topic or setting left unresearched, discussing why these choices have been made and what implications follow from these decisions for the research findings.

3 The theoretical framework they are operating within, and the broader values and commitments (political, religious, theoretical and so on) they bring to their work.

4 Critically assess their integrity as researchers and authors, by considering:
   • the grounds on which knowledge claims are being justified (length of fieldwork, the special access negotiated, discussing the extent of the trust and rapport developed with the respondents and so on);
   • their background and experiences in the setting and topic;
   • their experiences during all stages of the research, especially mentioning the constraints imposed therein;
   • the strengths and weaknesses of their research design and strategy.

5 Critically assess the data, by:
   • discussing the problems that arose during all stages of the research;
   • outlining the grounds on which they developed the categorization system used to interpret the data, identifying clearly whether this is an indigenous one used by respondents themselves, or an analyst-constructed one, and, if the latter, the grounds which support this;
   • discussing rival explanations and alternative ways of organizing the data;
   • providing sufficient data extracts in the text to allow readers to evaluate the inferences drawn from them and the interpretations made of them;
   • discussing power relations within the research, between researcher(s) and subjects and within the research team, in order to establish the effects of class, gender, race and religion on the practice and writing up of the research.

6 Show the complexity of the data, avoiding the suggestion that there is a simple fit between the social world under scrutiny and the ethnographic representation of it, by:
   • discussing negative cases which fall outside the general patterns and

categories employed to structure the ethnographic description, which often serve to exemplify and support positive cases;

- showing the multiple and often contradictory descriptions proffered by the respondents themselves;
- stressing the contextual nature of respondents' accounts and descriptions, and identifying the features which help to structure them.

All of these things are components of reflexivity and the process both assists the ethnographer in making claims in the text and helps the reader in assessing the credibility of those claims. Put in this way, reflexivity is a conventional scientific virtue and can be linked to realist ambitions to produce a single, authoritative account. And one that can be replicated. Seale (1999: 162) links reflexivity with specification of the methodological details that permits an audit trail by peers and thus possible replication of the results; a very realist ambition. But reflection on the above sort of issues also constitutes what van Maanen (1988) calls the 'confessional tales' that he says anti-realist ethnographers should now write when presenting their findings. Reflexivity thus accords with both extreme postmodern ethnography and the post postmodern position of 'subtle', 'analytical' or 'critical' realism, whereby ethnographers make strong statements about the social world while being sensitive to problems relating to representation and legitimation.

The presentation of ethnographic data

Writing up the results should not be restricted to the end of the research process, but should be an ongoing procedure; Wolcott (1990: 20) suggests that ethnographers even begin to write before entering the field, although what is written is clearly not the finished text. Nor is it separate from analysis and interpretation, in that writing clarifies thinking and thus assists both. Becker (1986: ix) declares that writing *is* thinking, so ethnographers should not wait to write until their thoughts are clear; they will become clearer by writing and rewriting. There is another reason for beginning writing early. Writing exposes gaps in knowledge, and if these are revealed early enough further data can be collected or adjustments made during the main period of fieldwork.

However, the process of writing up results is a contentious issue in the literature on ethnography. The fierce methodological divisions within ethnography are reflected in the debate about presentation, and the ethnographic text is a battle site. The first attempts to deconstruct ethnographic practice focused on the issue of representation in the text, and the battle is still being fought. Three issues are important in a consideration of the presentation of ethnographic data: what to include in the account; how to write it; and what status the author claims it to have.

What to write

With respect to what to include in an account, Altheide and Johnson (1998: 296) identify a number of generic topics which ethnographers should use reflexively to structure their account:

- the context, i.e. history, physical setting and environment;
- number of participants, key individuals;
- activities;
- schedules and temporal order;
- division of labour and hierarchies;
- routines and variations;
- significant events;
- members' perspectives and meanings;
- social rules and basic patterns of order.

These topics do not necessarily assume the implantation on the account of a single, authoritative realist voice, but the postmodern, reflexive ethnographer would add to these:

- presentation of the polyphony of voices and perspectives in the field;
- reflexive identification of the shortcomings of the research design;
- the limits of method, data and textual account.

The balance between verbatim quotations and analysis is important to all ethnographers and needs to be managed deftly. The extracts of natural language that the data comprise need to be given in fulsome enough proportion to present a credible report, to illustrate and substantiate the interpretation and to allow readers to evaluate the explanation. For the realist ethnographer the extracts must be so detailed as to assist 'thick description'. Quotations are the stuff of ethnography, but they should not be overdone and become repetitive. Nor should ethnographers use quotations to make analytical points for them: the quotations should illustrate the analysis, not substitute for it. Yet quotations are not the only data in ethnography. Fetterman (1998: 12) describes his approach: 'I usually include charts, pictures, and, whenever possible, computer-projected screens along with my text.' Davies (1999: 117) discusses the use of visual data in ethnography and distinguishes visual media as data from visual media as text.

How to write

Accounts should be accessible to readers. The audience for the account may vary, from policy-makers and academics to sections of the lay public, so that accessibility is relative to the readers of the account. Use a vocabulary relevant to the audience, but always write in a straightforward and unpretentious manner and always engage their interest. Dey (1993: 247) gives the following advice: engage readers' interest through vivid description and drama, trace the evolution of the account to contextualize what is written, identify key themes of the account, write it coherently, use simple language and make concepts and theoretical connections clear and explicit. There are many books outlining the craft of writing (for example, Becker 1986; Wolcott 1990; Cuba and Cocking 1994; Woods 1999), which identify skills and techniques in the use of metaphors, clear and precise prose, proper sentence construction and the avoidance of abstract nouns, passive constructions and split infinitives and so on. They also contain good advice about editing and proof reading and how to get started. It is wise to write in the third person, since first-person style is a spurious attempt to suggest immediacy that disguises the account as a representation (although some realist ethnographers recommend we write in the first person for this very reason; see Woods 1999: 55). Use the past tense for the same reason.

Good writing style is important – postmodernists consider the aesthetics of the literary form used as an important measure in ethnography (since they have abandoned most other measures). Woods (1999: 64–7), however, offers a list of don'ts: do not use words subtly designed to persuade but with no evidential support, like 'most', 'often', 'it is commonly recognized'; avoid the misuse of jargon and excessive references; do not misuse quotations; be careful in the use of rhetorical devices like metaphors, irony and simile; do not construct 'straw persons'; and do not overclaim, be overzealous or sloppy. Metaphors have great potential (see Brewer 1991b, where I used the metaphor of Hercules, Hippolyte and the Amazons as an analogy to represent the interaction between policemen and women in the RUC). They can also be entertaining (see Box 4.5), but the metaphors should not run ahead of the data or be too lyrical, and they have the potential to backfire (Woods 1999: 70–1).

However, before writing comes planning. Wolcott (1990: 16) suggests the importance of what he calls 'The Plan'. There are three stages: developing a statement of purpose; writing a detailed outline or sequence for the account; and determining the basic story to be told and representational style to be used. I plan each chapter and every section of the chapter in fine detail before I start, although the creative process of writing leads to adaptations as the chapter proceeds. The use of word processors greatly facilitates planning, writing and editing; it is quicker, allows easier editing and correction, and permits the insertion of graphics. Above all, word processors facilitate a non-sequential writing strategy, allowing sections to be stored, moved around, inserted here and there as the organizational structure of the text changes. Flexibility in writing-up is essential and the computer enhances this.

The status of the writing

Ethnographers are divided on the status they claim for their text. Realists of the positivist or humanistic kind 'tell it like it is', employing an authoritative

Box 4.5

I was asked once to write a report on a meeting for the university's news-letter. To enliven the account I used metaphor. You can judge whether or not it backfires.

I was relaxing the other night, an activity which still only partly fills me with guilt despite the RAE, TQA and all the other acronyms which spell work, when I saw yet another television news item on the *Titanic*. Local fascination with the disaster is explicable, since Ulster was responsible for building the ship, but the universal appeal of the *Titanic* after such a time is an interesting sociological issue. Strange that this should come to me while at Council. I have often wondered how many profound ideas or great research projects begin as drifts of thought in meetings, and how many fail to survive past the agenda. What were other people musing about, I wondered, as we yet again went through the internal restructuring of the university's management and academic framework; I noticed someone with eyes closed, no doubt thinking about something . . . Those who can always be relied on to ask questions at Council did so again: Council is, after all, what sociologists call an 'orchestrated encounter', with its own ritualised behaviour. We spent the first hour discussing the new structure as an item of 'matters arising', but I have come to realise that part of the ritual is that issues early in the agenda provoke the lengthiest discussion. Council learnt that it was to be reduced in size. I learnt that I would no longer be a member. We were also told we would be saying goodbye to other things too, not least perhaps the Deans' Business Group and perhaps the word 'teach', replaced in some quarters, it seems, by 'deliver'. But while some things 'downsize', to use yet more modern parlance, others grow in scale: after some discussion, the Central Students Progress Committee was permitted to increase its membership. And it was then that I thought of the *Titanic*, wondering whether some people really did rearrange the chairs after the iceberg had struck. The President described our iceberg in detail, in the form of the Report of the Planning and Resources Committee. We received the news in sullen and shocked silence, our bow potentially holed below the waterline by budget cuts, (alleged) escalating security costs in Northern Ireland, and the RAE allocations. A vigorous debate then ensued about who gets access to the lifeboats. Will it be women and children first? It was alleged that central administration direct a disproportionate amount of money to themselves, when any money earned is totally by the hard work of teachers and researchers. Someone from an active and successful research department wondered whether they should continue to be required to subsidise less research active departments. We were reminded that some departments provide subsidies through teaching and their high student numbers. Someone asked for 'compassion' in the treatment of departments which did not do well in the RAE – now there's a word I expect was heard a lot as desperate people on the *Titanic* negotiated access to the lifeboats – others called for developmental money to assist the departments with low RAE ratings. We were reminded, of course, that there is only so much that the high achievers in the RAE can do without new money being spent on them to help them continue to be good. The President sympathised with the dilemma and said there was a need for balance: who would be a Captain, I thought. We heard about the need for a reinvigorated scheme to encourage the research inactive to retire – no lifeboat for them, they had 'not pulled their weight', someone said. I must have been imagining when I thought I heard someone say cast them overboard. But seats in the lifeboat do have to be earned, and the introduction of performance-related appraisal was mooted. Clearly not women and children first then. A discussion of religion and morality is not something one expects at Council these days, but it proved lively and long. As a Christian I found myself agreeing with the atheist and not the Scots Presbyterian in believing that it is not the purpose of universities to uphold religion but rather to defend universalistic codes of conduct which embody moral principles. When I heard the codes described as the 'language of polytechnics' I gave a long and audible sigh and drifted away trying to recall the tune the band was playing when the ship sank. It was almost as if I could hear the refrain, but I couldn't quite put a name to it. The rest of the meeting went apace and we were finished in just over two hours. I later went to the pool, overcome by the conviction that it does no harm these days to know how to swim.

representational style reflecting their assumed privileged understanding of the field. The account suggests that there is a single telling – this is how 'it is' – which the text faithfully and accurately represents. The realist text thus claims a definitive status. This is ridiculed by postmodern, reflexive ethnographers, who dispute the assumption that there is one reality to represent and only one telling of it. Multiple versions of reality exist, and the ethnographer's is not definitive. The text, in this view, must either stress the partial and limited nature of the ethnographer's account or capture the polyphony of voices in textual form. In extreme postmodern positions, the ethnographer must refrain from even offering an account or reading of the material. In some this takes the form of unedited, unselected interview transcripts, without commentary by the ethnographer (for example, Dwyer 1982), very similar to some oral histories. Others remove the author's voice by allowing readers to interact with the material using the latest computer technology to compile their own text and reading. The covers of the book are not even solid any more but melt into cyberspace as material is placed on the Internet or CD-ROMs and readers negotiate a personal route through it. Less extreme anti-realists, subscribing to post postmodern methodologies like subtle realism (Hammersley 1990), analytical realism (Altheide and Johnson 1998) or the ethnographic imagination (Brewer 1994), retain some level of authority and definitiveness for the ethnographer's text. These divisions are worth elaborating so that the features of the 'realist', 'postmodern' and 'post postmodern' text can be distinguished.

The realist text

The most identifiable feature of the realist text is thick description and extensive verbatim quotation. In positivist type ethnography this thick description is balanced by analyst-constructed taxonomies and typologies and other analytical models, but it is there nonetheless; humanistic type ethnographies may restrict themselves to it. Verbatim quotations abound to convey a sense of immediacy to the reader and provide authenticity and support for the analyst's account. Thick description and verbatim quotation are thus rhetorical devices used to establish the authority of the author's voice. Other rhetorical devices are used to persuade readers of the authenticity of the account. For example, a sense of ethnographic 'presence' is constructed, by which authors stress their closeness to the data and their insider status among members. This is sometimes reinforced by creating rhetorically a sense of exoticism by means of which the author portrays the setting and the people as alien and strange to the reader, not understandable to anyone lacking the author's special access and privileged vision. This is as true for the 'nuts and sluts' urban ethnography as for anthropological studies of foreign cultures. Another rhetorical device in the realist text is to write in such a way as to imply an impersonal and impartial author, in the field but not of it, able to rise above their location and involvement with participants to write objectively and dispassionately (on the rhetorical turn in ethnography see Hammersley 1993a, b).

It is just such a kind of text that the post-positivist and postmodern ethnographers deconstructed. Their major objection was that such rhetoric was used to pretend to represent the world in a way that implied certainty, objectivity and exhaustiveness. Moreover, realist ethnographers of the naive kind were seen as 'constructing a text'. By the conventions for textual performance and the use of literary and rhetorical persuasive devices (on which see Atkinson 1990, 1992), the text was artfully managed to enhance its persuasive force. Sociologists again borrowed this from anthropology, where Marcuse and Cushman (1982) and Clifford and Marcuse (1986) first identified the procedures used to 'write culture' (although Atkinson published on this at the time; see Atkinson 1983). Naive realists may believe they write objectively, accurately 'telling it like it is', but their rhetorical devices share much in common with fiction writing or, at best, travel books (Hammersley 1993a: 23).

The post-modern, reflexive text

Associated with criticism of conventional forms of ethnographic writing, postmodern ethnographers experiment with new textual forms, although new literary forms do not have to be grounded in postmodernism. There are at least three new literary forms. The first is to write an account that is not concerned with truth or representing accurately the phenomenon but merely its aesthetic quality (for example, Tyler 1986) or its political effect (for example, Denzin 1998). If naive realist texts are fictional, let us write fiction explicitly. As Tyler (1986: 126) argues, the postmodern text must evoke 'an emergent fantasy of a possible world, in a word poetry'. Taking this advice, some ethnographers now write up data as poems (see Richardson 1992, 1994) or 'ethno-drama' (see Paget 1995). Another experimental form is for the ethnographer to write in dialogue with himself or herself, so that the text is an account of the data interspersed with the ethnographer reflexively commenting on what he or she has just written (for example, see Mulkay 1985; Woolgar 1988a; Ashmore 1989). Trevor Pinch (writing as Pinch and Pinch 1988) offers perhaps the best example, although its own rhetorical approach is irony (see Box 4.6).

   The third experimental form is the collaborative text constructed between the ethnographer, the reader and the social actors in the setting. Feminist ethnographers always urged greater participation of the female subjects they studied in the final analysis, but this tended to be met by various member validation strategies or greater researcher reflexivity. Collaborative texts experiment with textual form, and if they end up as messy, fragmented and rather complicated accounts, this is being faithful to the complexities and contours of everyday life (Coffey *et al.* 1996: 5). This lies behind the thrust to use *hypertext* as a qualitative computer package to permit non-linear and non-sequential presentations of data (see Coffey and Atkinson 1996; Coffey *et al.* 1996). The presentation of text is non-sequential, for the account is not written as a single stream of information fixed in linear form, but sets up a number of alternatives for readers to explore the data in a sequence they themselves determine. This requires the data to be on a CD-ROM or other high capacity electronic storage media so that readers conduct their own

---

Box 4.6

Extract from T. Pinch and T. Pinch, Reservations about reflexivity and new literary forms or why let the devil have all the good tunes, in S. Woolgar (ed.) *Knowledge and Reflexivity* (London: Sage 1988), p. 178.

This paper is somewhat unusual in a volume concerned to elaborate such exotica as reflexivity and new literary forms. It is designedly written as a text which is critical of both these recent developments in the sociology of science.
No, I beg to disagree. In the first place, there is nothing unusual in having a critical text in such a volume, but, even more importantly, the text is not even critical. This is because it is written in an unconventional fashion and thereby supports the move towards new literary forms.
I knew I should never have agreed to joint authorship.
Yes, you were reluctant to put both our names on the paper . . .
. . . In having two authors and agreeing to let you interrupt me throughout the text I wanted to construct a text which was not dissimilar from others to be found in this volume . . .
Okay, on with the introduction . . .

Introduction
In this paper, I want to examine critically the recent turns taken with the sociology of scientific knowledge . . .

---

investigation of the data and construct their own text. Thus, readers hit buttons that mark a point in the text and go direct to the unedited and unselected field notes, interview transcripts and other sources. Other links can be developed to allow readers to develop their own cross-references, picking a path through the data as they determine. Readers now need access to a computer rather than a good library, and there are problems of confidentiality and anonymity, as well as copyright. Edited versions of data are more ethical, although this perhaps infringes the postmodern spirit behind this form of interactive text. There are few examples of this sort of interactive text, although some ethnographers have supplemented their conventional monograph with a CD-ROM element.

Post postmodern texts

In a persuasive argument, Hammersley (1993a: 25) contends that the rhetorical turn in ethnography does not imply postmodernism, and thus does not undermine either validity as a measure of the quality of the data or the authority of the ethnographer's voice. Rhetorical deconstruction of the text remains consistent with those methodological positions that retain an element of realism, whether of the subtle, critical or analytical kind. As Seale (1999: 178) notes, the attempt to delete the author from the text, although required by the logical demands of some strands of postmodernism, is an impossible task. Marcus (1994: 563), who was among the first to deconstruct the ethnographic text, believes we have gone too far and are in a post postmodern phase. Reactions to postmodern texts have set in elsewhere, and Hammersley (1995) argues that experimental textual forms can confuse and obscure a line of argument. We need look no further than Pinch and Pinch (1988) and Box 4.6 to show this. Hence, he urges that all ethnographic texts should adopt a standardized format, outlining: the focus of the study and its rationale; the cases investigated; the methods used; the claims made; the evidence used to support them; and the general conclusions (Hammersley 1993a: 30). And preferably in that order.

Beyond this, Hammersley argues that ethnographers should adopt an authoritative voice in their texts as long as it is fallibilistic and limited in character. They can purport to produce knowledge that is beyond reasonable doubt, but it will never be final or absolutely certain. Thus, ethnographic texts can still reasonably claim to represent reality, but they must be explicitly identified as fallible representations and necessarily selective of the phenomena to which they refer (Hammersley 1993a: 30). Furthermore, such texts can and should provide the reader with the information necessary to assess the validity of the data and their relevance and plausibility (which are the standards of assessment within subtle realism). In this view, there is nothing wrong with ethnographers using rhetorical devices associated with conventional texts, such as evocative narratives, creating a sense of 'presence' and immediacy, extensive quotations and the use of exemplary types and vignettes. Indeed, these devices can be of considerable value as evidence and illustration (Hammersley 1993a: 32). Writing up results should thus still be done in a way that permits the rational assessment of the findings, and ethnographers should continue to provide accurate representations of the phenomena concerned while recognizing, in a reflexive manner, their own role in constructing them and not disguising the fact that this is a fallible and selective representation.

Conclusion

It is a commonplace to hear experienced ethnographers say that ethnography is easy to do, but difficult to do well. The analysis, interpretation and presentation of ethnographic data exemplify this truism: they are harder to do than at first sight, and to do them well requires careful and skilful attention. These

Uses of ethnography

Introduction

In this chapter we address some of the uses to which ethnographic data can be put. It is worth recalling that while ethnography is a methodology – an approach to research – it is also a method – a means of collecting data. The uses to which these data can be put demonstrate the utility of ethnography as an approach to research. Three particular usages are stressed in this chapter: the role of ethnography in generating knowledge; its role in theory generation, particularly in the development of grounded theory; and its application to issues of policy and policy making.

Knowledge generation

Ethnography is an attempt to understand society by the generation of knowledge in a rigorous and systematic manner, or, as Lofland (1996: 30) writes, it 'attempts to produce generic propositional answers to questions about social life and organisation'. Of course, it does this in a characteristic way, involving close association with and participation in the setting under study. As a result of this closeness to the field, an understanding is generated of the social meanings of the people involved in the setting; postmodernist ethnographers would stress at this point that it is only one possible understanding among several competing ones. Postmodernist or not, however, this ethnographic understanding is available to everyone. For in addition to academic investigators in universities or research centres, ethnographic understanding can be recommended to social workers, educationists, nurses and many more besides, who seek to become familiar with the social meanings of those people with whom they work. This means that ethnography can generate knowledge on a variety of subject matters relevant to different academic disciplines and to many occupations and working lives.

A focus on the knowledge generated by ethnographic understanding leads to typologies that distinguish ethnography by the subject matter of the knowledge generated. Thus far in this volume, ethnography has been classified by the methodological bases on which it is founded – 'scientific', 'humanistic', 'postmodern-reflexive' and 'post postmodern' – and by the scope of its lens – 'big ethnography' equating the method with qualitative research generally and 'little ethnography' restricting it to field research. These are not the only axes along which to categorize types of ethnography. Another is the type of subject matter about which it generates data. Hence Berg (1998: 122), for example, distinguishes 'educational ethnography', 'ethnonursing research' and 'general ethnography', although this is hardly exhaustive of the subject matters on which ethnography generates knowledge, since it excludes such well known applications as 'street' or 'urban ethnographies' and 'work-based' or 'occupational ethnographies'. Gubrium (1988: 23–34) offered a more sophisticated typology of the uses to which ethnographic understanding can be put, distinguishing three kinds of subject matters: structural ethnographies, articulative ethnographies and practical ethnographies. Inasmuch as this is not a typology based on ethnography's methodological foundations but on the uses of its data, his classification does not coincide with those used here. Thus, 'scientific', 'humanistic', 'postmodern reflexive' and 'post postmodern' ethnographies are not matched with Gubrium's types of ethnography, for a 'structural', 'articulative' or 'practical' turn is feasible with any methodological basis to the ethnography, although postmodernists would tend to abjure structural ethnographies.

Structural ethnographies generate knowledge about the folk structures of the group or way of life under study, or what Gubrium (1988: 24) calls the subjective meanings by which the people in the setting interpret experience. Realities are discerned in their own right, subjective meanings are depicted and organized, and actions are described in a way that 'tells it like it is'. Knowledge is generated about the organization, classification and form of 'field realities'; that is, of 'native' social meanings in the field. This kind of knowledge can be useful because the meanings are traditionally hidden and have not been disclosed before, and thus the ethnographer adopts what Burgess (1984: 20) calls the 'undercover agent' model. This knowledge may also be useful because the meanings are intrinsically interesting in their own right or as representative of some broader social process, in which case the ethnographer is much like Burgess's (1984: 20) 'going native model', understanding the setting sufficiently well to be able to behave like an ordinary member. The example Gubrium uses to exemplify the type is Whyte's (1955) study of street life among young Italian men ('corner boys') in an American city, where the ethnographic understanding was used to address broad social issues around ethnicity, assimilation and youth culture.

A second kind of subject matter leads to what Gubrium calls 'articulative ethnographies'. While this type takes an interest in the subjective meaning of social actions in the field, it examines the sense-making procedures the people in the setting use to construct these meanings. The focus is, as Gubrium (1988: 27) writes, 'on how members of situations assemble reasonable understandings of things and events of concern to them. The "how" of folk interpretation is emphasized over the "what"'. This approach has been taken in much phenomenological and ethnomethodological inspired ethnography, which addresses the common-sense reasoning processes by which categories of people in a particular setting construct their version of reality and its subjective meanings. This sort of ethnographic understanding is generated partly to show that the process of common-sense reasoning is the most prevalent form of sense assembly that ordinary people engage in, and thus to confirm the phenomenologist's point that this is the primary frame of relevance for reality construction. But this is also done in part to reveal what sense people make of their particular world and thus to describe and analyse various aspects of the social world. In this case, ethnographic understanding is used to generate knowledge about the social world as it is interpreted and made sense of by people, the usefulness of which depends on the interest in the group or the effects of their common-sense reasoning for wider social life. A great deal of this kind of ethnographic research has been done on policing, contrasting the official rule book's way for doing police work and the 'routine' or common-sense ways within police occupational culture. The effect is to reveal the role of discretion in police work in the way that formal rules are imaginatively used or even contravened in order to carry out the job of policing. Sometimes the effects of practical common-sense reasoning can be negative, as with anti-Catholicism in Northern Ireland (Brewer 1998), where it sustains sectarianism among conservative evangelicals (see Box 5.1).

The third kind of subject matter ethnographic understanding is used to generate is what Gubrium calls practical ethnography, in which ethnographers take the 'advocate research model' (Burgess 1984: 20) to improve and better the behaviour conducted in the setting or way of life of the people there. It is not enough in this type of ethnography to describe the folk structures of 'natives', or to display their sense-making and reasoning processes;

Box 5.1

Extract from J. D. Brewer, *Anti-Catholicism in Northern Ireland 1600–1998: the Mote and the Beam* (London: Macmillan, 1998), with Gareth Higgins, pp. 176–81.

Anti-Catholicism involves a practical reasoning process in which anti-Catholics draw on their stock of socially available common sense knowledge to understand the world. Four features characterise the common-sense reasoning process that supports and sustains anti-Catholicism, called distortion, deletion, distance and denial. Distortion occurs when evidence is turned around, manipulated or even invented in order to fit a generalisation about Catholicism; deletion involves the removal of evidence from deliberation and consciousness when it contradicts or complicates the generalisation; denial occurs when evidence against the generalisation is falsified by denying events or circumstances occurred; and distance occurs when evidence against the generalisation is avoided, ignored and overlooked. Distortion, deletion, distance and denial clearly appear together and many common sense notions can only be sustained because distortion, deletion, distance and denial mutually reinforce each other in sustaining antipathy toward Catholicism and Catholics. Their mutual reinforcement of antipathy results in a cognitive map which is very closed and self-contained, and one that is immutable and resistant to change. The closed and self-contained character of the cognitive map of anti-Catholicism is reinforced by various religious and secular artefacts and behaviours which sustain and support anti-Catholicism. These range from the Bible version they read, the King James version being the preferred version for anti-Catholics, the church to which they belong and the ministers to whom they listen, the hymns which they sing, the other Christian groups and organisations with which they have fellowship, the secular newspapers they buy, the political parties and politicians they support, the marching organisations to which they belong, the area where they live, the places where they shop, send their children to school and spend their leisure, and their places of work, entertainment and pleasure. All these can reinforce the closed cognitive map of anti-Catholicism because they are the mechanisms by which the stocks of anti-Catholic ideas and notions are socially transmitted and disseminated to the group, or because they involve sectarianised forms of social interaction which prevent or restrict contact with Catholics, ensuring that common sense stereotypes, ideas, maxims and beliefs are not undercut by personal experience. These artefacts and behaviours ensure that people's anti-Catholic notions are immune to empirical test in day-to-day life and, instead, are reinforced continually by the social dissemination and transmission of anti-Catholic common sense knowledge. The cognitive map of anti-Catholicism structures how anti-Catholics perceive, understand and 'know' the Catholic Church and its members, ensuring that relations with them, if there are any, are affected by a stock of anti-Catholic common sense notions, such that this common sense knowledge about Catholicism is reproduced in a self-fulfilling way. In short, the cognitive map remains closed, self-contained and impenetrable.

the point is to intervene in the setting and improve the position of the people studied. Ethnographic understanding in this case is generated in order to have practical applications in policy and is purposely designed to influence policy makers. No longer knowledge for knowledge sake, no longer description or articulation of reasoning simply because the phenomenon is interesting in its own right. Ethnographic understanding in practical ethnography is about advocacy of the interests of the subjects or changing the setting to improve the conduct of social action there. As a result of commitment to feminist methodology, for example, feminist ethnographies are enjoined to assist the lives of the women under study. But as we shall see below, there are many other examples of 'applied ethnography' which impinge on social and public policy.

Sometimes, ethnographies can have elements of all three of Gubrium's types, for the distinctions are not watertight. The example of my ethnography of routine policing in the RUC is instructive (Brewer 1991a). After having engaged in a structural ethnography, describing the accomplishment of routine policing by rank and file members of the RUC, and also undertaken an articulative ethnography by trying to display the common-sense reasoning processes behind this accomplishment, I concluded the ethnographic text with suggestions for police reform to enable them better to police Northern Ireland's divisions (see Box 5.2).

To conclude this section on the uses of ethnographic data, ethnography generates knowledge; sometimes knowledge for knowledge's sake because the knowledge is interesting in its own right, sometimes knowledge for a practical purpose. This purpose can be to build theory or engage in empirical generalization, and these empirical or theoretical inferences can themselves have practical effects, one of which is to affect public policy. Theory-building and applications to policy making are among the important uses of ethnography, to which we now turn.

Box 5.2

Extract from J. D. Brewer, *Inside the RUC: Routine Policing in a Divided Society* (Oxford: Clarendon Press, 1991), with K. Magee, pp. 258–9, 277.

> Up to this point, our ethnography of routine policing has been a mixture of the first and second kinds [structural and articulative ethnographies]. We have portrayed some of the feelings, beliefs, views, folk structures and symbols held by a group of policemen and women, and have done so using their own words [hence structural ethnography]. 'Routine policing' is a term which describes a type of police work and a quality of the way in which it is accomplished. The research displayed both the ordinariness of routine police work and the taken-for-granted, commonsensical and mundane processes of reasoning which infuse the accomplishment. This requires an articulative ethnography. At this juncture we wish to go beyond the narrow framework of the ethnographic data and explore some general questions. We will address three issues: what the essential features of policing in divided societies are; whether 'normal policing' is possible in a divided society; and whether or not policing in Northern Ireland can be improved. The last issue comes within the domain of a practical ethnography . . . We feel it important to end by turning our ethnography towards the practical type, which seeks to better conduct and improve the everyday life that has been explored. Ten principles seem to us to be crucial in determining whether or not the police in ethnically divided societies are used as a force for peace.

Theory-building in ethnography

A social theory is a set of interrelated abstract propositions about human affairs and the social world that explain their regularities and properties. Theoretical statements differ from descriptive statements in that they are abstract propositions that go beyond description by attempting to explain some feature of society. Theoretical statements may, or may not, form part of a fully fledged social theory. Theories can be distinguished by their level of generality. General theories offer abstract propositions about social action or society as a whole, while theories of the middle range either make propositions about more limited aspects of human and social affairs or the propositions are less abstract. The place of theory in ethnography is contested, especially among ethnographers themselves. The generation of theory is sometimes listed as one of the criteria by which to judge ethnographic data. Lofland (1974: 108), for example, considers the development of a generic conceptual framework as the main form of evaluation, enabling ethnographers to identify patterns in a wide variety of social phenomena. Athens (1984) also considered that ethnographic data should be judged in part according to the extent to which they generate formal theories. So confident was Woods (1985) that ethnography had done its job in describing the social world that he said it needed to enter its 'second phase' and develop coordinated theoretical statements.

Some ethnographers have sought to produce what are called **nomothetic** studies, which aim at abstract generalizations and focus on the discovery of general patterns and the structural regularities in everyday behaviour. This often leads to theoretical statements of high abstraction, if not a fully developed social theory. A good example of the former is Goffman, who produced statements of high theoretical abstraction without ever producing a fully fledged social theory. Goffman's elaborate theoretical claims about, for example, 'interaction rituals' and 'frames' of social behaviour were made on the basis of ethnographic observations of behaviour in public places (Goffman 1963, 1969, 1971) but never constituted a social theory. In contrast, ethnomethodology constituted a distinct and highly abstract – even obtuse – social theory that was premised on Garfinkel's elaboration of the routine nature of everyday life from ethnographic observations of such things as conversations, record keeping and the accounts of behaviour given by transsexuals (Garfinkel 1967). This was captured with a vocabulary that was once described as elephantine, and far removed from that of the people whose behaviour was being studied. Labelling theory is another example of a distinct social theory emerging from ethnographic data (as noted in Hammersley 1992: 91), in which it is argued that deviance increases among those people labelled and treated as deviant. However, even where fully fledged theories are developed from ethnographic data, they are never 'general theories' but 'theories of the middle range'. That is, they do not explain society or social action on a grand scale but some more limited aspect thereof (like deviance), and do not have universal applicability.

At the other extreme to nomothetic ethnographies are those that are called **ideographic,** in the sense of seeking to explore the unique features of an individual case in order to discover what social meaning it has for the participants. They eschew high abstraction and theory to focus on capturing people's social meanings and lived experiences in terms people themselves use. Using the more familiar nomenclature of this volume, ideographic ethnographies represent 'naive realist' ethnography. Experience is studied from within, through the use of 'thick description', and the particularities of the setting are drawn, not its general features. Theoretical inferences from ideographic ethnographies thus tend to be limited, and revolve around the claim that 'thick description' itself leads to 'theoretical description'.

Whether ethnography is a particularizing or a generalizing method is a longstanding debate among practitioners (see Denzin 1989: 20–1), and the claim by ideographic-style ethnographers, who are naive realists in their methodology, that they do in fact generate theory is contested; it is obvious that nomothetic ones do, even if the theory is disliked or disputed. In his critique of naive realist ethnography, Hammersley (see especially 1992: 11–31) attacks their claim to engage in 'theoretical description'. By this he means their claims to draw theoretical inferences from 'thick descriptions'. Clearly such 'thick descriptions' are not theories in themselves, but they can use theoretical and conceptual categories and are infused with theoretical assumptions (whether or not this is recognized by the ethnographer). 'Thick descriptions' can also be used to test theory by applying it to concrete cases that are studied ethnographically. Indeed, Geertz's (1975: 27) outline of 'thick description' made clear that theoretical elaboration and refinement was made possible by means of testing ideas through their application to cases studied by the process of 'thick description'. Ethnography may not be the best way to test or apply theory, or, at least, the claim to do so needs to be qualified because of the limits arising from the small-scale scope of ethnography, although Hammersley (1992: 174–82) accepts that it is possible to select cases that subject a theory to the severest possible test. This is by what is called 'theoretical sampling', wherein cases (be they people, groups, sub-groups or settings) are purposely selected in order to provide the best possible test of some theory or theoretical statement. This can be by selecting optimal cases. A good example is the selection by Goldthorpe and colleagues (1968) of Luton car workers to test the claim of embourgeoisement among the working classes in the early 1960s, since they were among the wealthiest and most secure workers at the time and those most likely to be experiencing embourgeoisement. A similar process of theoretical sampling governed my choice of 'Easton' district in Belfast to examine the effects of civil unrest on the RUC's routine policing, for one needed to select a case where normal policing could be expected. However, theory testing can also be done by selecting the least optimal case, for falsification can best be achieved by selecting a case that is least favourable to the theory, although, as Hammersley (1992: 182) notes, there have been few attempts at systematic falsification by means of ethnography.

Leaving aside the testing of theory, most criticism is reserved for claims that ethnography *generates* theory. Martyn Hammersley is among the most vociferous; above all in his objections to 'thick description' what concerns him the most is the claim that it facilitates the generation of theory. In social science, theory is used to explain patterns of behaviour or some social structural regularity; the theories can be general theories of social action or society as a whole, or be of the middle range, in explaining less general patterns and regularities or patterns and regularities among more small-scale aspects of social life. Hammersley (1992: 91ff) disputes the idea that ethnography can generate theory in its general or middle range sense. 'Theoretical statements' are possible if the research design permits generalizations to be made, in the sense that ethnographic data do permit the formulation of abstract explanatory propositions, but developing universalistic theories is different. He doubts whether universal claims can be derived from single cases, even when such cases exemplify a type, and it is impossible to use single cases to draw inferences about the truth or falsity of a universal law, although few ethnographers still believe that there are universal laws in social action.

Nonetheless, two approaches exist for ethnographers to try to generate theory of the middle range kind, although both survive merely as badges of honour to which lip service is paid. The first is analytic induction, discussed in Chapter 4 as a technique for the analysis of ethnographic data. If employed properly, the advocates of analytic induction believed that it was possible to develop universal laws of human behaviour from the in-depth analysis of individual cases. This was part of a highly positivist enterprise within ethnography in the post-war period (Seale 1999: 83), which involved five stages: definition of the problem; the construction of a hypothetical explanation for it; examination of cases to support the hypothesis; reformulation of the hypothesis on the basis of this testing until no negative cases can be found; the construction of a universal generalization. Seale (1999: 85) notes that such an approach now looks extremely out of place given the doubts about the existence of universalistic laws in human social behaviour. Less anachronistic as an approach to theory generation is grounded theory, although it is equally rare in application as analytic induction, despite the renewal of enthusiasm in grounded theory as a result of computer software packages like *NUDIST* which claim to generate theory along the lines of grounded theory. As Bryman and Burgess (1994: 5) note, some packages for computer-assisted qualitative data analysis were designed with grounded theory in mind, but Glaser and Strauss's notion of grounded theory is still essentially 'an approving bumper sticker' (Bryman and Burgess 1994: 6), cited often but practised more rarely.

Its intent is the same as analytical induction, but its operation different. In its practice, grounded theory rejects the positivist approach to theory generation within analytical induction, whereby data are collected in order to verify or falsify some theoretical proposition, which is then revised and tested further against more data. Strauss and Corbin (1998: 158) described its operation thus: 'grounded theory is a general methodology for developing theory that is grounded in data systematically gathered and analysed. Theory evolves during actual research and it does this through continuous interplay between analysis and data collection.' It plays on two closely related associations. The first is between analysis and data, the second between theory and data. Grounded theory requires the use of inductive analysis, in which analysis is built up from the ground rather than imposed from above. As we have seen in an earlier chapter, qualitative data analysis involves a number of stages, like the development of conceptual categories, typologies and classification systems. Inductive analysis requires that the analysis during these stages always be embedded in the data themselves, so that the analytical categories emerge from the data, are faithful to it and, if not couched in the terms people in the field themselves use, at least capture people's voices accurately. This kind of analysis permits the development of theoretical statements that connect together the analytical categories with the social world they describe in some explanation of the patterns and regularities. Thus, explanatory propositions are grounded in the data. In short, theoretical statements should be grounded in the data. What is more, fully fledged social theories can be discovered from the data by linking together a series of theoretical statements into an explanatory schema of greater complexity and abstraction as long as the propositions are grounded in the data. Grounded theory is an approach, according to its proponents, which facilitates the transformation of theoretical statements into fully fledged theories. The procedure for doing this was outlined in 1967 by Glaser and Strauss (also see Glaser 1978, 1992; Strauss 1987; Strauss and Corbin 1990, 1998). This timing was significant, for it emerged during a very anti-positivist phase in social science and when the qualitative approach was taken to excess. Grounded theory is the antithesis of the 1960s 'Californian way of subjectivity', as Gellner once ridiculed ethnomethodology, for grounded theory is noteworthy for its scientific orientation, its commitment to middle range theorizing and its opposition to reducing ethnography to mere description (even of the 'thick' kind). Yet the similarity between grounded theory and 'thick description' has been noted by many (for example, Seale 1999: 94), for both unravel the many layers of interpretation and meaning involved in some piece of social behaviour, although the ambition to render the description into middle range theoretical statements distinguishes grounded theory.

The practice of grounded theory is quite simple to describe, and some computer software packages now make it easier to do. Data are grouped into codes, which represent the categories that appear in the findings. The properties of the codes are identified, leading to further refinement and revision of the codes to account for variations in the properties that have been identified. Data must be examined for new or different properties that require reformulation of the codes or new codes altogether. This is done by the general method of constant comparative analysis (which is why the approach is sometimes called the constant comparative method), in which codes are constantly compared to instances of data in increasing forms of elaboration and refinement. In this way, categories emerge from the data that constitute explanatory propositions to account for the patterns and regularities represented by the categories. These in turn lead to the development of theoretical statements and, perhaps, a fully fledged theory (referred to as 'higher order grounded theory) if the theoretical statements and propositions can be generalized to other related settings or groups. The key to the process of developing grounded theory – to develop either theoretical statements or fully worked social theories – is theoretical sampling (see Glaser and Strauss 1967:

45ff). In the context of grounded theory, this involves the ethnographer selecting what next to collect data on as a result of the codes, categories and theoretical ideas that have been developed from the data thus far. So, 'the analyst jointly collects, codes, and analyses his data and decides what data to collect next and where to find them, in order to develop his theory as it emerges' (Glaser and Strauss 1967: 45). Ethnographers thus develop codes, as the simplest theoretical tool for indexing, categorizing and explaining the data, and then gather further data from different groups or settings to exemplify, extend, develop or modify the codes, leading to the eventual refinement of the theory. Needless to say, these codes must be grounded in the data and be faithful to the meanings they describe and explain.

In later work, Strauss and Corbin (1990, 1998) extend the coding procedure. They distinguish open codes (the simple naming of categories as they appear in the data), axial codes (identifying those categories that relate to others in the data) and selective codes (core codes or categories that subsume or explain others). Only the first constitutes a coding exercise as properly understood, since the others are really explanatory propositions that elaborate on open codes and are part of the process of theory generation. They are kinds of 'theoretical codes', which conceptualize how the substantive codes relate to each other as elements in an integrated theory. In distinguishing grounded theory from other coding procedures or other forms of inductive analysis, Strauss and Corbin (1998: 166) make the point that without this theoretical coding the analysis does not constitute grounded theory. They also suggest the development of a 'conditional matrix', which puts in diagram form the connections between the codes and the aspects of the social world they represent – something which qualitative computer software can now do on the screen.

The process of constant comparison could be endless given the possibility of discovering negative cases or cases with properties that constantly require some revision of the theory, so Glaser and Strauss (1967: 61) introduce the notion of 'theoretical saturation'. Saturation occurs when no additional data are being found which develop the properties of the code or category. This is not the same as saying that no such data are ever possible theoretically, so saturation is always imperfect. What it requires is that the ethnographer is confident that they have searched strenuously for groups or settings that stretch the code by looking with integrity for as diverse a data set as possible. 'Saturation is based', they write, 'on the widest possible range of data on the category' (Glaser and Strauss 1967: 63). Ethnographers thus complete the research when it seems unlikely that analysis can be taken any further, not when it appears that all data are collected or, even worse, after a fixed time period in the field. Theoretical developments thus dictate data collection, not any other contingency.

Grounded theory has many critics. Glaser (1992) has himself criticized the way it has developed in a positivist and technical direction by the stress on verification and the programmatic and rule-following procedures that have emerged within it over the years. But if for Glaser it has become a Frankenstein's monster, more complicated than envisaged, for others it is an illusion of a different kind. On the one hand (for example, see Hammersley 1992: 20–1) is the claim that it is illusionary because it fails to deliver on the promise to discover theory in the manner of 'good science', as Strauss and Corbin (1990: 25) put it. Another is that it cannot be applied to all kinds of ethnographic data (Brown 1973). Postmodernists, with an in-built tendency to deconstruct myths as illusions, argue that it is a narrow analytical procedure that prioritizes coding as the principal step. This is reinforced by their objections to the computer software packages, like *NUDIST*, that promise the allure of theory building on the basis of grounded theory procedures (see Coffey *et al.* 1996). Coffey and Atkinson (1996) argue for more subtle procedures to tease out the layers of meaning and interpretation in the data, which they find in various forms of textual and discourse analysis. Grounded theory also offends postmodernist sensibilities by constructing a single authoritative voice that gives an 'exclusive' interpretation of the data. Thus, they seek ways of representing data that do not constrain and confine it to analysts' codes, which is the premise of grounded theory. The solution is found in other computer software packages like hypertext, which allow readers to make their own links between the data and thus to construct their own text and reading (see Coffey *et al.* 1996). For this reason, Denzin (1998: 330) considers grounded theory to be out of touch with the postmodern moment in ethnography. Moreover, its commitment to realism as a methodology makes it blind to its own limitations: because the data on which any grounded theory is based are themselves already theory laden, the eventual theory is only discovering itself. In postmodern terms, grounded theory discovers only the author's theoretical assumptions and biases. Humanistic ethnographers, conversely, question the obsession with theory that is explicit in grounded theory, and dislike its affinities with positivism. Strauss and Corbin have mounted a defence against both claims. In relation to the latter, they state that theory is important in order to bolster social sciences from attack (Strauss and Corbin 1998: 168). With respect to postmodernism, they claim that grounded theory is compatible with such sensibilities because multiple perspectives can be sought in the research (p. 172). Although it remains the case that these multiple voices are interpreted by the researcher, their own voice is 'questioned and provisional' (p. 173) and the resulting grounded theory is recognized as only one plausible account among others (a plausibility they see as capable of being tested and strengthened by further research). These notions fit the post postmodern ideas of someone like Hammersley, who also considers plausibility as one of the criteria left by which to judge ethnographic research after postmodernism's deconstruction of ethnography.

Theory and practice are not incompatible uses of ethnographic data. Strauss and Corbin (1998: 175) argue that grounded theory is relevant to both the study of the process of policy making and the development of specific policies, although it is perhaps best suited to the former. The example they cite is their study of policy making in the United States health care system (Strauss and Corbin 1990). The link between theory and practice is stressed by others. Pollard (1984: 183) believes it possible to conduct studies that are relevant to both theory development and policy, a view echoed by Janet Finch in her account of policy research, where she writes that good theoretically grounded ethnography is likely to enhance the capacity of ethnography to impact on policy (Finch 1986: 171).

Applied ethnographic research

The application of ethnography to policy is one of the most important uses of ethnographic data, and it is a usage over which there are fewer disputes among ethnographers themselves. But it was not always thus. The old 'political arithmetic' tradition of British social science, epitomized by the work of Rowntree, the Webbs, and their Fabian heirs at the London School of Economics in the first part of the twentieth century, was purposely policy oriented, but qualitative techniques were only of secondary importance given the positivist methodology and fact-gathering mentality that underlay it (Finch 1986: 224). However, the attack on positivism within the social sciences in the 1960s negatively affected the policy orientation of British social science by shifting the focus to theory and by undermining the validity of empirical work (Abrams 1981; Payne *et al.* 1981). Thus, policy-oriented social scientists in Britain bemoaned their paltry influence on policy compared to North American counterparts, who were more closely associated with policy makers and better able to shape the policy agenda, and had been doing so for a much longer time (see the complaints of Bulmer 1982b). Humanistic ethnographers in particular rejected a policy orientation, partly because of their anti-positivism and the association of policy research with empiricism, and partly because the traditional sociological roots of ethnography in the Chicago School treated it as a tool for basic not applied research, concerned with contributing knowledge on human society without necessarily any immediate practical purpose (Hammersley 1992: 135; on the Chicago School's ambiguous contribution to policy research generally see Carey 1975; for Hammersley's own account of the Chicago tradition see Hammersley 1989). This preference for basic research existed among ethnographers despite the tradition in the United States of applied anthropology. It was in this historical context that policy makers in the United Kingdom showed considerable bias towards quantitative research by relying almost exclusively on quantitative information in policy making. This preference amounted almost to an obsessive dislike of qualitative data (see Box 5.3).

Box 5.3

Senior Researcher in the British Home Office, quoted in R. Clarke, The effectiveness of graduate education in sociology: employment and central government research, *Sociology*, vol. 15, no. 4, 1981, pp. 525–30.

> More important is an appreciation of the need to provide hard evidence. This needs to be in statistical form and, in my view, numeracy and a liking for numbers is an essential requirement for a successful policy oriented researcher. In this connection it must be said that the current vogue among sociologists for informal, qualitative methods is distinctly unhelpful. The kind of evidence provided by these means has to compete with other professionals – prisoner governors, probation inspectors, Her Majesty's Inspectors of Constabulary – who will inevitably command greater authority by virtue of their position and experience than will the young and 'green' research worker. The latter need 'hard' evidence if they wish to be taken seriously.

How much the situation has changed. There has been a growing application of ethnography, and qualitative methods generally, to policy making in areas such as education, health, social policy and social work. There are now textbooks directed towards the practice of applied qualitative research (Walker 1985) and other programmatic claims (see Rist 1981, 1984; Finch 1986; Wenger 1987a, b). Commercial market research companies, as well as political parties, extol the virtues of focus group interviews and other qualitative methods, and government-funded research on both sides of the Atlantic has ethnographic components (Atkinson and Hammersley 1998: 121). Advocates now urge the use of condensed fieldwork in order to fit in with the urgency required by policy makers (in education see Atkinson and Delamont 1985) and recognize that in applied settings fieldwork is often non-continuous (Fetterman 1998: 36), although some traditional ethnographers bemoan the loss of principles in the rush to become useful and applied (for example, Wolcott 1980).

Two changes have occurred to explain the penchant for applied ethnography: ethnographers became interested in affecting policy, and policy makers and research funders lost confidence in relying exclusively on quantitative data. Several processes explain these changes. Ethnographers – and qualitative researchers generally – became interested in applied research for several reasons. This moment is one in which 'user' involvement in research is essential in order to receive funding. The mission statement of the Economic and Social Research Council in the UK emphasizes the necessity of social science research 'meeting the needs of the users of its research, thereby enhancing the United Kingdom's industrial competitiveness and quality of life' (cited in Rappert 1999: 706). There are several initiatives that stress the user value of research, such as the out-reach to business and the community by the Higher Education Funding Council for England. The research agenda is now one in which users of research – business, government, charities, local agencies, voluntary associations – assume an important position, something reinforced by the effects of the Research Assessment Exercise, where research in measured in part on the basis of its effects on non-academic users (Rappert 1999: 716). This is part of the ethos of accountability that ensures that funders of research want user applications for the money they expend and researchers have to oblige. Qualitative researchers can thus no longer eschew a policy orientation.

More positively, ethnographers are now enjoined to consider 'relevance' as one of the criteria by which to judge ethnographic data. In part the attention given to 'relevance' follows from the stress on accountability, for publicly funded research in Britain is increasingly required to be relevant to wealth creation and enhancement of the quality of life (see Rappert 1999: 705). However, it also fits the postmodern moment in ethnography, which believes that relevance is all that is left by which to judge data once all other measures are deconstructed and shown to be part of a realist plot. In this view, research cannot be neutral and its value orientation should be made explicit, with the data judged against this orientation. Thus, data are judged by their relevance to the values and political engagements that underpin the research, although postmodernists also argue that ethnographic data can be judged by the aesthetic effects of the prose used in the text. Thus, ethnography is measured in terms of its political effects rather than its capacity to formulate truth statements or generalizations, and relevance is for the groups of people studied and who are emancipated or empowered by the research, not other academics. Bloor (1997: 222) notes that, in extremity, the postmodern position denies the utility of policy research, for it rejects the Enlightenment idea that planned intervention is capable of bringing desirable social change, or that scientific knowledge can facilitate this, or that social science produces such knowledge. But even some postmodernists see empowerment and emancipation as relevant to public policy. Relevant research in these postmodern terms is designed to improve the position of the subjects in the setting, which requires engagement with policy makers. One of the most enthusiastic postmodern ethnographers, for example, in outlining what he called 'Interpretative Interactionism' as a general methodological position in qualitative research (Denzin 1989: 10), saw it as focusing exclusively on the relationship between people's private troubles – Denzin cites 'wife beating' and alcoholism as examples – and the public policies and public institutions created to address them.

The post postmodern ethnography represented by Hammersley's (1990,

1992) notion of subtle realism or Altheide and Johnson's (1998) 'analytical realism' also valorizes 'relevance', but in less dramatic form. Under these methodological positions, postmodernism constrains but does not destroy the possibility of truth-like statements and generalizations, leaving it feasible that some truth-like statements can impact on social and public policy. Hammersley criticizes the politicization of social research and the emancipatory and political agendas of ethnographers (see especially Hammersley 1995), but he believes that public relevance is still important. Relevance for Hammersley (see 1990: 107–17; 1992: 72–7) is measured by the impact of the research on an audience different from the subjects of the research and is shown in ways other than their empowerment and emancipation. Much of the output of ethnography is concerned with particular events in particular places, interesting only to a limited audience. However, theoretical inferences and empirical generalizations can be drawn from properly designed ethnographic research to enable a broader range of audiences to find the data relevant, such as practitioners, policy-makers and other social researchers. Thus, the data can be relevant because the topic impacts on an issue of public concern, affects the professional conduct and behaviour of practitioners, contributes to debates and a literature among academics or practitioners, or exemplifies some methodological or theoretical issue or approach. Ethnographic research can thus be highly relevant to a number of audiences, including policy makers, and contribute to topics of public importance and concern. This demand for 'public relevance' further encourages the popularity of 'applied ethnography' among ethnographers.

There is another trend behind the popularity of applied ethnography: government and public bodies now make more use of ethnographic data. There are several reasons for this. One is the development of practitioner ethnography (see Hammersley 1992: 135–55). Graduates who are trained in or acquainted with ethnography, reflecting changes in undergraduate methods teaching away from empiricism, are ending up in public bodies as practitioners. The development of policy-related practitioner ethnography, done by nurses, teachers and health and social workers as part of their own professional practice and development, facilitates the growth of applied ethnography. Ethnographic data are thus not only closely tied to the needs of practitioners; they themselves collect it. There is a danger that practitioner ethnographers may come to believe that ethnography is only of value inasmuch as it serves the needs of practitioners, or that only practitioners can do policy relevant ethnographic research, but these dangers are not inherent.

A variation on practitioner research is the involvement of practitioners in the design, implementation, analysis and writing-up of the ethnography, so that they cooperate in the research rather than do it themselves. It is possible to involve policy makers in this way too. Not only is this likely to improve the relevance of the data for policy, it demonstrates to policy makers the rigour with which the ethnographer approached the research process and thus enhances the reputation of ethnographic research among funders and sponsors. Policy makers can participate in the design of the research, even accompany the ethnographer in the field, and sit in on discussions among the research team with the subjects of the research, thereby gaining first-hand experience of the research process and direct appreciation of the setting and the actors' perspectives. Policy makers are mostly very busy and the research is likely to be marginal to their day-to-day work, so applied ethnographers need to be flexible in their arrangements, liaise closely with civil servants and be succinct and clear in their meetings with policy makers. Involving policy makers as practitioners during fieldwork can have advantages in allowing them to identify what they would like investigated further in subsequent fieldwork visits.

Improving the reputation of applied qualitative research reinforces the growth of applied ethnography because it increases the chances of policy makers using ethnographic data in policy decisions, which in turn makes them more likely to support and fund future ethnographic research. As more qualitative data are proved to be useful to policy makers, so more are likely to be commissioned – and governments and public bodies are now sponsoring a lot of qualitative research. The endemic empiricism of many policy makers, reflected in their exclusive reliance on 'hard' data and 'facts', has been replaced by a recognition of the place of 'soft', 'rich' qualitative data in accessing real lives and real situations. One further reason for this is the privatization of much policy-related research effort. Private consultants and specialist research consultancies now undertake a lot of research for government and public bodies, and their professional predisposition to use focus groups and other qualitative methods as quick and cheap exposures to people's opinions and situations has increased the favour in which qualitative methods are held among policy makers, although Rappert (1999: 717) reminds us that this is not necessarily good research. In short, applied ethnography is popular because policy makers and ethnographers want it done.

Models of applied qualitative research

The popularity of applied ethnography among ethnographers and policy makers conceals a tension in the usage of ethnographic data between ethnographic research designed with the express purpose of addressing policy and that whose findings are used coincidentally as part of a body of knowledge drawn on to inform policy decisions. The former is genuinely 'applied' research; the latter is 'pure' or 'basic' research that has an intended or unintended policy effect. This highlights the fact that there are different kinds of policy research. In a classic formulation, Bulmer (1982b) identified three models of applied research. The 'empiricist model' involves researchers in collecting factual information at the request of policy makers to inform their decisions. Some forms of practitioner ethnography come within this model. Leaving aside the methodological point about whether 'facts' are there to be collected immune from value commitments, political agendas or theoretical biases, this model accords the policy makers the power to determine what they want information about and thus to shape, even distort, the policy agenda. In the 'engineering model', Bulmer argues, policy makers identify the problems that require solution, towards which researchers are required to work if publicly funded. Again, policy makers set the research agenda by defining the problems that require solution, foreclosing alternative formulations of the problem or the investigation of different problems. Practitioner ethnography and private sector ethnography are better suited to this model.

The third type of policy research is endorsed by Bulmer and called the 'enlightenment model'. In this case, researchers keep one step removed from policy makers in order to retain their critical and independent gaze, while remaining committed to being relevant in policy terms. Researchers offer 'enlightening' and alternative formulations of problems, offer new perspectives on past policies, problems and solutions, and engage in research designed to impact policy in a general and indirect manner rather than specifically (Hammersley 1992: 131–2). As Davies (1999: 59) points out, research in the enlightenment model shapes policy incrementally by adding weight to the volume of information and is not geared to the short-term goals of policy makers dealing with a specific problem or wanting to introduce a specific intervention strategy. Traditional forms of ethnography, independent of policy makers, best fit this model. However, Davies (1999: 60) rightly warns that the retention of intellectual and critical independence comes with a cost. Policy makers are unlikely to have the time to sift through a large body of cumulative knowledge and consult the debates and literature deriving from it before garnering what is of practical relevance to them. In reality, she writes, 'researchers are much more likely to have some input into policy formation when they do research directed towards particular policy issues and sponsored by organisations involved in making and implementing social policy' (Davies 1999: 60). At the very least, ethnographers must be prepared to interact with policy makers and make their findings accessible to them by presenting them in a format and language they can understand. Hence the advice to use diagrams, maps and non-technical jargon, to hone oral presentation skills and to write 'executive summaries' in the text to enable policy makers to get to the kernel of the recommendations quickly (some of this advice can be found in Walker 1985: 177–95). In practice, therefore, the other models of policy research, with all their attendant difficulties, are likely to have a greater impact on policy than the 'enlightenment model'. Thus it is not surprising that Wenger (1987a) should term the relationship between research practice and policy as problematic (for discussions of how problematic it can be see the other contributions in Wenger 1987b).

In Bulmer's formulation of the three models of policy research, the relationship researchers have with policy makers veers between the same two poles: one in which the researchers follow an agenda set by policy makers at the risk of losing their critical independence; another where researchers retain intellectual and critical distance but at the risk of lessening their impact on policy. Nas *et al.* (1987) outline what they call the 'praxeological approach', which broadens our understanding of the relationship between researchers and policy makers by extending the definition of what constitutes applied research. Four types are identified. 'Thematic research' focuses on a particular substantive area within academic disciplines, such as medical sociology, ethnic and race relations, or education studies, and involves researchers working on theoretical or empirical issues which have some public relevance. No policy effect may be intended and its relevance to policy is only very indirect and will involve little association with policy makers. 'Evaluative research' has a more specific policy focus and is characterized by the intent to collect evidence on the effects of an intervention strategy or policy. This may or may not be done at the behest and under the guidance of the original formulators of the policy and thus may or may not involve the suspension of the researchers critical perspective. The third type they refer to as 'policy research', in which the researcher gathers and analyses data designed to be used by policy makers in their decisions, and thus normally done under the sponsorship, commission or employ of policy makers themselves. The policy maker sets the agenda in a top-down manner. In contrast, 'action research' is bottom-up and is done in association with a target population whose situation requires improvement and change. The research is intended to feed back into planning and policy, although the achievement of policy change depends on policy makers' awareness of the information and their readiness to use it.

Ethnographic research can be applied in all four senses. In the weakest meaning of applied research, ethnography can be used to explore the themes within a substantive sub-disciplinary area. A great deal of ethnographic research is applied in this sense, since most of it is conducted within the framework of a substantive focus, whether this be education, race relations, police studies, medicine or whatever. Even those ethnographers who object to the growth of practical or applied ethnography are applied in this sense. However, it is 'applied ethnography' only in a very tangential sense, since there is no explicit intent to affect policy or conduct policy-related research. Ethnography can be more directly applied by engaging in evaluative research, such as the evaluation of a specific policy intervention, as in Smith and Cantley's (1985) use of ethnographic methods to evaluate a particular psychogeriatric unit introduced by a local health authority. Practitioner ethnography shows how it can be 'applied' in the sense of engaging in policy research, and there are many examples of action research undertaken ethnographically, where ethnographers engage directly with a target group – gypsies (Okely 1983), female victims of domestic violence (Dobash and Dobash 1979), working-class truants from school (Corrigan 1979) – to try to influence policy makers to change the situation experienced by the target population. Because ethnography by definition involves close participation with the subjects under study, it is particularly relevant to action research, and applied ethnographic research of the other kinds often shifts its characteristics towards an action research approach because of the engagement and identification with the lives, experiences and problems experienced by people in the setting.

Another typology of policy-related research was outlined by Robert Walker (1985), one of the earliest pioneers of applied qualitative data. In later work (Walker 1988) he identified four types of applied research: contextual, diagnostic, creative and evaluative. 'In brief', he writes, 'contextual research is concerned with what exists and diagnostic research with why it exists. Evaluative research is concerned with appraising policy after implementation or judging between policy options ahead of implementation. Creative research informs the development or formulation of plans or actions' (Walker 1988: 10). They are not equally amenable to qualitative methods. Walker argues that most 'fact gathering' about what a situation is like requires quantitative methods, with qualitative methods being used only where the topic or the research subjects constrain the use of quantitative methods, although it is possible to imagine that disclosure of the actors' own perceptions about what the situation is like would be more suitable to qualitative methods. Qualitative methods can also be important in the initial identification of problems before further exploration on a larger scale. Diagnostic research explains the reasons why a situation or problem is like it is, and again the role of qualitative methods is limited to grounded theory approaches that might proffer an explanation or the actors' own accounts of why things are as they are. Walker contends that qualitative methods come into their own with evaluative policy research, especially, he writes (Walker 1988: 13), if pluralistic evaluation is required, involving the assessment of policies or intervention strategies from the perspective of the multiple actors involved in the setting. Qualitative research copes with the flexibility and complexity of the social world better than quantitative methods, allowing it to respect and cope with diversity and recognize the multiple ways in which people understand and react to interventions and policies. However, it is in the creative type of policy research that qualitative methods are supposed to excel (Walker 1988: 14). Qualitative methods, it is claimed (Rist 1981; Finch 1986), assist in reorienting the policy maker in imaginative ways by redrawing the boundaries of problems, responding creatively with new questions and isolating the levers of change (Finch 1986: 180). They do so by allowing policy makers and the target population to be involved in the research process, in the form of action research, enabling the redirection to evolve during the research, and by being flexible enough to allow last minute adjustments to suit the emerging plans of policy makers.

These different models of policy research illustrate the varied ways in which qualitative research can have practical applications. It is clear from this outline that in practice the models are very similar, ensuring that the characterizations of the contribution of applied qualitative research which are contained with them are very alike. The same basic contrasts appear in these models.

- Qualitative researchers can affect policy by engaging in indirect studies that add to the cumulative knowledge needed by policy makers, or they can undertake directed studies feeding straight into a policy initiative or intervention strategy.
- They can undertake studies of the policy process and the way policies emerge creatively, or of the specific policies that emerge from that process.
- Qualitative researchers can have close cooperation with policy makers, perhaps even involving them as research participants, or they can maintain an intellectual and critical independence.

These choices put traditional ethnographers in a difficult position. Some of the key principles of the method and practice of ethnography have to be sacrificed to give ethnography an applied and practical bent. As we have seen, applied ethnography can involve changes in fieldwork practice by requiring shorter periods spent in the field, and risks losing the ethnographer's critical perspective; it can diminish the ambition to generate theory and dilute the focus on actors' meanings in a social setting. Thus, some ethnographers refuse to engage in policy research at all. Those who are aware of the compromises applied ethnography involves but still wish to have an impact on policy tend to opt for certain choices in the above antinomies. They prefer to keep their critical distance from policy makers, engage in studies that are policy-relevant in a general rather than specific way and focus on the process of policy making as much as on addressing particular policies.

The contribution of ethnography to policy research

The main features of ethnographic data are their richness and depth. Breadth can be introduced if the research design permits theoretical inferences or empirical generalizations. The data themselves come in the form of extracts of natural language: long quotations from interviews, extracts from personal documents, notes of observations and so on. The usefulness of this kind of data depends on how important one feels it is to access the social meanings of people in a setting. Ethnography is premised on the belief that this is vital. Thus four imperatives for research follow, as outlined above:

- we need to ask people what meanings they give to the social world;
- we need to ask them in such a way that they can tell us in their own terms;

- we need to ask them in depth because these meanings are often taken for granted and deeply embedded;
- we need to address the social setting that gives substance and context to these meanings.

These imperatives can make a significant contribution to policy research. As Walker (1988: 9) wrote, 'qualitative methods can get to the parts of some policy problems that quantitative ones cannot reach, and vice versa.' Ethnography can offer the following to policy makers:

- it can help to provide the world view and social meanings of those affected by some policy or intervention strategy;
- it can help to provide the views of those thought to be part of the problem that the policy or intervention strategy is intended to address;
- it can be used to evaluate the effects of a policy or intervention strategy as these effects are perceived and experienced by the people concerned;
- it can be used to identify the unintended consequences of policy initiatives and strategies as they manifest themselves in the experiences of people;
- it can be used to provide cumulative evidence that supplies policy makers with a body of knowledge that is used to inform decision making;
- it can be used to supplement narrow quantitative information and add flesh to some of the statistical correlations and factual data used to inform decision making.

There is a contrast in this list between ethnography as the principal method of data collection and as an adjunct to quantitative research. It is widely recognized that ethnography and other qualitative methods can be used as a form of pilot testing for the questions to be used in a mass survey or as a sensitizing technique to collect the prior information that enables the research team to devise the answers to the closed questions from which respondents are asked to select. It can help to determine how concepts are to be operationalized in the research and clarify hypotheses to be tested. The use of ethnography as the principal source of evidence is less widely recognized. However, in 1979 the Research and Development Committee of the Market Research Society compiled a report on the use of qualitative methods and recommended their use as the principal method in limited circumstances (cited in Walker 1985: 17–18). This revolutionary shift in attitude towards qualitative research reflected the pressures on private research companies and consultants for seemingly quicker and less expensive methods to enable them to meet the growing demand for research among central and local government and other public bodies. The report recommended the use of ethnographic and qualitative methods as the principal research approach in two limited circumstances.

- when the information is new and unfamiliar;
- when the information requested is too subtle or complex to be elicited by questionnaires and other quantitative techniques.

The use of questionnaires in a survey, for example, requires that the researchers know the questions to ask and are able to predict the range of answers from which people are asked to select. When this prior knowledge is missing, ethnographic and qualitative research can legitimately be used as the primary source of data. When the information is complex and subtle, more sensitive methods need to be used to access it. It was impossible to ask policemen and women in the Royal Ulster Constabulary what their feelings were about being targets of paramilitary violence, and how they confronted and coped with the prospect of violent death and maiming, by means of a questionnaire which used closed questions and asked them to tick which response from the selection I had given them came nearest to their feelings. To approach the subtlety and complexity of the topic in this way would do travesty to the topic and be offensive to the subjects. What I did instead was use ethnographic methods, involving natural conversations and in-depth interviews, to examine how the men and women talked about their danger and threat (see Brewer 1991a: 163–78). There is another dimension relevant to this point. Where the topic is subtle and complicated, major research questions may emerge during the course of the study itself, so that the original ideas and formulations have to be refocused or even overturned as the research unfolds. The advantage of ethnography, and qualitative research generally, is that its flexibility can accommodate these reorientations. A questionnaire, painstakingly drafted on the drawing board before data collection begins, cannot be redrafted if in the course of the research one finds that the wrong questions have been asked or important questions omitted. The lack of standardization within ethnography is an advantage in this instance (see Finch 1986: 161).

There are other situations in which ethnography can be the primary source of data beyond those identified by the Market Research Society:

- when actors' social meanings are required in order to move beyond the causal explanations derived from statistical explanations;
- when a longitudinal element is required in order to study social processes over time;
- when the subjects of the research or the topic are not amenable to study by quantitative means.

Some ethnographers claim that the approach can expose the limits of statistics and statistical evaluations (Denzin 1989: 11). Less tendentiously, qualitative research can illuminate statistical relationships by throwing into relief the social meanings of the actors described in them. A good example is the statistical correlation between truancy from school and social class. To move beyond the link between working-class status and truancy, one may want to understand the rationality and meanings of the working-class kids who bunk off school. Paul Corrigan, in *Schooling the Smash Street Kids*, shows that in terms of the social meanings of the children themselves, truancy is a rational and purposeful act in the face of a school curriculum they find irrelevant, boring and meaningless (Corrigan 1979). Understanding this allows policy makers and educationists to focus attention on the contents of the school curriculum rather than the social class of the truants as a way of solving the problem.

Ethnographic research routinely involves a longitudinal element because it involves sustained contact with subjects in the setting over a prolonged period of time. To build longitudinality into quantitative research is prohibitively expensive because it involves a repeat study at a second time juncture, so ethnographic research is particularly suitable to studying social processes over time. This is particularly relevant to research evaluating the effects of policy changes and intervention strategies introduced during fieldwork, allowing classic 'before' and 'after' assessments. Ethnographic research is also useful given certain sorts of respondents. It is the only method possible with respondents who are inarticulate and have few communication skills, restricting data to participant observation, or when the research population is too small and difficult to locate. Ethnography is also important when the respondents are unlikely to respond to requests for sensitive material asked in standardized closed questions, such as certain elite groups who might not bother to reply to mailed questionnaires coming through the letterbox but who may agree to in-depth interviews. High-status groups ought not to be sent mailed questionnaires but should receive a personal touch. Ethnographic methods are useful as the primary source of data when the group is controversial and may not submit to research or in some other way be resistant to it, in which instance covert observation may be possible if ethical constraints have been reconciled.

Qualitative methods are particularly useful where the topic, setting or respondents are sensitive and controversial, as are many of the public concerns that are rooted in private troubles: AIDS, adoption, incest, domestic violence, sex abuse, mental illness and so on. It is also important to note here that some topics involve patterns of behaviour that cannot be meaningfully measured in a few standardized closed questions – rapes, poverty, fraud, muggings, morale and more (Walker 1985: 18) – so that they are best studied qualitatively. Rist (1984) argues that qualitative methods come into their own when the topic involves a multiplicity of actors with different perspectives: policy makers, clients and their relatives, welfare workers, professional care workers and the like. It is also useful when it is important to delve behind some official façade and public front to examine actual beliefs and behaviour. Hammersley (1992: 125) makes the point that qualitative methods are crucial for detecting deviations from the intended goals of some policy or intervention, exploring unintended consequences as experienced by the target population or the policy makers themselves. Table 5.1 summarizes the contribution that ethnography and qualitative methods generally can make to policy research.

It must be remembered, however, that encouraging policy makers to

Table 5.1   Applied ethnographic research

Stage of research	Role
Preliminary stage	Clarification of concepts
	Formulation of hypotheses
	Discovery of new and unfamiliar data
	Adjunct to quantitative information
Principal stage	When the topic is:
	complex and subtle;
	sensitive;
	controversial;
	immeasurable;
	concerned with change over time
	When the subjects are:
	inarticulate;
	elite;
	resistant to research;
	small in number;
	difficult to locate geographically

Source: derived from Walker (1985: 21).

recognize the contribution of ethnography and qualitative methods should not extend to denying the important contribution of quantitative evidence. Ethnography routinely involves a wide source of data as a result of the use of multiple methods, and thus might be more advantageous than any other single method, including questionnaires and surveys, but Hammersley (1992: 124) is right to remind us of three risks: over-exaggeration of the validity of ethnographic findings compared to other sorts of social research; simplistic notions that direct contributions to policy are possible from ethnographic studies; and exaggeration of the effect which research generally has on policy making. Thus, he argues against false notions of superiority for any kind of research approach, claiming that each has advantages depending on the topic, location and subjects of the research (Hammersley 1992: 127).

The warnings about too much enthusiasm in promoting the cause of applied ethnography are salutary. Studies of the policy-making process show that decisions are not necessarily based on careful consideration of the research (Rappert 1999: 708). The chase after 'relevance' and 'practical application' can cause an over-reliance on commercial funds for applied research, thus damaging academic freedom. Sponsors can limit the ethnographer's autonomy by delaying or preventing publication of findings critical of the sponsor (see the case of Miller (1988) and the former Northern Ireland Civil Service with respect to the topic of discrimination against

Catholics). Organizations that commission research sometimes dislike revelation of critical findings, and some require academic researchers to sign away their right to publish. So do public bodies from whom researchers are seeking permission to undertake research. For example, the RUC requires academic researchers seeking access to complete a confidentiality agreement (see Box 5.4) that includes questions about the applicant's addresses over the past ten years in the United Kingdom and outside, and the names and addresses of parents for the same period. Thus, greater participation by 'users' in commissioning and assessing research increases their control over the research agenda (by determining what they will or will not fund or give access to), increases their influence over the research process (by affecting the design of the project and data collection), and the dissemination of the results (by limiting publication).

Conclusion

Practitioner ethnographers and those working inside commercial research agencies, government and public bodies make a different sort of contribution from ethnographers working in an academic environment. Commissioned consultants working in a direct relationship with policy makers or in-house researchers working to a policy agenda can end up telling the commissioning agency what it wants to hear. There is an important distinction, therefore, between practitioner ethnography and the contribution of ethnographers working in academic environments, for the latter tend to adopt a critical and challenging attitude towards what Finch (1986: 224) calls 'the official view', and to produce findings not wholeheartedly embraced by officialdom. This critical stance means that academic ethnographers can, because of their close association with people's real lives, suggest alternative moral points of view from which a problem, policy or intervention strategy can be judged (on this see Becker 1967: 23–4). Through the use of data that capture personal experiences the differences between the perspectives of ordinary people and officialdom can be explored. This critical stance can be missing in practitioner ethnographer and forms of qualitative market research consultancy. This critical stance is important to all the usages to which ethnographic data can be put. Three in particular have been stressed in this chapter: the role of ethnography in generating knowledge; its role in theory generation, particularly in the development of grounded theory; and its application to issues of policy and policy making. The ethnographer's critical gaze on social life, his or her closeness to the people studied, the wish to get behind the façade and to critique official positions and claims, all ensure that academic ethnography is challenging and confrontational. It generates knowledge, social theories of the middle range and policy-related research evidence that puts the ordinary actors' perspective, even documenting the diversity of these perspectives, and

Box 5.4

CONFIDENTIALITY AGREEMENT AND THE TERMS AND CON-
DITIONS OF ACCESS TO THE RUC FOR RESEARCH PURPOSES

This is an agreement between _____ (hereinafter 'Recipient') and Force
Research on behalf of the Chief Constable of the Royal Ulster Constabulary (hereinafter 'Discloser') under which the Discloser may disclose and
the Recipient may receive certain confidential information for the sole purpose described in Appendix 'A' (hereinafter 'Information').

Confidentiality and Commitments

1 To consult with the Discloser on the detail of the proposed research and
   to seek the advice of the Discloser. This will involve submitting and
   agreeing a full research project specification.
2 To report to the Discloser any proposal to change the scope or content
   of the research and to advise the Discloser on the progress of the
   research.
3 From the date of the disclosure, the Recipient shall maintain the information in confidence and limit the use of that information to the purpose specified in Appendix 'A'. Recipient shall use a reasonable standard
   of care to avoid disclosure of information.
4 (a) Police will select focus groups based on criteria supplied by _____.
   (b) A schedule of questions will be provided for perusal prior to each
       focus group.
   (c) Communication with the RUC will be strictly through the desig-
       nated liaison officer.
5 The Recipient shall limit internal access to such information only to individuals, who have a need to know the information, and only with the prior
   approval of the Discloser.
6 (a) The Recipient shall not copy or reproduce, in whole or in part, any
       information without written authorisation of the Discloser, except
       as is necessary to fulfil the purpose stated in Appendix 'A'.
   (b) The Recipient shall submit the text of any proposed report, thesis,
       or other publication in connection with the research to the Dis-
       closer, permitting the Discloser the opportunity to comment on,
       and seek identification of any part of the text derived from official
       sources. This is to enable the Discloser to ensure that nothing pub-
       lished would be likely to cause embarrassment, for example, by the
       identification of any individual or institution.
   (c) The Recipient will ensure that no publication or communication in
       connection with the research through any channel of publicity will

take place, without the approval of the Discloser, with regard to content, format and timing of any such publication.

(d) The Recipient shall, on completion of the research, make all reasonable efforts to promptly return all tangible information and copies thereof.

Ownership and Publication of Information
Ownership and copyright of information supplied shall remain with the Discloser.

Storage of Information
The Recipient shall ensure that all information supplied by the Discloser will be stored securely when not in use, whether in paper, computer disk or any other format

General
1 The Discloser does not guarantee that the information to be supplied to the Recipient will be accurate and complete, unless otherwise agreed upon.
2 The Discloser accepts no responsibility for any expenses, losses or action incurred or undertaken by the Recipient as a result of the receipt of the information.
3 This agreement expresses the entire agreement and understanding of the Recipient and the Discloser, with respect to the subject matter thereof and supersedes all prior oral or written agreement, commitments and understandings pertaining to the subject matter.
4 This agreement shall not be modified or changed in any manner, except in writing and signed by both the Recipient and the Discloser. This shall also apply to any waiver of this requirement.
5 I accept that failure to comply with the above conditions may influence any future applications of a similar nature.
6 I recognise that failure to comply with the terms and conditions of the Data Protection Act (1984) is a criminal offence and contravention could lead to prosecution.
7 This agreement shall be governed by the substantive laws of the United Kingdom. The courts of Northern Ireland shall have exclusive jurisdiction over any dispute arising out of or in connection with this agreement. The Disclosure may also commence any court proceedings at the general place of jurisdiction or the registered principal office of the Recipient.

Reproduced with the permission of the RUC.

is thus always likely to reveal the complexity of situations and to challenge accepted views. Ethnographers should always aspire to be iconoclastic.

Suggested further reading

Bulmer, M. (1982) *The Uses of Social Research*. London: Allen and Unwin.
Finch, J. (1986) *Research and Policy*. Lewes: Falmer Press.
Rist, R. (1981) On the utility of ethnographic research for the policy process, *Urban Education*, 15, 48–70.
Wenger, C. (ed.) (1987) *The Research Relationship*. London: Allen and Unwin.
Walker, R. (ed.) (1985) *Applied Qualitative Research*. Aldershot: Gower.

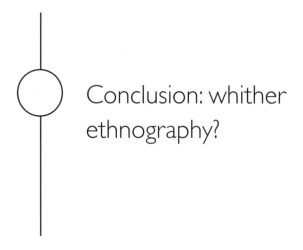

Conclusion: whither ethnography?

Introduction

Does ethnography have a future? Its roots are ancient; its future is uncertain. Travellers and outsiders of different kinds have for centuries lived among strangers and recorded their way of life. It became a specialist skill for social researchers at the beginning of the twentieth century. Since then, great consensus has emerged about its central features as a research method. As defined in this volume, ethnography is the study of people in naturally occurring settings or 'fields' by methods of data collection which capture their social meanings and ordinary activities. It involves the researcher participating directly in the setting, if not also the activities, in order to collect data in a systematic manner but without meaning being imposed on them externally. Defined in this way, it is one of the principal research methods in the social sciences, and foremost in the repertoire of qualitative researchers. Yet ethnography is under attack from within and without the qualitative tradition.

Among all the methods available to qualitative researchers it has been subject to the most criticism by ethnographers themselves and seen the greatest debate about its theoretical and methodological suppositions. The literature on ethnography is a battleground, and while in a sense it always was, the combatants have changed. Ethnography is no longer sniped at just from the outside by proponents of the natural science model of social research for failing to meet the cannons of science; its greatest critics are ethnographers under the sway of postmodern deconstruction. To some ethnographers, ethnography is no longer a privileged method to collect a special form of knowledge (in anthropology see Clifford 1983; Clifford and Marcus 1986; in sociology see Hammersley and Atkinson 1983; van Maanen 1988; Atkinson 1990; Hammersley 1990, 1992; Denzin 1997; Atkinson and Hammersley 1998; Richardson 1998). All accounts are constructions and the whole issue of which account more accurately represents social reality is meaningless (see Denzin 1992; Richardson 1992). They liken it to journalism, which always was the case among natural science critics, but now also to fiction, poetry or travelogues.

However, the postmodern critique of ethnography is not its only challenge. If postmodernism is a motif of contemporary social science, its twin is globalization. Globalization has become one of the conventional wisdoms of social science, in which it is claimed that the world is becoming smaller in scale as relationships become larger in scale. This is not a conundrum. Global relations and patterns now affect economic markets, consumption and lifestyles, cultural identities, politics, the environment, the military and culture artefacts, among other things. This makes the world a 'global village', wherein people live their lives on a larger scale than hitherto, travelling more extensively, watching and reading global media products, being at the mercy of events outside the control of their nation state and national economy, and subject to cultural homogenization. Globalization poses a threat to ethnography as serious as that of postmodernism. In the postmodern critique, ethnography is deconstructed so that its procedures and product are valueless; in the globalization critique it is left without a subject matter as a result of the disappearance of the local under global processes. Local 'fields' as sites for interesting and innovative social action and particularistic social meanings, which ethnography once explored, get subsumed under the homogenization that occurs with globalization. Globalization creates a cultural glob in which there is no space for difference, and thus for ethnography's stress on bounded fields as sites for localized social meanings.

Devoid of a subject matter and without practices that distinguish it from fiction or documentary travel writing, ethnography appears to have no future. However, this volume has throughout mounted a vigorous defence of ethnography from its postmodern critics. Post postmodern ethnography believes that it is still possible to make truth-like statements, even though these are contingent and conditional, and that it remains feasible to assess ethnographic representations of the social world by conventional criteria that give the data legitimacy. This defence will not be repeated here. Instead, the focus in the conclusion is on the implications globalization has for the practice and subject matter of ethnography. We ask whether ethnography has a future as a result of the threat posed by globalization; and it most certainly does. The argument mounted here involves giving ethnography back its subject matter, or, at least, showing that it was never threatened by globalization in the first place. Two examples from my previous ethnographic research are given to empirically focus these claims, the one concerning Ulster Loyalism (see Brewer 1998; Brewer and Higgins 1999), the other local crime management in Belfast (see Brewer *et al.* 1997, 1998). The attack implied by globalization is outlined first.

Globalization and ethnography

Globalization can be thought of as the widening, deepening and quickening of the worldwide interconnections in social, cultural, political and economic life (Held *et al.* 1999: 2). Some sociologists dispute that it is new and point to earlier periods of globalization, such as Western expansion in the nineteenth century; others are sceptical about its outcome and point to contradictory processes within it. A few deny that it is even occurring, at least to the extent that its enthusiasts claim. It is probably best to conceive of it as several processes rather than one, with different components in the various areas of social life which are experiencing global interconnectedness. And some of these processes have longer historical precedents than others, most notably political globalization through imperialism and the expansion of empires in the past. Nor are these processes producing a simple linear pattern of development towards the same end. But there are few areas of social life which escape the processes of globalization and there is an accelerating interdependence, wherein national borders are losing their significance and developments in one place impact directly on others as social, cultural, economic, military and political activities are stretched across frontiers.

Enthusiasts for globalization, known as 'hyperglobalists' by Held and colleagues (1999: 3–5), point to the demise of the local as relations and networks structure around global interactions. Activities are no longer organized around a territorial principle and thus become locally disembedded, diminishing the significance of locality and the particularities of place. New technologies of telecommunication and the emergence of international media corporations have generated cultural flows that exceed those of earlier epochs, and help to establish both a pattern of shared cultural belief over an extensive area and reciprocal interaction between separate places, so that cultural forms in one place influence those in another (see Mann 1986). The homogenization of mass consumption among the young also spreads cultural flows across the world (Featherstone 1990, 1991; Sklair 1995). The homogenization of culture further reduces the space for locality. National education systems, transnational media and global consumer markets all subvert localism. The emergence of 'global cities' seems to exemplify the disappearance of the local.

The loss of the local affects both identity and tradition. Identities are no longer seen as anchored in local social structures but constructed through the global mass media images that bombard people. People are no longer what their position in the social structure makes them: they are not defined by their position in the class structure or their identification with local or national territory; they are what they shop. Old identities are replaced by new ones developed around consumption patterns that are universalistic in their content. In such a circumstance, identity becomes translocal (something reinforced by the development of multicultural societies and diaspora communities). This idea is particularly associated with postmodern critiques of globalization, in which old identities have been replaced with 'hybrid' ones (Hall *et al.* 1992: 310; see also Hall and du Gay 1996), and where, in a state of hyper-reality, as Baudrillard describes it, people's identities are no longer anchored in social structures but constructed through lifestyle images in the mass media (see Sklair 1999: 329).

Furthermore, tradition is destroyed under the impact of globalization and the homogenization of culture. Globalization accelerates the decline in tradition that occurs under modernity and intensifies deroutinization (Giddens 1979: 220–1), by which is meant that tradition no longer underwrites the taken-for-grantedness of everyday life, which accordingly loses some of its routine character. Given the importance of this sense of routine to people, the weakening of its grip results in what Giddens calls 'ontological insecurity'. This is not the only feature of 'reflexive modernization', as he prefers to describe globalization (Beck *et al.* 1994). With the destruction of tradition comes the loss of local community and the stretching of action across time–space distances, so that the locale loses its centrality as a site for social action and emotional investment. Globalization involves the stretching of social action across frontiers, so that people are affected by 'action at a distance', where developments in one country have significant intended or unintended consequences for another. 'Distant others' thus come to affect individuals and 'overlapping communities of fate' emerge, where social situations across the globe are more closely entwined than historically has been the case. Globalization is thus closely associated with the disappearance of the local and of locally structured identities and tradition. People do not think or act locally, or identify with their locality. It is this disappearance of the local that bears on ethnography.

The practical limits of ethnography as a method, if not also its methodological preference for naturalism, require the survival of the local. Both its setting and its subject matter are local. Ethnography as a study is locally set, since it examines social meanings in a discrete and bounded locale. The requirement to participate in the activities under study and to share in the ways of life in the setting forces a restriction on studying a specific locality. It can do no other than engage in small-scale studies in physically and culturally bounded locales. Not only is its setting local, its subject matter is the local. Ethnography is characterized by small-scale studies to explore the social meanings of people in a particular setting. Such meanings are locally structured and embedded and thus are heavily shaped by the setting in which they occur. Ethnography is premised on the notion that the setting is in some way revealing because it displays social meanings which are either unique or special to it, or which might be representative of something more general and thus must be compared to similar local settings elsewhere. Either way, it is the features of social meanings in the local setting – their uniqueness or their potential for generalizations – which form the basis of the study. Ethnography has no rationale outside the survival of the local. It has neither a special place in which to locate its study nor a special subject matter. Under the globalization of society and the homogenization of culture, ethnography's role would merely be to chart the onward march of the cultural glob. In so doing there would be no real reason to focus on one setting over another, for the settings become amorphous equivalents. Ethnography's subject matter narrows to that of charting the features of the glob; even this will eventually disappear because such a task is finite.

No one can deny that globalization is occurring, but a critique of the globalization thesis shows that both tradition and locality survive, although in different forms than in earlier periods. Ethnography is thus left a future. As shown below in the two case studies, ethnography's role under globalization is to:

- chart the experience of people in a local setting to demonstrate how global processes are mediated by local factors;
- address the persistence of tradition;
- describe how traditional identities interface with globally structured ones.

In the face of globalization, tradition and locality are being reasserted. Two case studies will be presented to illustrate their persistence, showing the continued relevance of ethnography as the study of locally bounded and situated social meanings. The first case study concerns Ulster Loyalism.

Tradition, identity and Ulster Loyalism

Some commentators on the globalization thesis argue that tradition resumes its importance as a measure of identity because it challenges the globalizing forces that threaten people's localism and sense of personal difference. However, it does so in one or more of three new forms (see Giddens 1996c: 15ff). These forms are not mutually exclusive.

- Tradition can become fundamentalism. Religious, political and cultural fundamentalism offers a way of finding a place of authenticity in a changing world. That is, local practices, beliefs and traditions – and the identities they confer – can be defended with the vigour of fundamentalism,

because the tradition is seen as the sole thing of value in a universe of competing values, and held on to tenaciously as the last certainty in a changing, global world. Loyalty to one's tradition, and a belief in its certainty
and rightness, is held with a fundamentalist-like fervour. Thus, fundamentalist loyalty to tradition becomes a medium for structuring identity:
we are what the strength of our loyalty to our tradition makes us.

- Tradition can become relic. Local culture and identity can be reduced to
those relics, habits and routines associated with a traditional past, so that
the binding force of the group or neighbourhood is not culture but the
relic itself. The relic is invested with meaning as an expression of the past,
becoming a symbol of a community lost, rapidly going or under threat.
The performance of the routine, habit or relic becomes the main expression of identity. Thus, the relics, habits and practices associated with
former traditions become a medium for structuring identity: we are what
our cultural practices make us.

- Tradition can become collective memory. As sociologists see it, the historical past is never set in aspic, as if it was unchanging and fixed and a
matter of unambiguous record. Rather, the past is continuously reconsti-
tuted on the basis of the present, so that present concerns affect how the
past is recollected and understood. Tradition is the organizing medium of
collective memory, interpreting the past and organizing it according to the
concerns of the present. Tradition in this sense contains formulaic truths
that selectively interpret the past in order to serve the present, and while
it becomes a social glue that binds people together, the collective memory
distorts the past. Collective memory constitutes a form of identity in the
face of the postmodern fracture in identity, for it redefines notions of
'insider' and outsider' that the pluralism of postmodernity confuses. The
'other' is now anyone – everyone – who is outside the tradition and does
not share the collective memory. Moreover, the memory itself becomes
binding. The martyrs and long-since dead, who make up this past,
demand continued loyalty to it. To change the tradition is to dishonour
the past (selectively understood). Collective memory thus becomes a
medium for structuring identity: we are what our past (selectively understood) has made us.

As part of a study of anti-Catholicism in Northern Ireland from the plantation in the seventeenth century to the present day (Brewer 1998), I undertook some ethnographic research involving a series of in-depth interviews
with members of the conservative evangelical Protestant community in
Northern Ireland and various forms of documentary analysis. It was
the contention of that study that traditional identity concerns remain
important to Protestants in Ulster and contribute to the maintenance of anti-
Catholicism. Among other things, this sustains opposition to the peace
process. There is a tendency among many Protestants – not all – to construct

an identity to structure, manage and order their relations with Catholics, which is anti-Catholic and anti-Irish, while simultaneously, they confront a changing social world locally, nationally and internationally, which leads them to rely on distorted notions of tradition to define who they are, and who they are not.

So, an inherent tendency already to be anti-Catholic and anti-Irish becomes wrapped up with the tendency conservative evangelical Protestants in Ulster have: to define themselves in terms of the fundamental loyalty they show to Protestant traditions (the 'tradition as fundamentalism' idea); and/or to define themselves in terms of their dogged persistence in performing the cultural relics of a lost, dying or threatened Protestant tradition (the 'tradition as relic' idea); and/or to define themselves in terms of the collective memory of Protestantism in the past, to whose dead it would be disrespectful to jettison the memory (the 'tradition as collective memory' idea).

There are Protestants in Northern Ireland, especially in the conservative evangelical group, who at the moment are clinging tenaciously, doggedly, to the past, having to confront the social changes around them, challenging the structural forces which risk enveloping them, and for whom the familiar, routine traditions of old-style Protestantism and Unionism represent the only fixed thing in their lives. They see themselves as beleaguered and threatened, perpetually insecure and undermined, unable to trust anyone. Their feelings of ontological insecurity have been increased because the new circumstances they operate in politically, economically and socially as a result of the peace process require change, which can be psychologically difficult.

We therefore find three localized usages of tradition by Protestants today in Northern Ireland, giving a good example of what Giddens (1996c: 47) calls 'little traditions', which survive at the level of the local community despite (and even because of) aspects of globalization.

- Some Ulster Protestants are attracted to their tradition with a loyalty that approaches fundamentalism because it is the sole thing of value in a universe of competing values, and is held on to as the last certainty in an uncertain time. Their identity concerns are met by a fundamentalist loyalty to Protestant tradition. 'Not an inch' remains their shibboleth – the future goes backward to these Protestants; back to the familiarity of past traditions and identities.

- Some Protestants also persist in the performance of the habits, routines and relics of this tradition, despite their out-of-dateness, because these practices resolve their identity concerns. The right of the Orange Order to march in places where they are not wanted is perhaps the most obvious relic of a former tradition. The elision many Orangemen make between marching, territory and identity ensures that the right to march anywhere – even where they are not wanted – is seen as a cultural expression, an expression of their identity. To give up the right to march anywhere is to give up on that identity. To forgo the walk down Garvaghy Road in Portadown, in this mindset, therefore constitutes the end of Protestant witness in the North.

• Some Protestants use the collective memory of Protestant witness in Ireland since plantation, with its heroes, martyrs, innocents and legacy of much-spilt blood, as the standard by which to judge the future. No departure is permitted from the tradition which enshrines this collective memory, no compromise can be made with the memories of the long-since dead, 'not an inch', 'no surrender' and other shibboleths ensure conformity with the tradition. The 'guardians' of the tradition act to ensure its purity. All who believe thus are oblivious to the realization that this collective memory involves collective amnesia as well. It involves interpreting the past in ways which serve Protestant mythology and symbolism, distorting the historical record, ignoring uncomfortable pieces of evidence from the past and being thoroughly selective in the way they recollect Protestantism and its witness in Ireland. But collective amnesia is integral to collective memory, for no ambiguity is permitted in the way the past can be recalled, so as to avoid any ambiguity in the identity it constructs.

Identity matters to Ulster Protestants today. And while not all Protestants define themselves in terms of the sectarian past, a large number of conservative evangelical Protestants still construct their identity in this traditional way. This is so because traditional identities are a medium for structuring group relations with Catholics and a response to the way broad social processes are experienced locally. The case of Ulster Loyalism thus shows that local tradition survives, ensuring that ethnography has a role in displaying it and other 'little traditions' like it. This case study also highlights how local and global processes intersect, and we can turn now to a second case study that addresses this aspect of the globalization thesis.

The global–local nexus

As Sklair (1999: 330) wrote, globalization is not simply about the disembedding of the local by the global, it is also about the creation of a new global–local nexus, in which new relations develop between global and local spaces. Fragmentation and globalization are thus part of the same process. 'Globo-localism' or 'glocalization' are concepts used to express this (see Alger 1988; Sklair 1999). As globalization intensifies it generates pressure towards reterritorialization (see Held *et al.* 1999: 28), and reinforces the localization and nationalization of societies as a form of resistance to globalization, as a means to empower the powerless, and to reassert cultural and national difference. The emergence of new forms of national and independence movements (on which see McCrone 1998) is an illustration of this cultural and political fragmentation, as is the growth of various forms of fundamentalism, asserting the superiority of some particular religious, political or cultural identity (see Robertson 1992: 166–7). The upsurge in new social movements also highlights the new global–local nexus. Mobilizing on a range of issues, their motif is to think globally, since environmental, economic or social problems are often related to global factors, but to act locally, since the locale is people's immediate frame of relevance and concern. As another example, cultural products are consumed locally and locally read and can be transformed locally in the process, as Miller (1997) shows well in his study of patterns of mass consumption in Trinidad. In exploring the local–global nexus, Friedman (1990: 323) shows how local mediation affects the ways in which modern global processes affect group identity, with some groups consuming modernity to strengthen themselves and others using tradition to recreate themselves (much as Ulster Loyalists). This intersection between local mediations and global processes led Friedman (1990: 315) to argue that it is necessary to examine the relationship between local structures of desire and identity and the broader global economic and political context.

The local thus remains important, and the search for local variations and particularities via small-scale studies remains worthwhile. For example, there have been many creative local responses to the intrusion on local space of global processes, such as the formation of nuclear free zones (Algar 1988: 323), social movement protests to defend the local environment, the assertion of local culture and tradition, and mobilization locally on global problems, such as human rights, poverty, famine and disarmament. Local and national space is thus reformed, although not necessarily contiguously with former legal and territorial boundaries. Fragmentation is thus part of the same process as homogenization. Taking this on board, some proponents of the globalization thesis, like Giddens and Mann, recognize the transforming nature of these historically unprecedented changes but show the process to be replete with contradictions, such that the overall direction of these changes is uncertain (as pointed out by Held *et al.* 1999: 7).

The importance of local mediations of broader processes, and the associated survival of local cultures, meanings and peculiarities is demonstrated in an ethnographic study I and colleagues undertook into crime trends in Belfast, as part of a larger study of patterns of crime in the island of Ireland between 1945 and 1995 (Brewer *et al.* 1997). Criminology increasingly understands crime as part of a global process. Modernity, however, is at once both a globalizing and localizing process because it throws into sharper relief the differences that remain locally under broad social transformations, and criminology must also stress the importance of locality and place on crime ('environmental criminology' gives fullest expression to the importance of place on crime; for summary statements see Bottoms 1994; Bottoms and Wiles 1996). The case study described below considers the continuing importance of locality and place.

Local crime management in Belfast

During a twelve-month period between 1994 and 1995, the author was part of a research team that looked at crime trends in both parts of the island of Ireland for a fifty-year period. One dimension of the research covered an ethnographic study of two parts of Belfast, one largely Catholic, the other largely Protestant, with the intention of examining people's experiences of crime, their levels of fear of crime and how they responded to the crime that did occur. This focus illustrated how crime in Belfast was differentially experienced among people and places and how crime statistics were socially constructed by the public's willingness to report crime to the police. Data were collected by in-depth interviews and other ethnographic methods (the methodology is outlined in Brewer *et al.* 1997: 124–7). The data presented here do not focus on criminal activity in Belfast but the related issue of crime management, which is much neglected in the criminological literature (discussed in greater detail in Brewer *et al.* 1997: 165–97; 1998). This is of particular importance in Northern Ireland because crime management is contested. 'Official' crime management by the RUC is challenged by 'popular' or local forms, and a consideration of 'popular' crime management in Belfast confirms the marked differences that exist in the local experiences of crime within one city, let alone in Ireland as a whole compared to other industrialized societies. It illustrates that some areas within the same city have had different fortunes under modernity, making them better able to respond to or cope with criminogenic processes. The local experience of crime in Belfast is that the criminogenic tendencies of social change are being mediated in some localities by social processes which reflect the persistence of social control, slowing the rate of social breakdown, with obvious effects on crime and its management. In terms of the debate about the future of ethnography under globalization, crime management in Belfast shows the survival and persistence of the local and thus the continued role of ethnography to disclose it.

In effect, very traditional communities have persisted in the North, based on the traditional forms within which its modernization occurred in earlier decades. This helps to explain why Belfast, for example, has a lower crime rate per 100,000 of population than Liverpool or Manchester, despite a quarter-century and more of civil unrest, although it is higher than Dublin's. It is not just the case, therefore, that the persistence of traditional communities in Belfast displaces crime elsewhere (which it does); it also helps relatively to suppress it and thus counteract the criminogenic tendencies that exist in the city. These traditional social forms have a profound effect on crime management. By the local management of crime, we mean those structures in the local neighbourhood and community which have a role in preventing and suppressing crime and offer alternative ways of dealing with it once committed. Not all localities in Belfast contain these structures, so that popular crime management is a localized phenomenon, structured by processes embedded primarily in the communal structures and class dynamics of certain neighbourhoods, such as extended family kinship patterns, a strong sense of neighbourliness and a vivid sense of locality and community identity. It is within these social processes that 'popular' crime management is sociologically embedded.

Senses of community and neighbourhood identity are very localized, contingent upon the frames of reference people use, the locality in which they live and personal experiences of the quality of relationships that exist in their neighbourhood. Local experiences of community were mediated by class, being stronger in the inner city and working-class neighbourhoods in our study areas, and by the senses of community that survived in these localities. Social change, population relocation and housing redevelopment have affected localities in varying degrees, and have not everywhere destroyed a sense of community and local identity.

People from most West Belfast neighbourhoods portray the areas as having a strong sense of community. Community is not experienced in the same way as it was in the past, but most people in West Belfast, save the elderly, recognize that it has not been lost. This sense of community is on the whole weaker in parts of East Belfast, where there is a sense of greater social change, housing relocation and social dislocation. Neighbourhoods there have not lived under the same sense of siege. Far greater numbers of residents from the East Belfast study area reflected on a decline in the sense of community in their neighbourhood. A resident said, 'I think the community spirit is not as strong now. People tend to keep themselves to themselves. Years ago everybody minded everybody else's business. If you saw a child misbehaving you disciplined it.' However, there are localities in East Belfast where people commented that community structures had survived. Some people live in working-class neighbourhoods where the old streets have not been redeveloped. One resident described his area: 'a lot of good living people, close knit families, not a lot of movement, so people have been here for several generations, there is a stable social fabric.'

Local crime management is rooted in the social processes related to community and local identity, neighbourliness and an extended family kinship pattern. These processes provide, first, for the survival of a local moral economy. The values of this moral economy were expressed most frequently in the form that 'you don't steal from your own'. This runs entirely counter to local crime surveys in Britain, which show that most crime is committed by locals from the neighbourhood. In summarizing results from crime surveys,

Maguire (1994: 256–6) argued that most crime in Britain is predatory, it involves a continuing relationship between offender and victim, and the most vulnerable are people in council-owned dwellings primarily from people like themselves. Members of a mother and toddler group on a large housing estate in West Belfast explained, however, that 'you would get people in the private estates to talk more about crime, they're more burgled than we are. Off the record, we are sort of cocooned from criminals, they don't steal from their own.' An East Belfast worker with young offenders repeated the view: 'individuals who commit the crime have a lot of respect for the area that they live in, they don't break-in in their own area.' This moral economy therefore rules out crime in certain close-knit areas, at least by its own local criminals, displacing it elsewhere. But it also rules out crime against certain categories of people who are protected by the local moral economy. Thus, several people identified that crimes against children, the elderly and church property were defined as beyond acceptable bounds locally. An East Belfast community worker said of his neighbourhood: 'this is a parochial community around here and if the crime is against a pensioner, nobody will be spared. I have known a case where a parent actually contacted the police when they found out that their son had broken into a pensioner's house.'

This moral economy only works for criminals who are from the area and who share the code. Local crime is often perpetrated by outsiders who are escaping the constraints of the moral economy in their area or by people who do not subscribe to the code. The anti-social behaviour by local youths inflicted on elderly people, for example, seems to suggest that the values are not shared by all. Changes are occurring in the moral economy as structural adaptations to the changed circumstances young unemployed people find themselves in, and some people comment on the decline in the ethical code of local lags. But even if local criminals defy the code, the existence of a moral economy results in greater outrage, with its knock-on effects of increased effort to apprehend them by the community itself or by the paramilitaries, or successfully overcoming resistance to involving the police in official crime management.

Another factor involved in local crime management that arises from the survival of community structures is the existence of a 'local grapevine', a network of informal contacts which passes on knowledge about perpetrators, the whereabouts of stolen property and the sorts of people who can best apprehend or provide immediate satisfactory justice in the absence of reporting it to the police. The grapevine is also the mechanism by which the local moral economy is socially disseminated. As a resident from West Belfast said, 'if a crime happened against an old person or a child, maybe if it happened in [name of area], everybody would be talking about it.' A young adult from West Belfast indicated how the grapevine worked even on a large estate. 'Although this is a large estate, there is always somebody who knows something, always somebody. There is not too many people that keep things to themselves. There is always "did you hear about that", and then it works its way around the grapevine.' The grapevine ensures that knowledge is passed on to victims or even the relatives of perpetrators, which is where neighbourliness and an extended family kinship network particularly come in useful in local crime management. A very young girl, associated with a youth club in West Belfast, described how this network of contacts constrained her. Referring to possible victims of crime she said, 'they would always know who you are or know your ma or something. This is a close knit community and people often do tell your ma or friends of your ma sees you.'

This permits do-it-yourself policing. Many respondents told of how they responded as victims when they knew the perpetrator as a result of the local grapevine. Some went straight to the paramilitaries, some to the police. Others, however, used the neighbourhood's network of informal contacts to confront the parents. A member of a women's group in West Belfast explained how she would respond: 'you wouldn't like to see a child get punished in a beating, you wouldn't like to see your own harmed, so we went around and let the parents know.' A woman from East Belfast said the same, 'you would just go to the family'. Do-it-yourself policing thus depends for its efficacy precisely on the survival of neighbourhood networks.

Because a sense of community survives, the neighbourhood is able to be readily mobilized to manage crime locally. One of the resources that can be mobilized is the remnant of legitimate authority which community representatives still possess, such as teachers, priests and pastors, and community and youth workers. This authority has diminished compared to the past, since many people experience social change as a decline in respect for authority among the young, but the data reveal that many of these figures are still drawn into the management of crime. A youth worker in East Belfast, for example, explained how local people have come to her to deal with specific incidents concerning youngsters rather than go to the police. Clerics repeated the point. A priest in West Belfast said he was like a policeman sometimes, being called out before the RUC: 'the people wouldn't ring the police, they'd ring you directly, you got out and you went and dealt with it.' Other community resources that can be mobilized in local crime management are the skills, finances and manpower of community organizations in the development and servicing of local initiatives against crime.

Social changes wrought by twenty-five years of civil unrest have therefore clearly not eroded some forms of social control in certain parts of Belfast, furnishing effective mechanisms for popular crime management in some localities. Social change has facilitated local crime management in another way because different mechanisms have developed as adaptations to new structural conditions. Most notable of these new mechanisms are the paramilitary organizations. Their role in local crime management is heavily conditional upon the social processes associated with community structures. These networks disseminate the information that makes paramilitary policing possible and efficacious, and provide the push for the paramilitary organizations to engage in it in the first place.

Some respondents extolled the contribution made by the paramilitaries to the relatively low crime rate in their area: 'I think it is to the credit of the IRA that crime has been kept so low, because it has nothing to do with the RUC, absolutely not.' In East Belfast the paramilitaries were described by several people as the unofficial police force. 'The paras get things done', said one youth worker, 'things are done.' Some of the policing methods by which paramilitaries 'get things done' depend in part upon social processes associated with community structures in local neighbourhoods. One method is that of 'shaming', particularly associated with Republican paramilitaries, which requires for its effectiveness that communal disgrace will be experienced as a constraint by offenders. In West Belfast people have been forced to stand in public places (especially outside churches and supermarkets) with placards; some are tied to lamp posts to ensure they stay put. There is also a primitive 'house protection scheme', whereby paramilitary organizations place a sticker in the window of a house warning that criminals enter at their peril. Mostly, however, people perceive force as the main policing method of the paramilitaries. Some people perceive that this force comes in proportional degrees depending on the circumstances of the crime and the criminal background of the perpetrator, although others claim it to be quite arbitrary (on the gradation in paramilitary punishment beatings see Thompson and Mulholland 1995). These informal disciplines almost appear as a form of customary law in a situation where state law is deemed to be without legitimacy or effect, making them similar to disciplines used by indigenous groups in North America and Australasia.

Local crime management is thus a phenomenon embedded in communal structures that are localized to specific places in Belfast, depending upon experiences of class, communal development, population relocation and other social transformations locally. Civil unrest, however, has also played its part in differentiating local experiences of crime management. In certain neighbourhoods 'the troubles' have had the effect of inhibiting the processes of social dislocation and community breakdown. In some areas, where it is most intense, civil unrest has produced a voluntary ghettoization by restricting geographic mobility and population relocation, producing socially homogeneous districts in religious, ethnic and class terms. In-group solidarity has been reinforced by conflict with an out-group. This cohesion is reflected in structures such as the survival of extended kinship networks, close-knit neighbourhood structures and a sense of living in solidaristic communities, with their own local moral economy. Other ethnographies of crime in working-class neighbourhoods, for example, show them to be less vibrant and communal than equivalent localities in our study areas (see, for example, Williams 1989; Robins 1992). Some of this is also due to benevolent housing policy (Northern Ireland has not seen the infamous tower block to any great extent) or employment restrictions on geographic mobility. Northern Ireland is also small, so families tend not to be disrupted even where geographic mobility occurs. For all these reasons, some localities in Belfast have not experienced social dislocation and breakdown.

Conclusion

Ethnography can defend itself against its two most important challenges. It is still possible to collect objective, reliable knowledge because the postmodernist attack does not deconstruct it to the point of complete relativism and scepticism (for a former postmodernist arguing that we have gone too far see Marcus 1994). Some ethnographers have responded to the thrust of the postmodern critique in order to defend the practice of ethnography by developing a type of post postmodern ethnography. Methodologically they have defined an alternative range of positions to naive realism, such as analytical realism (Altheide and Johnson 1998) and subtle realism (Hammersley 1990, 1992), which make it feasible to consider and evaluate truth statements; and they have identified guidelines for good practice, which make it possible to collect ethnographic data in a systematic and rigorous manner (Silverman 1989; Brewer 1994).

In the context of the debate about ethnography's future, what is equally important is that ethnography is also left a subject matter to research. Since it is suited to studying localities in a small-scale manner in order to investigate their particular dynamics, the globalization of society and the homogenization of culture potentially robs it of the specificity of the local. Without the survival of the local, ethnography would be reduced to documenting the onward progress of globularity. However, since global processes are always mediated locally, often being transformed in the process according to the particularities of the locale, a space for ethnography remains along with that for locality.

Two ethnographic case studies have been used to demonstrate this claim. Tradition survives under postmodern, global conditions, because local groups use their traditional culture and identity as a resistance to globalization and homogenization, or reassert traditional identities as part of local conflicts. The case of Ulster Loyalism is thus only slightly different from all the ethnic nationalisms currently fragmenting Europe and elsewhere. The case of crime management in Belfast illustrates the ways in which locality survives to affect crime and its management in parts of Belfast, ensuring that modern society is experienced differently in some parts of Belfast, to facilitate informal social control and thus crime management by the community itself. These arguments demonstrate that there is a role left for ethnography, especially for ethnography done systematically and rigorously. In this post-modern, global moment, ethnography can still demonstrate how local processes are transformed under the pressure of globalization and show how these global processes are themselves mediated by local factors to create localized variations and particularities. Along with the persistence of locality and local specificity in social meanings, a form of ethnographic realism survives in the postmodern, global world under the influence of post postmodern practice. Ethnography has a future.

Suggested further reading

Beck, U., Giddens, A. and Lash, S. (1994) *Reflexive Modernization*. Cambridge: Polity Press.

Featherstone, M. (1990) *Global Culture: Nationalism, Globalization and Modernity*. London: Sage.

Featherstone, M. (1991) *Consumer Culture and Postmodernism*. London: Sage.

Held, D., McGrew, A., Goldblatt, D. and Perraton, J. (1999) *Global Transformations*. Cambridge: Polity Press.

Marcus, G. (1994) What comes (just) after 'post'? The case of ethnography, in N. Denzin and Y. S. Lincoln (eds) *Handbook of Qualitative Research*. London: Sage.

Miller, D. (1997) *Modernity: an Ethnographic Approach*. Oxford: Berg.

Sklair, L. (1995) *Sociology of the Global System*. Baltimore: Johns Hopkins University Press.

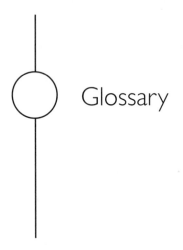

Glossary

Analysis: In ethnography this can be defined as the process of bringing order to the data, organizing what is there into patterns, categories and descriptive units, and looking for relationships between them.

Anti-realism: This is an approach to knowledge that attacks *realism* by disputing its two central tenets, denying that there is an externally knowable world that can be accurately and objectively represented and studied. It is associated with *postmodernism's* attack on the very idea of rationality, science and objectivity. Anti-realism influences the postmodern, reflexive type of *ethnography*, which seeks to marry some postmodern theories with the continued commitment to disciplined, rigorous and systematic ethnographic practice. It does this by distinguishing 'naive realism' from more acceptable forms, such as 'subtle realism', 'critical realism' and 'analytical realism'.

Case study: A case can be defined as any phenomenon located in space and time about which data are collected and analysed, and can comprise single individuals or a group, particular events or situations, a specific organization, a social institution, neighbourhood, national society or global process. Case studies can address the micro situation of a single person in everyday life or the macro situation of a nation state in the global world. Case studies are distinguished, therefore, by the focus on the instance of the phenomenon, not by the method used to study it. While not all case studies are qualitative, all ethnographic research involves case study. There are intrinsic, instrumental and collective case studies, differentiated by the degree of empirical generalization they permit.

Credibility: This involves an assessment of whether any truth claim is likely to be accurate given the nature of the phenomenon, the circumstances of the research and the characteristics of the researcher. Associated with the *postmodern* and *anti-realist* critique of the criteria by which ethnographic data are evaluated.

Deduction: This is an approach to the formulation of truth claims and statements which deduces general statements from a theory or law, from which hypotheses are formed, which are then tested against prediction and observation. This is what is known as the hypothetico-deductive method and involves nomological-deductive explanation. It is associated with *positivism* and forms part of the natural science model of social research. It is the opposite of *induction*.

Ethnography: This can be defined as the study of people in naturally occurring settings or 'fields' by methods of data collection which capture their ordinary activities, involving the researcher participating directly in the setting, if not also the activities, in order to collect data in a systematic manner but without meaning being imposed on them externally. Ethnography is not one particular method of data collection but a style of research that is distinguished by its objectives, which are to understand the social meanings and activities of people in a given 'field' or setting, and an approach, which involves close association with, and often participation in, this setting. To access social meanings, observe behaviour and work closely with informants and perhaps participate in the field with them, several methods of data collection tend to be used. 'Little' ethnography describes 'ethnography-understood-as-fieldwork', to which this definition relates, while 'big' ethnography equates it with the whole qualitative method and describes 'ethnography-understood-as-qualitative-research'. Ethnography-understood-as-fieldwork comes in various types. 'Scientific ethnography' involves the application of some features of scientific method to the above sort of study; 'humanistic ethnography' concentrates on the search for the meaning of social action and life from the perspective of the people concerned and is uninterested in the values and rhetoric of science; 'postmodern reflexive ethnography' adopts a critical approach to ethnography and seeks to ground its practice in *postmodernism's* ideas about the impossibility of definitive 'objective' study. Less extreme versions exist as a type of 'post postmodern ethnography', which although it attacks *realism* is strongly committed to *realism's* ambition to disciplined, rigorous and systematic ethnographic practice.

Gatekeepers: These are individuals that have the power to grant access to the field, such as gang leaders, tribal chiefs and heads of organizations and bureaucracies like headteachers and police chiefs. These constitute formal gatekeepers. At lower levels, there are usually a number of informal gatekeepers who can affect access, sometimes positively (being more open and forthcoming than the formal gatekeeper), sometimes negatively (by objecting to the permission given on their behalf by someone else and trying to limit what is seen and heard).

Generalizability: This means the applicability of the data to other like cases (also sometimes called 'external validity').

Ideographic: This is a style of research which assumes that each individual case is unique and which thus opposes generalizations and abstractions. It is the opposite of *nomothetic* research.

Induction: This is an approach to the formulation of truth claims and statements which argues that general statements, if they are to be made at all, should emerge from the data themselves and not be imposed on the data by prior conceptions and theoretical assumptions. It is associated with *naturalism* and an approach to theory formation known as 'grounded theory'. It is the opposite of *deduction*.

Interpretation: In ethnography this involves attaching meaning and significance to the *analysis*, explaining the patterns, categories and descriptive units, and the relationships that exist between them.

Meaning: This describes the beliefs, feelings, moods, perceptions and interpretations of people. The study of these meanings is normally associated with the idea that the social world is partly (or wholly) constructed and reconstructed by people on the basis of these meanings. This forms a defining element of *naturalism*. People are seen as 'meaning endowing', by which is meant they have the capacity to endow meaning to the world, and people are seen as discursive, by which is meant they possess the ability to articulate these meanings.

Method: These are procedural rules, which, if followed properly, certify the knowledge as reliable and objective. There are methods of data collection, defining the procedural rules for collecting data, methods of data analysis, defining the procedural rules for the analysis and interpretation of data, and methods of research enquiry, defining the procedural rules for formulating elements of the enquiry, such as hypotheses, concepts and theories.

Methodology: This describes the broad theoretical and philosophical framework within which methods operate and which give them their intellectual authority and legitimacy. Examples would be *positivism* and *naturalism*. The *philosophy of social research* argues that researchers have a preference for a particular methodology, which predetermines the use of those methods that the particular methodology validates and legitimates.

Naturalism: This is an orientation concerned with the study of social life in real, naturally occurring settings; the experiencing, observing, describing, understanding and analysing of the features of social life in concrete situations as they occur independently of scientific manipulation. These naturally occurring situations are also sometimes called 'face-to-face' situations, mundane interaction, micro-interaction or everyday life. Stress is laid on experiencing and observing what is happening naturally rather than hypothesizing about it beforehand, mostly by achieving first-hand contact with it, although researchers minimize their effect on the setting as much as possible. Stress is also laid on the analysis of people's 'meanings' from their own standpoint.

Nomothetic: This is a style of research that seeks to develop abstract generalizations about phenomena. It contrasts with *ideographic*.

Participant observation: This is a method in which observers participate in the daily life of a people under study. Classic or traditional participant observation involves the acquisition of a new role to study in an unfamiliar setting. The utilization of a role one already possesses in order to study in a familiar field is sufficiently different as sometimes to be called 'observant participation'.

Philosophy of social research: Not to be confused with the philosophy of social science, this is a term employed by John Hughes and examines the theories of knowledge (*methodologies*) which locate and explain the practice of research.

Plausibility: This involves an assessment of whether any truth claim is likely to be true given our existing knowledge. It is associated with the *postmodern* and *anti-realist* critique of the criteria by which ethnographic data are evaluated.

Positivism: This is a methodological position that believes in the application of natural science methods and procedures to the study of social life. It results in the natural science model of social research, which involves the notion that the social sciences address similar problems to the natural sciences, that social scientists confront a social world similar in most respects to the natural world, can focus on causal explanations and can use *deduction*.

Postmodernism: This is a set of theories that argue in relation to knowledge that objective truth is unattainable. The search for objective truth is deconstructed and shown to dissolve into various language games about 'truth'. All we have are merely 'truth claims', which are partial, partisan and incomplete. Knowledge is therefore relative, and people should thus be sceptical about truth claims. Postmodernism thus encourages us to examine the contingent social processes that affect research and undermine the objectivity and truthfulness of the knowledge. This is seen as being achieved through *reflexivity*. It is associated with *anti-realism*.

Presentation: This is the process of writing up the data in textual form.

Realism: This reflects a methodological position which advances two claims: that there is an external world independent of people's perceptions of it (so that there is more to find out about the social world than people's meanings); and that it is possible to obtain direct access to, and 'objective' knowledge about, this world. It permeates *positivism* to the point where the two terms are used interchangeably. However, the second principle is also a feature of *naturalism*. Realism has always embedded ethnography. Scientific and humanistic ethnographies are realist, in the sense that both assume there is a knowable world that can be studied directly and accurately, the representation of which is feasible in ethnographic texts. The *anti-realism* of the postmodern, reflexive type of ethnography disputes realism's twin assumptions. However, post postmodern ethnographers do not rule out completely the possibility of rigorous and systematic practice, and ground their alternatives to realism in realist-type arguments. They attack only what they describe as 'naive realism', offering instead alternatives like 'subtle realism', 'analytical realism', 'critical realism' or 'the ethnographic imagination', which shy away from the complete relativism and scepticism of postmodernism ethnography.

Reflexivity: This involves reflection by ethnographers on the social processes that impinge upon and influence data. It requires a critical attitude towards data, and recognition of the influence on the research of such factors as the location of the setting, the sensitivity of the topic and the nature of the social interaction between the researcher and researched. In the absence of reflexivity, the strengths of the data are exaggerated and/or the weaknesses underemphasized. It is associated with the idea that ethnographic representations of reality are partial, partisan and selective, and thus with *anti-realism* and *postmodernism's* dispute that there is a perfectly transparent or neutral way to represent the social world (or the natural one). It is a fundamental part of both types of postmodern, reflexive ethnography.

Relevance: This describes the evaluation of ethnographic findings by their relevance to issues of public concern. Associated with the *postmodern* and *anti-realist* critique of the criteria by which ethnographic data are evaluated. Ethnographic research could be judged by whether and how well they resolve some social problem, or achieve emancipation for some oppressed group (such as women) or release from some constraining situation or setting (such as discrimination experienced by ethnic minorities). Many feminist ethnographers are particularly concerned to ensure that their practice ends up with the emancipation of women rather than the production of valid knowledge for its own sake. Hammersley defines two aspects of public relevance: the importance of the topic in terms of public issues, and the contributions of the findings to existing knowledge.

Reliability: This describes the extent to which measurements are consistent when replicating a study using the same instruments under the same conditions.

Research design: This is the strategic plan of the project, setting out the broad structure and features of the research.

Research process: This refers to the series of actions involved in producing the end result of the study. In ethnography, it is necessary to see this as a series of coordinated actions rather than distinct hermetic stages, which do not necessarily occur in sequence and which require flexibility.

Sample: In ethnographic research, to sample means to select the case or cases for study from the basic unit of study where it is impossible to cover all instances of the unit. In some rare cases, where the unit is small or unusual, it is possible to include a universal study of the unit, but complete coverage is mostly impossible. In these circumstances, a sample is drawn from the universe of units. In probability sampling, each instance of the unit has the same probability of being included in the sample; in non-probability sampling there is no way of estimating this probability or even any certainty that every instance has some chance. Most ethnographic research uses non-probability sampling. Sampling can be done of the fields in which to site the ethnography and of the units of study within them.

Theoretical sampling: This is the procedure in which cases, be they people, groups, sub-groups or settings, are purposely selected in order to provide the best possible test of some theory or theoretical statement or the optimal opportunity to develop some theory or theoretical statement.

Theory: A theory is a set of interrelated abstract propositions about human affairs and the social world that explain their regularities and properties. **Theoretical statements** differ from descriptive statements in that they are abstract propositions that may, or may not, form part of a fully fledged theory. Theories can be distinguished by their level of generality. **General theories** offer abstract propositions about social action or society as a whole, while **theories of the middle range** make propositions about more limited aspects of human and social affairs, or less general propositions.

Thick description: This is seen as the 'special', 'privileged' sort of data that ethnographers collect because of their close involvement in the field. It is the account of life on the 'inside', and represents a thorough description, taking in the context of the phenomena described, the intentions and meanings that organize them and their subsequent evolution or processing. It is associated with both scientific and humanistic types of ethnography. The *anti-realism* of the *postmodern*, reflexive types of ethnography challenge the idea of thick description, arguing that it is just as selective and partial as all descriptions.

Triangulation: This term is associated with Norman Denzin and refers to the use of multiple methods, researchers and theoretical frameworks in order to extend the range of data.

Validity: This refers to the extent to which the data accurately reflect the phenomena under study (also sometimes called 'internal validity'). *Ethnography* has traditionally been seen as collecting data with high validity but low *reliability*, although the attack on ethnography by *anti-realism* and *postmodernism* challenges whether there are any agreed criteria by which to evaluate ethnographic data. New criteria are suggested, such as *relevance*, and validity is redefined to include *plausibility*, *credibility* and evidence tests.

Vignette: This term has a double meaning. In one sense it describes a data collection technique, in which researchers present subjects with a hypothetical situation or scenario and ask them to write down how they or a third person would respond to it. It is particularly useful in dealing with very sensitive material. Its other meaning relates to the presentation of ethnographic data where some aspect of the data is extracted and given special close analysis or description to act as an exemplar of a broader process.

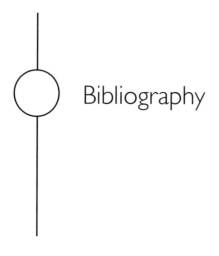

Bibliography

Abrams, P. (1981) The collapse of British sociology, in P. Abrams, R. Deem, J. Finch and P. Rock (eds) *Practice and Progress: British Sociology 1950–1980*. London: Allen and Unwin.

Ackroyd, S. and Hughes, J. A. (1981) *Data Collection in Context*. London: Longman.

Adler, P. A. and Adler, P. (1998) Observational techniques, in N. Denzin and Y. Lincoln (eds) *Collecting and Interpreting Qualitative Materials*. London: Sage.

Alger, C. (1988) Perceiving, analysing and coping with the local-global nexus, *International Journal of Social Science*, 117, 321–40.

Altheide, D. and Johnson, M. (1998) Criteria for assessing interpretive validity in qualitative research, in N. Denzin and Y. Lincoln (eds) *Collecting and Interpreting Qualitative Material*. London: Sage.

Anderson, D. (1978) Some organisational features of the local production of a plausible text, *The Philosophy of the Social Sciences*, 8, 113–35.

Ashmore, M. (1989) *The Reflexive Thesis*. Chicago: Chicago University Press.

Athens, L. (1984) Scientific criteria for evaluating qualitative studies, in N. Denzin (ed.) *Studies in Symbolic Interactionism, Volume 5*. Greenwich, CT: JAI Press.

Atkinson, J. and Drew, P. (1979) *Order in Court*. London: Macmillan.

Atkinson, P. (1983) Writing ethnography, in H. J. Helle (ed.) *Kultur und Institution*. Berlin: Duncker and Humbolt.

Atkinson, P. (1990) *The Ethnographic Imagination*. London: Routledge.

Atkinson, P. (1992) *Understanding Ethnographic Texts*. London: Sage.

Atkinson, P. and Delamont, S. (1985) Bread and dreams or bread and circuses: a critique of 'case study' research in education, in M. Shipman (ed.) *Educational Research*. Lewes: Falmer Press.

Atkinson, P. and Hammersley, M. (1998) Ethnography and participant observation, in N. Denzin and Y. Lincoln (eds) *Strategies of Qualitative Inquiry*. London: Sage.

Babcock, B. (1980) Reflexivity: definitions and discrimination, *Semiotica*, 30, 1–14.

Barnes, J. A. (1979) *Who Should Know What?* London: Penguin.

Barry, C. (1998) Choosing qualitative data analysis software, *Sociological Research Online*, 3(3): http://www.socresonline.org.uk/socresonline/3/3.html

Barter, C. and Renold, E. (1999) The use of vignettes in qualitative research, *Social Research Update*, 25.

Bauman, Z. (1990) *Thinking Sociologically*. Oxford: Blackwell.

Beck, U., Giddens, A. and Lash, S. (1994) *Reflexive Modernisation*. Cambridge: Polity Press.

Becker, H. (1967) Whose side are we on?, *Social Problems*, 14, 239–47.

Becker, H. (1970) *Sociological Work*. Chicago: Aldine.

Becker, H. (1986) *Writing for Social Scientists*. Chicago: University of Chicago Press.

Becker, H. (1998) *Tricks of the Trade*. Chicago: University of Chicago Press.

Bell, C. and Newby, H. (eds) (1977) *Doing Sociological Research*. London: Allen and Unwin.

Bell, C. and Roberts, H. (1984) *Social Researching*. London: Routledge.

Berg, B. (1998) *Qualitative Research Methods for the Social Sciences*. Boston: Allyn and Bacon.

Berger, P. (1963) *Invitation to Sociology*. New York: Doubleday.

Bhasker, R. (1989) *The Possibility of Naturalism*. Hemel Hempstead: Harvester.

Blaikie, N. (1993) *Approaches to Social Inquiry*. Cambridge: Polity Press.

Blumer, H. (1969) *Symbolic Interactionism*. Englewood Cliffs, NJ: Prentice Hall.

Bloor, M. (1997) Addressing social problems through qualitative research, in D. Silverman (ed.) *Qualitative Research: Theory, Method and Practice*. London: Sage.

Boden, D. and Zimmerman, D. (1991) *Talk and Social Structure*. Cambridge: Polity Press.

Bogden, R. and Biklen, S. (1982) *Qualitative Research for Education*. Boston: Allyn and Bacon.

Bogden, R. and Taylor, S. (1975) *Introduction to Qualitative Research Methods*. New York: Wiley.

Bottoms, A. (1994) Environmental criminology, in M. Maguire, R. Morgan and R. Reiner (eds) The *Oxford Handbook of Criminology*. Oxford: Oxford University Press.

Bottoms, A. and Wiles, P. (1996) Explanations of crime and place, in J. Muncie, E. McLaughlin and M. Langan (eds) *Criminological Perspectives*. London: Sage.

Bowden, R. (1989) *Statistical Games and Human Affairs*. Cambridge: Cambridge University Press.

Brewer, J. D. (1984a) *Mosley's Men: The BUF in the West Midlands*. Aldershot: Gower.

Brewer, J. D. (1984b) Looking back at fascism: a phenomenological analysis of BUF membership, *Sociological Review*, 32, 742–70.

Brewer, J. D. (1988) Micro-sociology and the 'duality of structure': former fascists 'doing' life history, in N. Fielding (ed.) *Actions and Structure*. London: Sage.

Brewer, J. D. (1990) Sensitivity as a problem in field research, *American Behavioral Scientist*, 33: 578–93.

Brewer, J. D. (1991a) *Inside the RUC: Routine Policing in a Divided Society.* Oxford: Clarendon Press.

Brewer, J. D. (1991b) Hercules, Hippolyte and the Amazons – or policewomen in the RUC, *British Journal of Sociology*, 42, 231–47.

Brewer, J. D. (1994) The ethnographic critique of ethnography: sectarianism in the RUC, *Sociology*, 28, 231–44.

Brewer, J. D. (1998) *Anti-Catholicism in Northern Ireland 1600–1998.* London: Macmillan.

Brewer, J. D. and Higgins, G. (1999) Understanding anti-Catholicism in Northern Ireland, *Sociology*, 33, 235–55.

Brewer, J. D., Lockhart, B. and Rodgers, P. (1997) *Crime in Ireland 1945–95.* Oxford: Clarendon Press.

Brewer, J. D., Lockhart, B. and Rodgers, P. (1998) Informal social control and local crime management in Belfast, *British Journal of Sociology*, 49, 570–85.

Brewer, J. D., McBride, G. and Yearley, S. (1991) Orchestrating an encounter: a note on the talk of mentally handicapped children, *Sociology of Health and Illness*, 13, 58–67.

Brown, G. (1973) Some thoughts on grounded theory, *Sociology*, 7, 1–16.

Brown, P. and Levinson, S. (1987) *Politeness.* Cambridge: Cambridge University Press.

Bruce, S. (1992) *The Red Hand.* Oxford: Oxford University Press.

Bruyn, S. (1966) *The Human Perspective in Sociology.* Englewood Cliffs, NJ: Prentice Hall.

Bryman, A. (1988) *Quantity and Quality in Social Research.* London: Allen and Unwin.

Bryman, A. and Burgess, R. (eds) (1994) *Analysing Qualitative Data.* London: Routledge.

Bulmer, M. (1980) Comment on 'The ethics of covert research', *British Journal of Sociology*, 31, 59–65.

Bulmer, M. (ed.) (1982a) *Social Research Ethics.* London: Macmillan.

Bulmer, M. (1982b) *The Uses of Social Research.* London: Allen and Unwin.

Burgess, R. (1982) *Field Research: a Sourcebook and Field Manual.* London: Allen and Unwin.

Burgess, R. (1984) *In the Field.* London: Routledge.

Burns, T. F. (1980), Getting rowdy with boys, *Journal of Drug Issues*, 80, 273–86.

Carey, J. (1975) *Sociology and Public Affairs.* London: Sage.

Carroll, R. (1982) Adequacy in interpretive sociology: a discussion of the meaning of Alfred Schutz's postulate of adequacy, *Sociological Review*, 30, 15–25.

Clifford, J. (1981) On ethnographic surrealism, *Comparative Studies in Society and History*, 23, 539–64.

Clifford, J. (1983) Power and dialogue in ethnography, in G. Stocking (ed.) *Observers Observed.* Madison: University of Wisconsin Press.

Clifford, J. (1988) *The Predicament of Culture.* Cambridge, MA: Harvard University Press.

Clifford, J. and Marcus, G. (eds) (1986) *Writing Culture.* Berkeley: University of California Press.

Coffey, A. and Atkinson, P. (1996) *Making Sense of Qualitative Data Analysis.* London: Sage.

Coffey, A., Holbrook, B. and Atkinson, P. (1996) Qualitative data analysis: technologies and representations, *Sociological Research Online*, 1(1): http://www.socresonline.org.uk/socresonline/1/1/4.html

Cohen, S. and Taylor, L. (1972) *Psychological Survival*. London: Penguin.

Cook, J. and Fonow, M. (1986) Knowledge and women's interests, *Sociological Inquiry*, 56, 2–29.

Corrigan, P. (1979) *Schooling the Smash Street Kids*. London: Macmillan.

Cuba, L. and Cocking, J. (1994) *How to Write about the Social Sciences*. London: HarperCollins.

Davies, C. (1982) Ethnic jokes, moral values and social boundaries, *British Journal of Sociology*, 33: 383–403.

Davies, C. A. (1999) *Reflexive Ethnography*. London: Routledge.

Davis, D. (1986) Changing self-image: studying menopausal women in a Newfoundland fishing village, in T. Whitehead and M. Conway (eds) *Self, Sex and Gender in Cross-Cultural Fieldwork*. Urbana: University of Illinois Press.

Denzin, N. (1968) On the ethics of disguised observation, *Social Problems*, 15, 502–4.

Denzin, N. (1970) *The Research Act*. Chicago: Aldine.

Denzin, N. (1978) *The Research Act*, 2nd edn. New York: McGraw-Hill.

Denzin, N. (1982) On the ethics of disguised observation: an exchange, in M. Bulmer (ed.) Social Research Ethics. London: Macmillan.

Denzin, N. (1988) Blue velvet: postmodern contradictions, *Theory, Culture & Society*, 5, 461–73.

Denzin, N. (1989) *Interpretive Interactionism*. London: Sage.

Denzin, N. (1992) Whose Cornerville is it anyway?, *Journal of Contemporary Ethnography*, 21, 120–32.

Denzin, N. (1994) Postmodernism and deconstructionism, in D. R. Dickens and A. Fontana (eds) *Postmodernism and Social Enquiry*. London: University College London Press.

Denzin, N. (1997) *Interpretive Ethnography*. London: Sage.

Denzin, N. (1998) The art and politics of interpretation, in N. Denzin and Y. Lincoln (eds) *Collecting and Interpreting Qualitative Materials*. London: Sage.

Denzin, N. and Lincoln, Y. (1998) Entering the field of qualitative research, in N. Denzin and Y. Lincoln (eds) *Strategies of Qualitative Inquiry*. London: Sage.

Dey, I. (1993) *Qualitative Data Analysis*. London: Routledge.

Dingwall, R. (1977) *The Social Organisation of Health Visitor Training*. London: Croom Helm.

Dingwall, R. (1980) Ethics and ethnography, *Sociological Review*, 28, 871–91.

Ditton, J. (1977) *Part-Time Crime*. London: Macmillan.

Ditton, J. and Williams, R. (1981) The fundable versus the doable, University of Glasgow, Background Papers no. 1.

Dobash, R. E. and Dobash, R. (1979) *Violence against Wives*. New York: Free Press.

Douglas, J. (1972) Managing fronts in observing deviance, in J. Douglas (ed.) *Observing Deviance*. New York: Random House.

Douglas, J. (1976) *Investigative Social Research*. London: Sage.

Douglas, J. (1980) Introduction to the sociologies of everyday life, in J. Douglas, P. A. Adler, P. Adler, A. Fontana, C. R. Freeman and J. Kotarba, *Introduction to the Sociologies of Everyday Life*. Boston: Allyn and Bacon.

Douglas, J. (1985) *Creative Interviewing*. London, Sage.

Durkheim, E. (1951) *Suicide*. London, Routledge and Kegan Paul (first published 1905).

Dwyer, K. (1982) *Moroccan Dialogues*. Baltimore: Johns Hopkins University Press.

Easterday, L., Papademas, D., Schorr, L. and Valentine, C. (1977) The making of a female researcher, *Urban Life*, 6, 333–48.

Ellen, R. (1984) *Ethnographic Research*. New York: Academic Press.

Emmison, M. (1988) On the interactional management of defeat, *Sociology*, 22, 233–52.

Erikson, K. (1967) A comment on disguised observation in sociology, *Social Problems*, 14, 366–73.

Erikson, K. (1968) On the ethics of disguised observation: a reply to Denzin, *Social Problems*, 15, 505–6.

Erikson, K. (1982) On the ethics of disguised observation: an exchange, in M. Bulmer (ed.) *Social Research Ethics*. London: Macmillan.

Featherstone, M. (1990) *Global Culture: Nationalism, Globalization and Modernity*. London: Sage.

Featherstone, M. (1991) *Consumer Culture and Postmodernism*. London: Sage.

Fetterman, D. (1998) *Ethnography*. London: Sage.

Fielding, N. (1981) *The National Front*. London: Routledge and Kegan Paul.

Fielding, N. (1982) Observational research on the National Front, in M. Bulmer (ed.) *Social Research Ethics*. London: Macmillan.

Fielding, N. (1993) Ethnography, in N. Gilbert (ed.) *Researching Social Life*. London: Sage.

Fielding, N. and Lee, R. (1991) *Using Computers in Qualitative Research*. London: Sage.

Fielding, N. and Lee, R. (1998) *Computer Analysis and Qualitative Research*. London: Sage.

Filstead, W. (1970) *Qualitative Methodology*. Chicago: Markham.

Finch, J. (1983) *Married to the Job*. London: Allen and Unwin.

Finch, J. (1986) *Research and Policy*. Brighton: Falmer Press.

Finch, J. (1987) The vignette technique in survey research, *Sociology*, 21, 105–14.

Fonow, M. and Cook, J. (1992) *Beyond Methodology*. Buckingham: Open University Press.

Fontana, A. and Frey, J. (1998) Interviewing: the art of science, in N. Denzin and Y. Lincoln (eds) *Collecting and Interpreting Qualitative Materials*. London: Sage.

Fox, J. and Lundman, R. (1974) Problems and strategies in gaining access to police organisation, *Criminology*, 12, 52–69.

Friedman, J. (1990) Being in the world: globalisation and localisation, *Theory, Culture & Society*, 7, 311–28.

Garfinkel, H. (1967) *Studies in Ethnomethodology*. Englewood Cliffs, NJ: Prentice Hall.

Geertz, C. (1975) Thick description, in C. Geertz, *The Interpretation of Cultures*. London: Hutchinson.

Gellner, E. (1975) Ethnomethodology: the re-enactment industry or the Californian way of subjectivity, *Philosophy of the Social Sciences*, 5, 431–50.

Giddens, A. (1974) *Positivism and Sociology*. London: Heinemann.

Giddens, A. (1979) *Central Problems in Social Theory*. London: Macmillan.

Giddens, A. (1984) *The Constitution of Society*. Cambridge: Polity Press.

Giddens, A. (1996a) In defence of sociology, *In Defence of Sociology*. Cambridge: Polity Press.

Giddens, A. (1996b) What is social science?, *In Defence of Sociology*. Cambridge: Polity Press.

Giddens, A. (1996c) Living in a post-traditional society, *In Defence of Sociology*. Cambridge: Polity Press.

Glaser, B. (1978) *Theoretical Sensitivity*. Mill Valley, CA: Sociology Press.

Glaser, B. (1992) *Emergence versus Forcing*. Mill Valley, CA: Sociology Press.

Glaser, B. and Strauss, A. (1967) *The Discovery of Grounded Theory*. Chicago: Aldine.

Goffman, E. (1961) *Asylums*. London: Anchor Books.

Goffman, E. (1963) *Behaviour in Public Places*. New York: Free Press.

Goffman, E. (1969) *Strategic Interaction*. Philadelphia: University of Pennsylvania Press.

Goffman, E. (1971). *Relations in Public*. New York: Basic Books.

Goffman, E. (1981) *Forms of Talk*. Philadelphia: University of Pennsylvania Press.

Gold, R. (1958) Roles in sociological field observation, *Social Forces*, 36, 217–33.

Goldthorpe, J., Lockwood, D., Bechhofer, F. and Platt, J. (1968) *The Affluent Worker*, 3 Volumes. Cambridge: Cambridge University Press.

Gouldner, A. (1970) *The Coming Crisis of Western Sociology*. London: Heinemann.

Gouldner, A. (1973) *For Sociology: Renewal and Critique in Sociology Today*. London: Penguin.

Gubrium, J. (1988) *Analysing Field Reality*. London: Sage.

Hall, S. and du Gay, P. (1996) *Questions of Cultural Identity*. Buckingham: Open University Press.

Hall, S., Held, D. and McGrew, A. (1992) *Modernity and Its Futures*. Cambridge: Polity Press.

Hammersley, M. (1989) *The Dilemma of Qualitative Method: Herbert Blumer and the Chicago Tradition*. London: Routledge.

Hammersley, M. (1990) *Reading Ethnographic Research*. London: Longman.

Hammersley, M. (1992) *What's Wrong with Ethnography?* London: Routledge.

Hammersley, M. (1993a) The rhetorical turn in ethnography, *Social Science Information*, 32, 23–37.

Hammersley, M. (1993b), Ethnographic writing, *Social Research Update*, 5.

Hammersley, M. (1995) *The Politics of Social Research*. London: Sage.

Hammersley, M. and Atkinson, P. (1983) *Ethnography: Principles in Practice*. London: Tavistock.

Hammersley, M. and Gomm, R. (1997) Bias in social research, *Sociological Research Online*, 2(1): http://www.socresonline.org.uk/socresonline/2/1.html

Hammond, P. (1964) *Sociologists at Work*. New York: Basic Books.

Harding, S. (1987) *Feminism and Methodology*. Milton Keynes: Open University Press.

Harvey, D. (1989) *The Condition of Post Modernity*. Oxford: Blackwell.

Harvey, J. (1994) Researching major life events, *Studies in Qualitative Methodology*, 4, 137–70.

Held, D., McGrew, A., Goldblatt, D. and Perraton, J. (1999) *Global Transformations*. Cambridge: Polity Press.

Heritage, J. (1997) Conversational analysis and institutional talk, in D. Silverman (ed.) *Qualitative Research: Theory, Method and Practice*. London: Sage.

Hertz, R. (1997) *Reflexivity and Voice*. London: Sage.

Hill, M. (1997) Research review: participatory research with children, *Child and Family Social Work*, 2, 171–83.

Hobbs, D. and May. T. (1993) *Interpreting the Field*. Oxford: Clarendon Press.

Holdaway, S. (1982) 'An insider job': a case study of covert research, in M. Bulmer (ed.) *Social Research Ethics*. London: Macmillan.

Holdaway, S. (1983) *Inside the British Police*. Oxford: Blackwell.

Holstein, J. and Gubrium, J. (1998) Phenomenology, ethnomethodology and interpretive practice, in N. Denzin and Y. Lincoln (eds) *Strategies of Qualitative Inquiry*. London: Sage.

Homan, R. (1980) The ethics of covert research, *British Journal of Sociology*, 31, 46–59.

Homan, R. (1982) On the merits of covert research, in M. Bulmer (ed.) *Social Research Ethics*. London: Macmillan.

Homan, R. (1991) *The Ethics of Social Research*. London: Longman.

Hornsby-Smith, M. (1993) Gaining access, in N. Gilbert (ed.) *Researching Social Life*. London: Sage.

Huberman, A. and Miles, M. B. (1998) Data management and analysis methods, in N. Denzin and Y. Lincoln (eds) *Collecting and Interpreting Qualitative Materials*. London: Sage.

Hughes, J. (1998) Considering the vignette technique and its application to drug injecting and HIV risk and safer behaviour, *Sociology of Health and Illness*, 20, 381–400.

Hughes, J. A. (1976) *Sociological Analysis*. London: Nelson.

Hughes, J. A. (1990) *The Philosophy of Social Research*. London: Longman.

Hunt, J. (1984) The development of rapport through the negotiation of gender in fieldwork among the police, *Human Organisation*, 43, 283–96.

Hymes, D. (1962) The ethnography of speaking, in J. Fishman (ed.) *Readings in the Sociology of Language*. The Hague: Mouton.

Jacobs, J. (1979) A phenomenological study of suicide notes, in H. Schwartz and J. Jacobs (eds) *Qualitative Sociology*. New York: Free Press.

Janesick, V. (1998) The dance of qualitative research design, in N. Denzin and Y. Lincoln (eds) *Strategies of Qualitative Inquiry*. London: Sage.

Jenks, C. and Neves, T. (2000) A walk on the wild side: urban ethnography meets the *flâneur*, *Cultural Values*, 4, 1–17.

Kelle, U. (1995) *Qualitative Computing: Using Software for Qualitative Data Analysis*. Aldershot: Avebury.

Kelle, U. (1997) Theory building in qualitative research and computer programs for the management of textual data, *Sociological Research Online*, 2(2): http://www.socresonline.org.uk/socresonline/2/2.html

Kirk, J. and Miller, M. (1986) *Reliability and Validity in Qualitative Research*. London: Sage.

Krausz, E. and Miller, S. (1974) *Social Research Design*. London: Longman.

Krieger, S. (1983) *The Mirror Dance: Identity in a Women's Community*. Philadelphia: Temple University Press.

LeCompte, M. and Goetz, J. (1982) Problems of reliability and validity in ethnographic research, *Review of Educational Research*, 52, 31–60.

Lee, R. (1994) *Doing Sensitive Research*. London: Sage.

Lee, R. (1995) *Dangerous Fieldwork*. London: Sage.

Leonard, M. (1994a) *Informal Economic Activity in Belfast*. Aldershot: Avebury.

Leonard, M. (1994b) The politics of sensitive research, *Sociology Review*, 3(4), 29–33.

Liebow, E. (1967) *Tally's Corner*. Boston: Little Brown.

Lincoln, Y. and Denzin, N. (1994) The fifth moment, in N. Denzin and Y. Lincoln (eds) *Handbook of Qualitative Research*. London: Sage.

Lincoln, Y. and Guba, E. (1985) *Naturalistic Inquiry*. London: Sage.

Lofland, J. (1971) *Analysing Social Settings*. Belmont: Wadsworth.

Lofland, J. (1974) Analysing qualitative data: first person accounts, *Urban Life and Culture*, 3, 307–9.

Lofland, J. (1996) Analytic ethnography: features, failings and futures, *Journal of Contemporary Ethnography*, 24, 30–67.

Lofland, J. and Lofland, L. (1984) *Analysing Social Settings: a Guide to Qualitative Observation and Analysis*. Belmont: Wadsworth.

Lonkila, M. (1995) Grounded theory as an emerging paradigm for computer-assisted qualitative data analysis, in U. Kelle (ed.) *Computer-Aided Qualitative Data Analysis*. London: Sage.

Luff, D. (1999) Dialogue across the divides: 'moments of rapport' and power in feminist research with anti-feminist women, *Sociology*, 33, 687–704.

MacAuley, C. (1996) *Children in Long Term Foster Care*. Aldershot: Avebury.

McCrone, D. (1998) *The Sociology of Nationalism*. London: Routledge.

Maguire, M. (1994) Crime statistics, patterns and trends: changing perceptions and their implications, in M. Maguire, R. Morgan and R. Reiner (eds) *The Oxford Handbook of Criminology*. Oxford: Oxford University Press.

Maguire, M., Morgan, R., and Reiner, R. (1994) *The Oxford Handbook of Criminology*. Oxford: Oxford University Press.

Mann, M. (1986) *The Sources of Social Power*. Cambridge: Cambridge University Press.

Marcus, G. (1980) Rhetoric and the ethnographic genre in anthropological research, *Current Anthropology*, 21, 509.

Marcus, G. (1994) What comes (just) after 'post'? The case of ethnography, in N. Denzin and Y. Lincoln (eds) *Handbook of Qualitative Research*. London: Sage.

Marcus, G. and Cushman, D. (1982) Ethnographies as text, *Annual Review of Anthropology*, 11, 25–69.

May, T. (1998), Reflexivity in the age of reconstructive social science, *International Journal of Social Research Methodology*, 1, 7–24.

May, T. (1999), Reflexivity and sociological practice, *Sociological Research Online*, 4(3): http://www.socresonline.org.uk/socresonline/4/3may.html

Miles, M. (1983) Towards a methodology for feminist research, in L. Stanley and S. Wise (eds) *Breaking Out: Feminist Consciousness and Feminist Research*. London: Routledge.

Miles, M. B. and Huberman, A. (1994) *Qualitative Data Analysis*. London: Sage.

Miller, D. (1997) *Modernity: an Ethnographic Approach*. Oxford: Berg.

Miller, R. L. (1988) Evaluation research 'Ulster style': investigating equality of opportunity in Northern Ireland, *Network*, 42.

Miller, R. L. (2000) *Researching Life Histories and Family Biographies*. London: Sage.

Mills, C. W. (1959) *The Sociological Imagination*. London: Penguin.

Moore, R. (1977) Becoming a sociologist in Sparkbrook, in C. Bell and H. Newby (eds) *Doing Sociology Research*. London: Allen and Unwin.

Moore, R. (1978) Sociologists not at work – institutionalised inability, in G. Little-john, B. Smart, J. Wakeford and N. Yuval-Davies (eds) *Power and the State*. London: Croom Helm.

Morgan, D. (1972) The British Association scandal, *Sociological Review*, 20, 185–206.

Mulkay, M. (1985) *The Word and the World: Explorations in the Form of Socio-logical Analysis*. London: Allen and Unwin.

Oakley, A. (1981) Interviewing women: a contradiction in terms, in H. Roberts (ed.) *Doing Feminist Research*. London: Routledge and Kegan Paul.

Okely, J. (1983) *The Traveller-Gypsies*. Cambridge: Cambridge University Press.

Okely, J. (1994) Thinking through fieldwork, in A. Bryman and R. Burgess (eds) *Analysing Qualitative Data*. London: Routledge.

Paget, M. (1995) Performing the text, in J. van Maanen (ed.) *Representation in Ethnography*. London: Sage.

Parker, H. (1974) *View from the Boys*. Newton Abbot: David and Charles.

Patrick, J. (1973) *A Glasgow Gang Observed*. London: Eyre Methuen.

Pawson, R. (1999) Methodology, in S. Taylor (ed.) *Sociology: Issues and Debates*. London: Macmillan.

Payne, G. (1979) Social research and market research, *Sociology*, 13, 307–14.

Payne, G., Dingwall, R., Payne, J. and Carter, M. (1981) *Sociology and Social Research*. London: Routledge.

Perakyla, A. (1997) Reliability and validity in research based on transcripts, in D. Sil-verman (ed.) *Qualitative Research: Theory, Method and Practice*. London: Sage.

Philips, D. (1973) *Abandoning Method*. San Francisco: Jossey-Bass.

Pinch, T. and Pinch, T. (1988) Reservations about reflexivity and new literary forms, in S. Woolgar (ed.) *Knowledge and Reflexivity*. London: Sage.

Platt, J. (1981) The social construction of 'positivism' and its significance in British sociology, in P. Abrams, R. Deem, J. Finch and P. Rock (eds) *Practice and Progress: British Sociology 1950–1980*. London: Allen and Unwin.

Pollard, A. (1984) Ethnography and social policy for classroom practice, in L. Barton and S. Walker (eds) *Social Crisis and Educational Research*. London: Croom Helm.

Porter, S. (1993) Critical realist ethnography: the case of racism and professionalism in a medical setting, *Sociology*, 27, 591–609.

Porter, S. (1995) *Nursing's Relationship with Medicine*. Aldershot: Avebury.

Powdermaker, H. (1966) *Stranger and Friend*. New York: Norton.

Pryce, K. (1979) *Endless Pressure*. London: Penguin.

Punch, M. (1989) Researching police deviance, *British Journal of Sociology*, 40, 177–204.

Nas, P., Prins, W. and Shadid, W. (1987) A plea for praxeology, in C. Wenger (ed.) *The Research Relationship: Practice and Politics in Social Policy Research*. London: Allen and Unwin.

Ragin, C. C. (1987) *The Comparative Method*. Berkeley: University of California Press.

Rahman, N. (1996) Caregivers' sensitivity to conflict: the use of vignette methodol-ogy, *Journal of Elder Abuse and Neglect*, 8, 35–47.

Rainwater, L. and Pittman, D. (1966) Ethical problems in studying a politically sensitive and deviant community, *Social Problems*, 14, 357–66.

Rappert, B. (1999) The uses of relevance: thoughts on a reflexive sociology, *Sociology*, 33, 705–24.

Reinharz, S. (1992) *Feminist Methods in Social Research*. Oxford: Oxford University Press.

Renzetti, C. and Lee, R. (1993) *Research Sensitive Topics*. London: Sage.

Reynolds, P. (1982) Moral judgements, in M. Bulmer (ed.) *Social Research Ethics*. London: Macmillan.

Richards, L. (1999) Qualitative computing: the next stage in teaching and developing software, *SocInfo Journal*, 4, 11–18.

Richards, L. and Richards, T. (1991) Computing in qualitative analysis, *Qualitative Health Research*, 1, 234–62.

Richards, T. and Richards, L. (1994) Using computers in qualitative research, in N. Denzin and Y. Lincoln (eds) *Handbook of Qualitative Research*. London: Sage.

Richards, T. and Richards, L. (1998) Using computers in qualitative research, in N. Denzin and Y. Lincoln (eds) *Collecting and Interpreting Qualitative Materials*. London: Sage.

Richardson, L. (1991) Postmodern social theory, *Sociological Theory*, 9, 173–9.

Richardson, L. (1992) The consequences of poetic representation, in C. Ellis and M. Flaherty (eds) *Investigating Subjectivity*. London: Sage.

Richardson, L. (1994) Nine poems: marriage and the family, *Journal of Contemporary Ethnography*, 23, 3–14.

Richardson, L. (1998) Writing: a method of inquiry, in N. Denzin and Y. Lincoln (eds) *Collecting and Interpreting Qualitative Materials*. London: Sage.

Rist, R. (1981) On the utility of ethnographic research for the policy process, *Urban Education*, 15, 48–70.

Rist, R. (1984) On the application of qualitative research to the policy process, in L. Barton and S. Walker (eds) *Social Crisis and Educational Research*. London: Croom Helm.

Rist, R. (1998) Influencing the policy process with qualitative research, in N. Denzin and Y. Lincoln (eds) *Collecting and Interpreting Qualitative Materials*. London: Sage.

Roberts, H. (ed.) (1981) *Doing Feminist Research*. London: Routledge and Kegan Paul.

Robertson, R. (1992) *Globalization*. London: Sage.

Robins, D. (1992) *Tarnished Vision: Crime and Conflict in the Inner City*. Oxford: Oxford University Press.

Rosenham, D. (1973) On being sane in insane places, *Science*, 179, 250–8.

Schutz, A. (1964) *Collected Papers, Volume 1*. The Hague: Martinus Nijhoff.

Schutz, A. (1967) *The Phenomenology of the Social World*. Evanston, IL: Northwestern University Press.

Schwartz, B. (1973) Notes on the sociology of sleep, in A. Birenbaum and E. Sagarin (eds) *People in Places: the Sociology of the Familiar*. London: Nelson.

Schwartz, H. and Jacobs, J. (1979) *Qualitative Sociology*. New York: Free Press.

Seale, C. (1999) *The Quality of Qualitative Research*. London: Sage.

Silverman, D. (1985) *Qualitative Methodology and Sociology*. Aldershot: Gower.

Silverman, D. (1989) Six rules of qualitative research: a post-Romantic argument, *Symbolic Interaction*, 12, 215–30.

Silverman, D. (1993) *Interpreting Qualitative Data*. London: Sage.

Silverman, D. (1997a) Towards an aesthetics of research, in D. Silverman (ed.) *Qualitative Research: Theory, Method and Practice*. London: Sage.

Silverman, D. (ed.) (1997b) *Qualitative Research: Theory, Method and Practice*. London: Sage.

Sklair, L. (1995) *Sociology of the Global System*. Baltimore: Johns Hopkins University Press.

Sklair, L. (1999) Globalisation, in S. Taylor (ed.) *Sociology: Issues and Debates*. London: Macmillan.

Smith, D. (1987) *The Everyday World as Problematic*. Boston: Northeastern University Press.

Smith, G. and Cantley, C. (1985) Policy evaluation: the use of varied data in a study of a psychogeriatric service, in R. Walker (ed.) *Applied Qualitative Research*. Aldershot: Gower.

Spencer, J. (1989) Anthropology as a kind of writing, *Man*, 24, 145–64.

Spradley, J. P. (1980) *Participant Observation*. New York: Rinehart and Winston.

Stake, R. (1998) Case studies, in N. Denzin and Y. Lincoln (eds) *Strategies of Qualitative Inquiry*. London: Sage.

Stanley, L. (ed.) (1990a) *Feminist Praxis*. London: Routledge.

Stanley, L. (1990b) Doing ethnography, writing ethnography: a comment on Hammersley, *Sociology*, 24, 617–28.

Stanley, L. (1993) On auto/biography in sociology, *Sociology*, 27, 41–52.

Stanley, L. (1996) The mother of invention: necessity, writing and representation, *Feminism and Psychology*, 6, 45–51.

Stanley, L. and Wise, S. (eds) (1983) *Breaking Out: Feminist Consciousness and Feminist Research*. London: Routledge.

Stanley, L. and Wise, S. (1990) Method, methodology and epistemology in feminist research processes, in L. Stanley (ed.) *Feminist Praxis*. London: Routledge.

Stein, S. (1999) *Learning, Teaching and Researching on the Internet*. London: Addison-Wesley.

Stocking, G. (ed.) (1983) *Observers Observed*. Madison: University of Wisconsin Press.

Strauss, A. (1987) *Qualitative Analysis for Social Scientists*. Cambridge: Cambridge University Press.

Strauss, A. and Corbin, J. (1990) *Basics of Qualitative Research*. London: Sage.

Strauss, A. and Corbin, J. (1998) Grounded theory methodology: an overview, in N. Denzin and Y. Lincoln (eds) *Strategies of Qualitative Inquiry*. London: Sage.

Suttles, G. D. (1968) *The Social Order of the Slum*. Chicago: University of Chicago Press.

ten Have, P. (1998) *Doing Conversation Analysis*. London: Sage.

Thompson, P. (1988) *The Voice of the Past: Oral History*, 2nd edn. Oxford: Oxford University Press.

Thompson, W. and Mulholland, B. (1995) Paramilitary punishments and young people in West Belfast, in L. Kennedy (ed.) *Crime and Punishment in West Belfast*. Belfast: The Summer School, West Belfast.

Tyler, S. (1986) Post-modern ethnography, in J. Clifford and G. Marcuse (eds) *Writing Culture*. Berkeley: University of California Press.

van Maanen, J. (1981) The informant game, *Urban Life*, 9, 469–94.

van Maanen, J. (1982) *Varieties of Qualitative Research*. London: Sage.

van Maanen, J. (1988) *Tales of the Field: On Writing Ethnography*. Chicago: University of Chicago Press.

Waddington, P. (1992) Problems of ethnography: the case of the police, *Reviewing Sociology*, 8, 26–32.

Walker, R. (ed.) (1985) *Applied Qualitative Research*. Aldershot: Gower.

Walker, R. (1988) We would like to know why: qualitative research and the policy maker, Policy Research Institute, The Queen's University of Belfast.

Wallis, R. (1977) The moral career of a research project, in C. Bell and H. Newby (eds) *Doing Sociology Research*. London: Allen and Unwin.

Wallis, R. and Bruce, S. (1983) Accounting for action, *Sociology*, 17, 97–111.

Warren, C. (1988) *Gender Issues in Field Research*. London: Sage.

Warren, C. and Rasmussen, P. (1977) Sex and gender in fieldwork research, *Urban Life*, 6, 359–69.

Wax, R. (1979) Gender and age in fieldwork and fieldwork education, *Social Problems*, 26, 509–22.

Weitzman, E. and Miles, M. (1995) *Computer Programs for Qualitative Analysis*. London: Sage.

Wenger, G. C. (1987a) Introduction: the problematic relationship, in G. C. Wenger (ed.) *The Research Relationship: Practice and Politics in Social Policy Research*. London: Allen and Unwin.

Wenger, G. C. (1987b) *The Research Relationship: Practice and Politics in Social Policy Research*. London: Allen and Unwin.

Westley, W. (1970) *Violence and the Police*. Cambridge, MA: MIT Press.

Whyte, W. F. (1955) *Street Corner Society*, 2nd edn. Chicago: University of Chicago Press.

Williams, A. (1990) Reflections on the making of an ethnographic text, *Studies in Sexual Politics*, no. 29, University of Manchester.

Williams, T. M. (1989) *The Cocaine Kids: the Inside Story of a Teenage Drug Ring*. Reading, MA: Addison-Wesley.

Willis, P. (1977) *Learning to Labour*. Farnborough, Gower.

Wolcott, H. (1973) *The Man in the Principal's Office: an Ethnography*. New York: Rinehart and Winston.

Wolcott, H. (1980) How to look like an anthropologist without actually being one, *Practising Ethnography*, 3, 111–27.

Wolcott, H. (1990) *Writing Up Qualitative Research*. London: Sage.

Wolf, M. (1992) *A Thrice Told Tale*. Stanford, CA: University of Stanford Press.

Wolff, M. (1973) Notes on the behaviour of pedestrians, in A. Birenbaum and E. Sagarin (eds) *People in Places: the Sociology of the Familiar*. London: Nelson.

Woods, P. (1985) Ethnography and theory construction in educational research, in R. Burgess (ed.) *Field Methods in the Study of Education*. Lewes: Falmer Press.

Woods, P. (1999) *Successful Writing for Qualitative Researchers*. London: Routledge.

Wooffitt, R. (1993) Analysing accounts, in N. Gilbert (ed.) *Researching Social Life*. London: Sage.

Woolgar, S. (1988a) Reflexivity is the ethnographer of the text, in S. Woolgar (ed.) *Knowledge and Reflexivity*. London: Sage.

Woolgar, S. (ed.) (1988b) *Knowledge and Reflexivity*. London: Sage.

Woolgar, S. and Ashmore, M. (1988) The next step: an introduction to the reflexive project, in S. Woolgar (ed.) *Knowledge and Reflexivity*. London: Sage.

Yearley, S. and Brewer, J. D. (1989) Stigma and conversational competence, *Human Studies*, 12, 97–115.

Zimmerman, D. and West, C. (1975) Sex roles interruptions and silences in conversations, in B. Thorne and N. Henley (eds) *Language and Sex*. Rowley, MA: Newbury House.

Index

About the author

John D. Brewer is Professor of Sociology at the Queen's University of Belfast. He is a Fellow of the Royal Society of Arts, and has been Visiting Fellow at Yale University, 1989, and Visiting Scholar at St John's College, Oxford, 1992. He taught formerly at the University of East Anglia and the University of Natal. He has extensive experience of qualitative research on a variety of topics and in many different locations, as well as considerable experience of writing up ethnographic data. He has used oral/life history methods with former policemen in the Royal Irish Constabulary and former members of the British Union of Fascists. He has used observational methods on the Royal Ulster Constabulary, documentary research on the South African Police, in-depth interview research on crime in East and West Belfast and among conservative evangelicals in Northern Ireland and conversation analysis on the talk of people with learning difficulties. Much of this has involved research on sensitive topics or in sensitive locations, and he has developed an acute awareness of the strengths and weaknesses of ethnographic data and their practical use. He has over twenty years' experience of teaching qualitative research methods to undergraduate and postgraduate students. He is currently writing a book on the sociology of the peace process in Northern Ireland and South Africa, to be published by Macmillan Press.

Books by the same author

After Soweto: an Unfinished Journey (Clarendon Press, 1986).
Anti-Catholicism in Northern Ireland 1600–1998: The Mote and the Beam (Macmillan, 1998), with Gareth Higgins.
Black and Blue: Policing in South Africa (Clarendon Press, 1994).
Can South Africa Survive? (Macmillan, 1989), editor.
Crime in Ireland 1945–95: 'Here Be Dragons' (Clarendon Press, 1997), with Bill Lockhart and Paula Rodgers.
Inside the RUC: Routine Policing in a Divided Society (Clarendon Press, 1991), with Kathleen Magee.
Mosley's Men: The BUF in the West Midlands (Gower, 1984).
Police, Public Order and the State (Macmillan, 1988 and 1996), with Adrian Guelke, Ian Hume, Edward Moxon-Browne and Rick Wilford.
Restructuring South Africa (Macmillan, 1994), editor.
The Royal Irish Constabulary: An Oral History (Institute of Irish Studies, 1990).